WHERE THE WORD ENDS

The Life of Louis Moreau Gottschalk

The Life of Louis Moreau Gottschalk

WHERE

THE WORD

ENDS

by Vernon Loggins

Louisiana State University Press

BATON ROUGE

BY VERNON LOGGINS

Chansons du Midi

The Negro Author

American Literature

I Hear America

Two Romantics

The Hawthornes

Copyright 1958 Louisiana State University Press
Library of Congress Card Catalogue Number: 58-7553
Printed in the United States of America by the
J. H. Furst Company, Baltimore, Maryland
Designed by William Nicoll

TO MABEL DANIELS

CONTENTS

ILLUSTRATIONS

Where the deepest word ends, there music begins with its supersensuous and all-confounding intimations.

—MELVILLE

Louis Moreau Gottschalk was the first American to manifest a marked genius for playing the piano and for composing piano music.

His life span—from May 8, 1829, to December 18, 1869—covered a little more than forty years. By the time he was thirteen he had mastered all that could be taught about the art of piano playing in his native New Orleans. At the end of his next eleven years—which he spent in Europe as a student of composition as well as of the piano—France, Switzerland, and Spain were at his feet, hailing him the peer of Franz Liszt. For the rest of his life he was in the New World, struggling to hold on to his artistic ideals in the face of misunderstanding, intolerance, and crudeness of taste.

He was more than a musician. He was from first to last a romantic, akin in spirit to Byron, Shelley, and Poe. He was a wit, a great talker, and a writer of talent: his *Notes of a Pianist*, compiled from his journals after his death, is one of the most fascinating of American diaries. He was an iconoclast, gracefully hurling his brickbats at abuses in religion, politics, and art. He was a man of pity—a prey to relatives, friends, and doting women: before he left Europe he had a string of dependents, and with the years the number grew.

His quixotic altruism turned out to be his tragic frailty. To earn the money necessary to satisfy those to whom he had made promises he was forced to give concerts in the New World, where not even a composer of the hardy stamina of a Bach or a Handel could have flourished a century ago.

The stamina of Gottschalk was of the delicate order. If he had remained where his genius was appreciated, he would no doubt stand today in the firmament of fame between Chopin, with whom his European contemporaries invariably associated him, and Debussy, over whom his music cast an influence.

Such an "inheritor of unfulfilled renown" was the American pioneer whose birth-to-death odyssey I shall trace in the following narrative.

WHERE THE WORD ENDS

The Life of Louis Moreau Gottschalk

Edward Gottschalk was married to Aimée Bruslé in the St. Louis Cathedral in New Orleans on Monday, May 26, 1828. The vicar of the Cathedral at that time was the most celebrated of all the Catholic clerics of Louisiana, Antonio de Sedella, a Capuchin friar known familiarly as Père Antoine. It was he who gave to Edward Gottschalk and Aimée Bruslé the nuptial benediction.

Like the architecture of the French quarter of New Orleans, Père Antoine was an inheritance from the Spanish regime. But he was not the Spanish bigot he had been during his early years in the New World. The older Creoles remembered that in the late 1780's he fought in vain to set up in Louisiana the Holy Office of the Inquisition. They also remembered that fifteen years later, after the purchase of the territory by the United States, he again fought in vain to keep New Orleans in the diocese of the Bishop of Havana. The younger generation, which included Edward Gottschalk and Aimée Bruslé, recalled only that Père Antoine was a man of God, dedicated body and soul to fulfilling the vows he took upon becoming a Capuchin.

He lived on the rue Dauphine, in a wooden hut which he had built with his own hands. On the stretch of turf in front of the kennel-like structure he had planted a date palm. By 1828 this tree was big enough to provide shade for the eighty-year-old friar as he sat on a stool in his doorway listening to the accounts of distress poured into his ear by this suppliant and that.

Every day he made his tour of visits to the sick. No man was more frequently seen walking the streets of New Orleans than tall thin Père Antoine, cowled and sandaled, his brown eyes shining, his white beard flying. Often on a mission of mercy he crossed Canal Street and entered a Protestant home in the Ameri-

3

can faubourg. To Père Antoine the sick were the sick, whatever their religion might be.

Marvelous tales were told of the physical endurance he manifested when one of the ever recurring epidemics of yellow fever struck New Orleans. It was said that he went without sleep for weeks at a stretch, spending every hour of the twenty-four in comforting the stricken, administering last rites, and burying the dead. No one, it was declared, ever saw him take food from the beginning of an epidemic to the end. It was said that so long as yellow jack loitered Père Antoine's strength was sustained by a flow of manna that entered his body with the air he breathed.

His parishioners laughed over his shrewdness in collecting silver for the poor at the three or four thousand marriages he had consecrated. Every participant—the groom, the bride, each parent, each relative of whatever degree, and each witness—was coaxed into contributing. All the money thus collected, down to the last picayune, went into Père Antoine's many, many charities.

When he opened his door to start for the Cathedral on Monday morning, May 26, 1828, his eyes fell upon several ragged old women kneeling at the foot of the date palm. At solemn Mass on three successive Sundays they had heard him publish the banns for the Gottschalk-Bruslé nuptials. Expecting his purse to be filled anew before the end of the day, they were already at his door to tell of their distress and plead for alms. Père Antoine knew that by the hour of his return a dozen other unfortunates would be kneeling beside them. As the women looked up, he raised his hand in blessing and then went on to the Cathedral to prepare for the arrival of the wedding party.

The bride, whom Père Antoine himself had christened Marie Aimée, was the daughter of Camille Bruslé, owner and manager of the bakery which for twenty-five years had supplied the French quarter of New Orleans with bread. The shop was on the rue de Chartres. From the windows of the oven room in the back Camille Bruslé could look upon the garden at the rear of his home, which fronted on the rue St. Louis. He was one of the thousands of refugees from Haiti in New Orleans. His father was a landholder with plantations in the vicinity of Cap François, a high-ranking magistrate and a militia officer of sufficient importance to be made a Chevalier of the Order of St. Louis. In the insurrection of the Negro slaves in the 1790's Camille Bruslé, alone of all his family, escaped massacre. He saved his life by joining the British force sent into the island to take advantage of the disorder and assume control. He proved to be so competent a soldier that in 1795 he was commissioned an ensign in the name of King George III. When he again became a civilian, he was in Jamaica. There, in 1800, he was married to Josephine Alix Deynaud, also a refugee from Haiti. About the time of the Louisiana Purchase the couple migrated to New Orleans. Camille Bruslé at once opened a bakery, leaving to three or four slaves the labor of kneading the dough and tending the ovens. For a decade now he had been rich enough to provide his family with such luxuries as seats at the Théâtre d'Orléans during the seasons of opera. Père Antoine, as well as the hundreds who sent servants every morning to the shop on the rue de Chartres for the day's supply of bread, respected the baker as a man of sobriety and honesty, ambitious for each of his many children.

The most aspiring among them was Aimée, born in 1808. Her visions of greatness often blinded her to reality. Still there was a strain of high seriousness in this beautiful and extremely intelligent twenty-year-old girl, and Père Antoine knew that he was in great measure responsible for it. He had prepared her for confirmation, he had delivered hundreds of moral discourses in her hearing, and he had again and again spoken directly to her heart in the confessional. As the molder of her faith, he knew that religion would always stand her first great interest in life.

A second interest, in music and literature, he had in no way discouraged. But he had left to one of his admired friends the responsibility of directing the girl's artistic development. This friend was Louis Moreau Lislet, a personage in early nineteenth-century New Orleans. Educated for the law in Paris, Monsieur Lislet had an important part in drawing up the Louisiana civil code. He too was a refugee from Haiti, and he was possibly a blood relative of the Bruslés or of the family of Madame Bruslé, the Deynauds. Aimée, who won his heart when she was a tiny girl, learned under his guidance how to make her hours at the Théâtre d'Orléans more than hours of passing pleasure. Taught by teachers he recommended, she was able to sing to her own piano accompaniment the soprano arias from such favorite operas as Méhul's *Joseph* and Boieldieu's *La Dame blanche*. Monsieur Lislet himself gave the young girl lessons in elocution, and she often entertained her friends with recitations from Corneille and Racine.

Père Antoine, whom she looked upon as a saint, would never have chosen Edward Gottschalk to be her husband. This Northman—born in London in 1795, one of the several sons of Lazarus and Jane Harris Gottschalk—was thirteen years older than she. Moreover Père Antoine and everybody else in New Orleans took him to be an Israelite. His name suggested a German Jewish origin, and he was decidedly Jewish in appearance.

Still he and the four brothers who accompanied him to New Orleans in the early 1820's identified themselves with the Protestants of the American faubourg. One of the brothers died in the yellow-fever epidemic of 1825. Another, Dr. Joseph Gottschalk, established himself as a physician in the French quarter, with an office and residence on the rue Conti. Each of the other three was associated with a house of business.

For a number of years Edward had been the senior partner in Gottschalk, Reimers & Co., owners and operators of a cloth shop on the rue Royale. In dress, manners, and speech he was an English gentleman, well educated. Before deciding to devote himself to business he spent two years as a student of medicine in Leipzig. His mastery of the German language was thorough. He spoke French with his fiancée's fluency, and could converse in Spanish with Père Antoine's ease. It was said that he was familiar with several other tongues. He had at least the aged friar's respect.

Where in the St. Louis Cathedral Père Antoine pronounced Edward Gottschalk and Aimée Bruslé man and wife has not been determined. There appears to be no record that the groom was ever received into the Roman Catholic Church. If he became a Roman Catholic in order to win the hand of Aimée Bruslé, the ceremony was performed before the great altar. If he merely promised to rear in the Catholic faith the children born of his union with Aimée, the scene of the ceremony was the sacristy. The witnesses for the groom, Thomas Franklin and Samuel Herman, were residents of the American faubourg. One of the witnesses for the bride was Monsieur Lislet; the other, Jacques Pitot, was a judge of a civil court.

After the vows had been taken and the benediction given, Père Antoine, with his accustomed jocularity, collected the donations. Then he saw the bride and groom leave for the house they had fitted up for themselves on the rue des Remparts, near Canal Street. In entering the certificate of marriage in the record book, octogenarian Père Antoine wrote in Spanish with a steadiness of hand a man of forty might have envied. He was ready then to go back to his hut and spend an hour or two in the shade of the date palm dropping into the outstretched hands of the needy the silver with which the pockets under his cassock were heavy.

He lived long enough to learn from Aimée that she was pregnant and to pray with her the prayers of the expectant mother. But before the year was out he was too feeble even to hear confessions. On January 18, 1829, the end came.

His death was looked upon in Louisiana, Catholic and Protestant alike, as a public calamity. All New Orleans went into mourning. The funeral rites were observed with a pomp hitherto unknown to the city. Such crowds assembled to witness the ceremonies as had gathered to welcome Lafayette in 1825 and General Jackson in 1828.

Throngs of the faithful, convinced within their hearts that Père Antoine was a saint, demolished the hut on the rue Dauphine. Even the slightest splinter of the wood was carried away to be preserved as a holy relic. No two in New Orleans appear to have agreed on what happened to the date palm. In the many legends which tell of its miraculous powers its actual history was lost.

The child born to Edward and Aimée Gottschalk on the eighth day of May following Père Antoine's death was the son destined to be the first American to win world-wide renown as a piano virtuoso, the first American composer to see his music accepted with high favor in Europe, and the first composer from anywhere to make serious use of American folk themes. As a youth he always laughed when his mother would tell him that he was exceptional because a saint in the flesh had prepared the way for his entrance into this world. But he never treated lightly Père Antoine's moral precepts, in which, as he well knew, his own moral sense had its origin.

He was given the names Louis Moreau, after Monsieur Lislet. For everyday use the second was considered sufficient. When a whole year and a half passed and he was still unbaptized, Creole gossips began to whisper, "That Jew Gottschalk has no respect for the usages of the Church!" The talk was hushed when on December 22, 1830, the christening rites were celebrated by a curate of the St. Louis Cathedral. Monsieur Lislet stood as godfather. The godmother was the wife of Aimée's favorite brother, Gaston Bruslé, a printer and bookseller.

Aimée was then in the last weeks of her second pregnancy. She bore the child, a daughter, on January 8, 1831. While she was in travail, her neighbors were noisily celebrating the sixteenth anniversary of the battle in which General Jackson saved New Orleans from British capture. The baptism this time was not delayed. The girl was christened Thérèse Aimée, the godmother being an unmarried aunt, Thérèse Emilie Bruslé.

The young family on the rue des Remparts was expanding as the husband and father desired. In Gottschalk, Reimers & Co. he was the partner to whom the important matter of investments was entrusted, and in his deals he had so far met with unusual success. He looked forward to the time when his private means would enable him to withdraw from the company and set up a brokerage business of his own. Projecting his dreams into the distant future, he saw himself the founder of a great New Orleans merchant family, growing richer and more powerful with each generation. Moreau, who would be his immediate successor as head of this great family, was already manifesting an amazing precocity. Day by day the father's pride in his son mounted.

Even as a child Moreau had the physical attractiveness that was to count greatly to his advantage in the years to come. His body was beautifully shaped, as was his mother's, and he had inherited her blue eyes and her way of smiling. But in his brown hair and facial contour he favored his father.

By the second summer after the birth of Thérèse, the summer of 1832, Moreau could say in either French or English anything he wished to say. Every word he heard on the lips of his parents somehow got into his vocabulary, and was straightway put to use. His French enunciation was that of a boy growing up in a cultivated family of Touraine. But his English showed a hint of an accent.

He knew definitely what he wanted, and without hesitation asked for it, always calmly. On occasion he was inclined to take advantage of his mother's affectionate disposition and argue for the right to some forbidden privilege. With his father he chanced no liberties; it was evident that here Moreau met a force to be respected, even revered. When Edward Gottschalk said no, however gently, the boy was at once submissive.

The Gottschalk house, long and narrow, was brick, faced with a gray stucco. The entrance was directly upon the sidewalk. Stretching across the front on the second and third floors, forming a roof over the sidewalk, were galleries enclosed with wrought-iron balustrades. Rambler roses and cypress vines, growing in big stone urns, protected the galleries from the afternoon sun.

Here, on the second or third floor, Moreau spent hours every day with his nurse, a gray-haired mulatto slave named Sally. Together he and she surveyed the wonders of the rue des Remparts. Looking southward, to their left, they could see the square where Canal Street cut across. Sally, always speaking in French, explained that this wide thoroughfare was the dividing line between the old New Orleans of the Creoles, in which Moreau lived, and the new New Orleans of the "foreigners," where he was often taken on their strolls. He understood perfectly what Sally meant when she said that he belonged to both areas. Facing the Gottschalk house, a block away, was the St. Louis Cemetery. By pointing out the tips of the ten or twelve tombstones so tall that they towered above the roofs of houses Sally taught the boy how to count.

A quarter of a mile beyond the cemetery the city ended and the savanna began. The tops of the moss-hung live oaks which dotted this swampy expanse were plainly visible from either of the Gottschalk galleries. Sally claimed that at the feet of these trees lay the skeletons of many runaway slaves who had gone into the savanna to hide. They died from hunger or snake bite, she said, or took their own lives when they heard bloodhounds on their trail. " These eyes of mine have many a time seen the sky above those trees black with vultures," she declared. The tone of her voice showed that, to her, the savanna stood for all that was wicked and horrible. To Moreau it represented a fascinating mingling of greenness, distance, and sadness. He was never to think of it without thinking also of a tune Sally often hummed, the mournful spiritual into which the Louisiana slaves converted the gay old English dance song " Skip-tum-lu, my Darling."

Northward on the rue des Remparts, beginning with the intersection with the rue de Toulouse, were the two long lines of little houses out of which came the beautiful ladies who especially delighted Moreau. Neither Sally nor his mother ever took him into the neighborhood of these houses, but he found out that they were white cottages, set back from the street and almost hidden by chinaberry trees, oleanders, crepe myrtle, and morning glories. If Sally ever so much as alluded to the ladies who lived in them, she said, crossly, " They're quadroons." Several times a day three or four of the enticing creatures, walking together, might be seen passing the Gottschalk house on their way to or from the shopping centers. They invariably dressed in gay colors, and walked with a rhythm so pleasing to Moreau that he would clap his hands in time with their steps. All the while he kept his eyes on their heads, on which they wore silk scarves pinched and puffed into the most fantastic shapes. He was so fascinated that he paid no attention when Sally explained that though these women of color were free they were forbidden by law to wear such hats and bonnets as his mother wore. Always when the beautiful heads disappeared around a corner the boy relaxed and looked up in disapproval at Sally's blue calico scarf. "Frown at it, m' p'tit, till your eyes get lost in their sockets," she would say. Then, drawing herself up in pride, she would add, "You don't see my head covered with the red a field woman has to wear!"

Mr. Gottschalk owned two other slaves, a housemaid and the woman who cooked. Both were very black and considerably younger than Sally. The three slept in the big room on the second floor at the rear of the house, and ate in the kitchen, directly below.

Moreau liked to steal into the kitchen when the slaves were at breakfast. They always talked while eating, and when they dropped their voices to a whisper the boy knew they were telling secrets and listened all the harder. Once he heard them speak of a Creole gentleman who sent his wife and children to France to prevent their interference with his attentions to a quadroon. Another time they talked excitedly about the quadroon over whom two American gentlemen killed one another in a pistol duel fought under the oaks near the Bayou St. John. In these whispered conversations Moreau frequently heard the name of the Bruslé uncle who managed the ballroom connected with the Théâtre d'Orléans. No other salon where white gentlemen could dance with quadroons demanded such strict decorum. Nevertheless Moreau's uncle witnessed many a tragedy of jealousy.

The boy never got the chance to listen long when the slaves' voices were low. Sally would always spy him out and, looking at him sternly, would say, "Here you are eavesdropping again! If you tell your maman and papa what you've just heard, I'm going to give you a little tan skillet with five handles, back where it hurts. Now you go out in the garden and pick some flowers for your maman."

Usually when Moreau got into the garden he found that playing street vendor was far more exciting than gathering nosegays. All around the banana trees and among the beds of mignonette and periwinkle he wandered, singing his imaginary wares in precisely the rhythms heard on the lips of sellers in the streets. If he was trying to dispose of his services as a chimney sweep, he held out make-believe brooms and sang,

> R-r-r-raminez la cheminée
> Du haut en bas!

When selling palmetto root for scouring floors, he chanted,

> Pal-met-to! Pal-met-to-o-o!

If he fancied that he was holding a pail of figs under his right arm, he sang,

> Six figues célestes,
> On a green leaf,
> On a green leaf!

He sang of popcorn tic–tac balls, pralines, pyramides de nougats, macaroons, candied oranges, and watermelons. If the make-believe basket on his head was piled high with yams, he chanted in the black vendor's patois,

> Quand patate la cuite,
> Na va mange li!
> Na va mange li!

When Sally came into the garden to see what mischief he was up to, he would pretend she was a buyer and start crying his wares all over again.

Of the many games he played by himself the one which excited him most was to go up to the third-floor gallery on Saturday afternoons and dance and sing to the beat of the drums coming from the Place Congo. This great open square of tramped earth was on the opposite side of the rue des Remparts beyond the neighborhood where the quadroons lived. It provided a drill field for the New Orleans unit of the Louisiana militia, and it was also a gathering place where hundreds of New Orleans slaves made merry on the one afternoon of the week they were not on duty to serve their masters. Moreau seemed to know by instinct when noon came on Saturday. Always at that hour he was up on the third-floor gallery listening for the first sound of the drums. As soon as the beats fell into a steady rhythm he began to march.

Louder and faster the beats grew, and the boy's march turned into a dance. The three slave women were always on the Place

Congo for the weekly gaiety, and when shouts began to accompany the drums Moreau sometimes thought he could hear Sally. But there was only one shout about which he could be sure, that of the best known of all the slaves of New Orleans, a one-armed giant of an African called Bras Coupé. There was no mistaking his voice when he thundered,

Dansez bamboula! Badoun, badoun!
Dansez bamboula, badoun!

As the hundreds of dancing slaves sang this snatch of song, the dancing boy sang it too. Over and over he would repeat the melody, until his mother would come, pick him up, carry him into the nursery, and lay him on his bed. In an instant he would be sound asleep. Though in mentality he was six or seven, in years he was only three.

Growing up on the rue des Remparts in the 1830's, he had no more than five chances out of ten of living to maturity. New Orleans—with its Théâtre d'Orléans, its American Theatre, its circuses, its cockpits, its fencing salons, its ballrooms where a visiting rich planter could dance with a quadroon one night and a lady of purest Caucasian origin the next, its white cottages where white gentlemen openly maintained their colored concubines, its dozens of brothels, its gambling houses, its Place Congo, and its luxurious hotels—was winning fame throughout the world as a city of pleasure, America's Gomorrah. Perhaps its people were epicurean because they were so conscious of the imminence of death. The mortality rate from diseases not epidemic was higher in New Orleans than in any other American city. When the victims of pestilence were also taken into account, the rate was appalling.

Every summer since Moreau's birth a yellow-fever epidemic struck New Orleans, severe in 1829 and 1830, light in 1831. The year the boy was three the summer months passed with less sickness than the city had known since Louisiana became American. But in the first week of September yellow jack returned in violent form. Within a few days an epidemic of unprecedented severity spread to every district of the city. It was believed that the effluvium causing the pestilence might be dispelled by the firing of cannon and the burning of tar. So all over New Orleans great guns boomed day and night, and at every street corner enormous vats of molten tar shot up flames. The autumn remained warm that year. Not until the last week of October could the Board of Health report a decline in the number of deaths.

By this time the people had a new fear to contend with. The newspapers reported that the Asiatic cholera, which within the past two years had ravaged certain cities in Europe, was now in Quebec. The inhabitants of New Orleans were asking one another, " Will our turn also come? " This question was answered sooner than anyone expected.

Before dawn on the morning of October 25 two boatmen, members of the crew of a foreign vessel anchored far out in the Mississippi, brought ashore two of their sick shipmates. The unfortunates were laid on the Levée at the foot of Poydras Street, flat on the cobblestones. While one boatman watched over them, the other went for a doctor. When the physician arrived on the scene, he found a crowd of the curious, who, on their way to work, had stopped to see what the trouble was. After examining the seamen, the doctor spoke two words. The crowd scattered. The words were, " Asiatic cholera! "

At eleven o'clock that morning, at the City Hospital, the two men died. Before the day ended the report of their fate struck terror to the heart of every person then in New Orleans.

The newspapers sold on the streets that evening gave instructions from the Board of Health. Those who might be received in the homes of relatives or friends in the country were permitted to leave provided they could travel by private conveyance. All public transportation—by river steamer, or by stagecoach, or by the railway covering the four and a half miles to Milneburg on Lake Pontchartrain—was declared stopped. No one could hope to find refuge in any neighboring city or town. A quarantine against any person coming from New Orleans would within a day or two be in force in even the hamlets of Louisiana, Mississippi, and Alabama. All houses of business in the city, except shops where medicines and other necessities might be bought, were ordered closed. Those who remained in the city were urged to stay at home and keep all doors and windows shut.

Among the thirty-five thousand thus confined were the Gottschalks of the rue des Remparts. Once a day Mr. Gottschalk braved danger and went to the Canal Street corner for a newspaper, the one means of communication between the health authorities and the people. Through this medium the Gottschalks learned that three days after the importation of the pestilence its victims averaged five hundred in every twenty-four hours. Certain news items seemed almost incredible. At breakfast one morning a family of thirteen gathered at table; at the hour for breakfast the next day not one of the thirteen was alive. A young couple just married succumbed to the choleraic cramps one evening at the same moment, died the next morning at the same moment, and were buried that afternoon in the same tomb at the Protestant Cemetery. The great public need, said the newspapers, was for men to dispose of the dead. On the Levée corpses were piled like cordwood, waiting to be carried out into the river, weighted, and dropped overboard. At each of the cemeteries were more piles of corpses, belonging to families unwilling to see their loved ones committed to the waters. The yellow fever was still at epidemic stage, but the newspapers had little to say of it, so greatly eclipsed it was by the new horror. The workers formerly engaged in firing cannon and keeping the vats of tar in flames were now burying the victims of cholera.

Those who fell from both pestilences during the twelve days between October 26 and November 6 numbered six thousand, a little more than one out of every six who remained in the city. "This," wrote a Protestant minister of New Orleans, the Reverend Theodore Clapp, a friend of Edward Gottschalk, "is the most appalling instance of mortality ever known to have taken place in any city of the world, ancient or modern."

Early on the morning of November 7 a cool wind swept down, ending at last the long-continued heat, drying the air, blowing away the stench of death, and bringing back hope. Three days later the Asiatic cholera vanished with the suddenness with which it had come. Then within a week or two the last case of yellow fever for the year was reported. By the beginning of December life in New Orleans was, to outward appearances, moving in normal manner. The big interest of the people seemed to be the opening of the opera season at the Théâtre d'Orléans.

The two plagues, with all their ravaging, claimed none of the Gottschalks, none of the Bruslés, and none of the intimate friends of Aimée and her husband. It seemed to them therefore an unjust irony that on December 3 apoplexy struck down Monsieur Lislet, who had reached his sixty-sixth year. He died a poor man, said the obituaries; but in his will he left a small legacy to his godson Moreau Gottschalk, now approaching the age of four.

That winter the boy learned the meaning of apprehension. Everybody knew that the cholera would return with hot weather, as in each of the European cities where it had struck. Thousands who had remained in New Orleans the preceding autumn and had come out of the twelve days of horror alive were making plans to leave in the early spring. Again and again Moreau heard his father and mother talk of what course they should follow. Finally they adopted a fatalistic attitude and decided to stay on the rue des Remparts. But their little son sensed the dread that pulled at their hearts.

The dread was increased when, on March 7, Aimée's father, aged sixty-three, died of a lung infection. Moreau at last had the opportunity to march in a funeral procession such as he had often seen crossing the rue des Remparts. Dressed in full mourning, he walked between his father and mother as they followed his grandfather's coffin from the Bruslé house to the Cathedral for the requiem Mass and then to the St. Louis Cemetery for the committal. The experience held no terror for the boy. He had heard too much about death for that.

For the rest of that spring his sad grandmother spent much of her time with the Gottschalks. Many an evening she sat before the fire in the nursery with Thérèse in her lap and Moreau stretched out on the floor at her feet. At the urging of the boy she would tell once more the story of the atrocities suffered by the Bruslés and Deynauds when the black slaves of Haiti rose in rebellion. Much as Moreau loved to listen to the gory account, he never got the details straight. He was to be always confused as to whether it was his great-grandfather Bruslé or his great-grandfather Deynaud who disguised himself as a mulatto witch woman in order to make his way through the black lines and join the French force trying to quell the insurrection. Whichever grandsire it was, he was ultimately shot by the rebels.

Once when Aimée entered the nursery just as her mother was telling of this horror she became hysterical. "Deaths! Deaths!" she cried. "Can't you talk to the children about something else?" Then she covered her face with her hands and walked out of the room sobbing. She knew that she was again pregnant.

She and her husband saw the day when they regretted with all their hearts their decision to remain in New Orleans that summer. By May 8, when Moreau became four, there were cases of yellow fever in the city. By the end of the month the disease had reached epidemic stage. On June 1 a case of cholera was reported. Within a week this graver plague was claiming several hundred lives every day, and the people were again shut in their houses. This time the Gottschalks were not spared. On June 9 little Thérèse fell victim to the cholera, and the next day her body was stacked with dozens of others at the gate of the St. Louis Cemetery to await turn for burial.

The child had scarcely breathed her last when Aimée, who was ending the third month of her new pregnancy, took the disease. In moments of consciousness between seizures of the choleraic cramps her mind was a prayer to Heaven that she might live to bear the child to replace her lost Thérèse. When finally the cramps ceased and her heart was still beating, the physician in attendance, her brother-in-law Dr. Joseph Gottschalk, pronounced her out of danger.

On December 14—weeks after the yellow fever and cholera, with a combined toll of five thousand deaths for 1833, had given way to cool weather—Aimée bore her baby, a girl. The infant was named Célestine.

At the beginning of the spring of 1834, when the people of New Orleans were again apprehensive over a joint return of the two plagues, Mr. Gottschalk made all arrangements for the removal of his family to the country. He explored the coast district east of New Orleans in the state of Mississippi, and in Pass Christian, a settlement made up of a few families of Creoles, found a place to his liking. A house was available, and he rented it and prepared it for occupancy. So on an early April morning in 1834, when Moreau was nearing the age of five, the four Gottschalks and their three slaves boarded the train at the foot of the rue des Champs Elysées. By rail they traveled to Milneburg on Lake Pontchartrain. There they changed to the Mobile mail steamer, and that afternoon arrived in Pass Christian.

The barnlike structure to which the landing pier was attached was a warehouse, general store, and post office, all together in one great room. The only other buildings in the settlement were a Roman Catholic chapel and ten or twelve crude private homes. The existence of Pass Christian at this period depended upon the upcountry farmers, who from time to time came into the settlement in ox-drawn caravans bringing for shipment hides, furs, dressed venison and turkeys, cotton, peanuts, and wild honey. The chapel was of service only on the infrequent occasions when a priest from New Orleans or Mobile landed from a steamer to spend a day and night hearing confessions, celebrating Mass, performing marriage ceremonies, and christening babies. The dwelling houses, all facing the sea, nestled in the forest of pines which extended many miles northward from the shore.

The Gottschalk house, a single floor set on pillars six feet high, was of the simplest construction. There was a wide gallery across the front. Sitting here, facing the stretch of beach which served as the main street of the settlement, one could see the waters of the bay and, far in the distance beyond an island of barren sand, the Gulf of Mexico. If the wind came from the sea, one could hear the rustling of pine branches and the lapping of the little waves of the bay. If it came from the forest, as was usual at night, it brought the perfume of magnolias and the song of mocking birds.

Mr. Gottschalk and Aimée realized that they had come into a paradise. In their first letters to relatives in New Orleans they prophesied that within ten or twelve years Pass Christian would be a favorite watering place for the plantation gentry of Mississippi, Louisiana, and Alabama and for the wealthy merchant families of New Orleans and Mobile.

Mr. Gottschalk was free to enjoy the richness of the natural beauty for no more than a week or two. The afternoon soon came when he said farewell to his wife and children, promised frequent visits, and returned to New Orleans to reassume his duties in the shop on the rue Royale.

With the father of her children back in the city which might on any day be turned again into a city of death and with no one outside her own household to talk to except persons of the most primitive mentality, Aimée found herself anxious and lonely. Mr. Gottschalk, who had been the most tender of husbands since the tragic June of the preceding year, had the forethought to order her piano shipped to Pass Christian. Every time she sat down at the instrument her heart welled with gratitude. For she discovered that singing and playing, far more than any other activity, relieved her mind of dark memories and dread.

Moreau had all his life showed interest in the music she made. At the age of two he patted his hands or kicked his feet or swayed his body to the rhythms. Now she noticed that when she was at the piano he came and stood at her right side. He watched her hands intently as they moved over the keys. Often he brought his head nearer, as if trying the better to hear all the nuances of the melodies. More than once when she was singing he lifted his fine little voice in an accompaniment, always reaching the high notes with true pitch. Then when he went out into the yard to look for Indian arrowheads, he was likely to repeat phrases from her songs all by himself.

Unlike most boys, he never seated himself at the piano to play at playing. He rarely sounded one of the keys. He seemed to look upon the instrument as his mother's sacred property.

Since coming to Pass Christian he had outgrown his old love for playing street vendor and dancing the bamboula. Solving the mysteries of the sea and the forest occupied most of his time. From the hour he got up in the morning till he went to bed at night he pestered his mother and Sally with questions. Several times every day he scanned the shore toward the west to see whether the Indians were coming. Late every spring, he was told, they came to Pass Christian to sell the baskets which they wove with the tough cane and palmetto found only in the Pearl River bottom.

One afternoon his mother spent an hour or two at the piano practicing an air from Meyerbeer's *Robert le diable*, an opera which had been the rage of Paris for the past three years but had not yet been heard in New Orleans. As usual Moreau was at her side. When she grew tired she went into the room adjoining the parlor to do some mending and left the boy to wander about as he pleased. She had been at her sewing perhaps ten minutes when she heard the piano. Someone was playing the air from *Robert le diable*—playing it fluently, expressively, and in exactly the tempo in which she had sung it. She dropped her sewing in fright. Besides herself there was no one within forty miles of Pass Christian who could do that. Had some friend from New Orleans come to surprise her? Or was she the victim of some grave aural disorder? Mystified, trembling all over, she went to the parlor door. Her eyes had to be trusted: the performer was Moreau.

He was standing at the keyboard, playing with his right hand. When he ended the melody and saw that his mother was watching, he said in a very matter-of-fact way, " I believe I can play another one." The tune this time was " Hail Columbia." He had gone through no more than the first few bars when Sally came in. Seeing at a glance what was taking place, she threw up her hands in terror. Then she dashed out toward the kitchen, and in a few seconds was back with the cook and the housemaid. The three slaves stood directly behind the boy, holding themselves close together. As the marching tune moved on, they began to shrug their shoulders to the rhythm. All the while the wonder in their eyes grew, and at the sounding of the last note they whispered as with one voice, " Zombie! " Aimée at the moment was ready to agree that only a supernatural force could have been responsible for what she had just heard and seen.

After Moreau played a dozen more of her songs, she and the slave women realized that this was simply one more evidence of the extraordinary precocity he had been manifesting all his life. But his mother soon noticed that he showed more pride in his ability to play tunes on the piano than in anything else he had ever done. He could hardly wait to perform for his father, who was coming on Friday. "When the Indians come I'll play for them too," he said.

Though the awaited Friday brought the Indians as well as Mr. Gottschalk, it was a day of disappointment for Moreau. When, in his best form, he played "Robin Adair" for his father, he was not told that he was a bright boy. Mr. Gottschalk merely said, "I suppose you're good enough to play for the redskins." When the Indians arrived, they were not a whole tribe, but only a dozen men. They were in neither war paint nor feathers; they were in nothing except cottonade breeches. Instead of dashing along the shore whooping and yelling, they trudged in slowly and silently, as if they were exhausted from their all-day walk. They could scarcely be seen for the stacks of baskets they carried—baskets of all sizes, on their heads, on long poles fastened horizontally to their shoulders, and in their hands.

They stopped and put down their burdens at the steps of the Gottschalk gallery, where the whole household was assembled to see them. The leader, who could speak a little English, said, pointing to himself, "Me, Sky Blue." Then, holding up in turn a basket of each size, beginning with the biggest, he gave the prices, which ranged from four bits to a picayune. Mr. Gottschalk bought several, and then invited Sky Blue to come into the house with his men.

The Indians, moving in their bare feet as noiselessly as cats, filed into the parlor. As Mr. Gottschalk led Moreau to the piano, Sky Blue looked at it in wonder and said, "Big box."

"A big box full of sweet sounds," said Mr. Gottschalk, motioning Moreau to play.

The boy, who had decided that after all the Indians were wonderful, dashed off in fast tempo "Hail Columbia." But at the end he got no applause except grunts of approval from the slave women. The faces of the Indians remained as expressionless as the pine boards of the wall.

Then Sky Blue, without speaking a word, stepped up to Moreau, bent down, and, feeling and pressing, gave the boy's muscles from the calves of the legs to the tips of the fingers a thorough examination. Evidently satisfied with his findings, he rudely pushed Moreau aside, and, standing before the keyboard, held out his arms so that everybody could see the might of his muscles. Then, with all his strength, he struck the keys with his right fist, again and again, from the low bass to the high treble. At the volume of sound he produced the other Indians burst into an uproar of laughter that could only be interpreted as triumphant. Above the din their leader shouted, "Boy, little pale face, make little noise. Sky Blue, big Indian, make big noise." Then, like victors walking from a field of battle, Sky Blue and his men, again burdened with their baskets, made their way into the forest to set up a temporary camp.

For most of their sales they depended upon passengers on the steamers that called at Pass Christian. Since a steamer rarely remained tied up at the landing for more than a few minutes, the Indians had little time to hawk their goods. The middle of autumn arrived and found them still in Pass Christian with a number of unsold baskets on their hands.

Though Sky Blue did not again extract a big noise from the big box, he became very friendly with the Gottschalks, indeed too friendly. He turned up for a visit nearly every day, and felt free to wander over the house as if he were a member of the family. One morning he happened into the kitchen, where Aimée, sleeves rolled up, was preparing a sweet for dinner. He liked the appearance of her arms, and decided to examine the muscles, as he had once examined Moreau's. When Aimée saw him coming toward her with his hands extended to do the feeling and pressing, she began to scream. The cook rushed in, grabbed a poker from the fireplace, and drove Sky Blue off the premises.

This experience convinced Aimée that there were more terrors for her in Pass Christian than there could possibly be in New Orleans. The Asiatic cholera had departed, and was now doing its ravaging in Mexico and Central America. The yellow fever the past summer had never once approached epidemic stage. That afternoon Aimée, the children, and the slaves, all with light hearts, left on the New Orleans steamer for the return to the rue des Remparts. The piano, on which Moreau had learned to use his left hand and make harmonies for his melodies, followed a day or two later.

What to do about his interest in music was the first problem the parents turned to after their life slipped back into the old routine. He must have lessons, they agreed. Then they tried to decide upon the right teacher. As they considered this one and that out of the large company of musicians which the Théâtre d'Orléans had attracted to New Orleans, they found themselves repeatedly coming back to François Letellier, the organist and choir master at the St. Louis Cathedral. He was reputed to be eccentric as a man and revolutionary as a pedagogue, but everybody talked about his great success in bringing out the best that was in a child. It was upon him that the choice finally fell.

He came from Paris the winter following Moreau's birth. His wife arrived on a later ship, bringing their two children. For five years now he had made occasional appearances in minor bass roles at the Théâtre d'Orléans, directed the music at the Cathedral, and given lessons in singing and in piano and organ playing to an ever-expanding number of pupils. He turned out musicians, it was said, not mere performers of a few pieces. His wife, also a singer and a pianist, assisted him in teaching; and it was usually to her that he entrusted a young beginner.

But when at Mr. Gottschalk's invitation he came to the rue des Remparts and heard Moreau play, he said without deliberating, " I myself will teach him." Then, in his blunt fashion, he stated his credo as a pedagogue. He believed in solfège, right at the beginning of the study of music and for a long, long time thereafter. The ability to sing perfectly a printed melody at sight should, he said, be every pupil's first great goal. He believed that the education of children of musical promise should be through the study of music alone. To keep such little ones penned in a schoolroom for hours every day was, he affirmed, a crime against nature. In learning how to read notes they learned incidentally how to read words, and in mastering numbers one year of solfège was worth five years of memorizing multiplication tables. The Greeks, the most cultivated of all peoples, got their education by studying the principles of rhythm, melody, and harmony. Why not the Americans? He believed in enjoying music. Gifted children, he said, should be encouraged to play by ear as much as they liked and on any instrument that pleased them. Finally, he believed in punctuality. "I shall be here every afternoon except Sunday at four o'clock," he said, "and I shall expect to find Moreau waiting for me." Then, as he threw his long sweeping black cape over his shoulders and picked up his big black hat, he added, "You must keep this piano well tuned."

Monsieur Letellier was as homely as he was brusque. His extreme height and his angularity made him seem to be all arms and legs. His hair was always tousled, and he wore a perpetual scowl. Though he was under forty, he talked and sang with an old voice. New Orleans, remembering Beaumarchais, had nicknamed him Don Bazile. Nevertheless New Orleans held him in high esteem.

In spite of his unattractiveness he fascinated children. After three or four lessons Moreau Gottschalk was in love with him. The boy found his music lessons far more exciting than his games. He looked forward all day to four o'clock in the afternoon, when, fair weather or foul, he heard Monsieur Letellier's vigorous knock at the front door.

Sometimes when he had done especially well at a lesson he was rewarded with the privilege of going to the Cathedral to hear the choir rehearse. Monsieur Letellier would help the boy into his scarlet woolen overclothes, perch him on a shoulder, and, stepping in great strides over the muddy plank sidewalks, carry him all the way to the Cathedral door. Neighbors, looking out their windows and seeing the two pass, began to say, "That little Gottschalk boy is getting to be as serious as old Don Bazile himself."

But there were hours when Moreau was far from serious. He was still a little boy on those evenings when his grandmother came to spend the night. Holding Célestine in her lap as she had once held Thérèse, she would sit before the fire in the nursery, with Moreau once more stretched out on the floor at her feet. Again at his insistence she would tell the story of the insurrection of the blacks on the island of Haiti.

When the narrative was well under way, Sally would come in, bringing an apronful of yams. She would place them on the hearth one by one, shovel hot ashes over them, and then settle down on a stool to listen while she waited for them to roast. When finally the grandmother would end her story with the account of her flight to Jamaica, Sally, always wearing her blue calico head scarf, would follow with a hundredth telling of her tales of the clown Compé Bouqui and the knave Compé Lapin. Sometimes in the middle of a sentence she would stop, shake her finger at the portrait of Napoleon above the mantel, and mutter an incantation. "That man's eyes are trying to bewitch me," she would say. "They follow me about this room when I dust." Then, sitting up straight and looking angry, she would make the sign of the cross, spit in the fire, and say, "But they're casting no spell on me!" Her face again calm, she would take up her tale where she had left off.

When she had told all the stories she knew, she would carefully turn the yams. It was then that Moreau would look up to his grandmother and ask about Bras Coupé, the big-voiced gigantic African whom he had heard on hundreds of Saturdays shouting "Dansez bamboula!" while leading slaves in their revels on the Place Congo. Madame Bruslé would then repeat a tale which was being told in one form or another throughout Louisiana.

No, Bras Coupé wasn't the kind of Negro to remain the property of the New Orleans doctor who paid two thousand dollars for him in the St. Louis Hotel slave market. One Saturday afternoon, after shouting himself hoarse on the Place Congo, Bras Coupé made his break for freedom, and he didn't stop until he was in the swamps of the Bayou Sarah country. He was still there, living a charmed life, fattening himself on the flesh of the men sent to capture him. Every day he rubbed his skin with an herb which made it so hard that no bullet, however powerful, could penetrate it. A rifle ball on hitting it would flatten and drop at his feet. All he had to do to kill a man was to look at him straight. A detachment of troops was sent into the Bayou Sarah swamps to get him, dead or alive. The soldiers never came back, and not a trace of a single one of them was ever found. Bras Coupé of course had got them under the control of his spells and then had devoured every last one of them, bones and all. God only knew what other depredations he'd work before he was captured and brought to the justice of a hangman's rope.

As Moreau listened to the cannibalistic details in this story and realized that Bras Coupé was still alive, he would press close against his grandmother's knees. But when she finished he was never too frightened to ask about the secret of Madame Lalaurie. At the mere mention of this name Sally would cross herself and Madame Bruslé would say, "That story is not for a little boy's ears."

Though Moreau knew that his father was one of the men who discovered what a terrible woman Madame Lalaurie was, the boy was unable to get any of his elders to tell him her secret. He had at least learned that she bought slaves for no other purpose than to torture them to death up in the attic of her mansion on the rue St. Philippe and that she always buried their bodies under the flagstones of her patio. Moreau's father and the men with him found out what was going on in the mansion the afternoon it came near burning down, just a few days before the departure of the Gottschalks for Pass Christian. Madame Lalaurie and her handsome mulatto coachman got away to no one knew where, but hangdog Monsieur Lalaurie was still in New Orleans, living in a cheap boardinghouse.

The fire-damaged mansion on the rue St. Philippe was deserted —except by the ghosts. Moreau had heard a lot about them. Sally had seen a skeleton hand trying to unlock the front door. She had also seen eyes without sockets or sockets without eyes, she couldn't tell which, peering out of one of the upstairs windows. While passing the mansion one Saturday afternoon when there was dancing on the Place Congo she heard a great clacking and clattering within the patio walls. Her explanation was that the skeletons of the murdered slaves buried there heard the call of the drums and rose from their graves to dance the bamboula.

After a year of Monsieur Letellier's guidance, Moreau no longer depended upon his grandmother and Sally for stories. He found them in books and newspapers and read them to himself, in French or English. Neither he nor anyone else was ever able to recall just how or precisely when he took the step from reading musical notes to reading words in two languages. It was obvious that there was justification for Monsieur Letellier's belief in education through music.

Moreau's skill in solfège after a single year of instruction was such that he could sing at sight, with true pitch and in exact tempo, any melody in his mother's store of music. And without a second glance at the printed notes he could play the melody on the piano and improvise a pleasing harmony.

In his second year of lessons solfège continued to be the subject of first importance. But by the time this year was ended he was able also to read at sight simple compositions on either the piano or organ.

He had not quite reached the end of this second twelve months under Monsieur Letellier when he accomplished a feat which gave his father and mother a foretaste of fame in the family. The day was Sunday, November 7, 1836, when Moreau was just seven and a half. He was in the Cathedral, with his grandmother Bruslé, waiting for the celebration of high Mass. To his surprise an usher came and told him that Monsieur Letellier wished to see him at once in the choir loft. As he approached the organ, he found his teacher scowling more menacingly than ever. " I've just received word," he said, "that my bass soloist can't be here today. I've got to take his place, and you've got to take mine. Now sit down and play this Mass, and see that you make no mistakes. I'll be standing beside you to manipulate the pedals." Moreau carried out this command so creditably that of the great congregation in the Cathedral that morning only the few in the choir loft knew that Monsieur Letellier was not as usual at the organ. The story of the impromptu performance was told in hundreds of homes in New Orleans. The press reported it as an accomplishment the like of which had never before been known in the New World.

Mr. Gottschalk was very proud of his son and happy over the public acclaim. His heart beat all the faster when on a crowded street he heard someone call out, " There goes the father of that little seven-year-old organist! "

But he attached little real significance to the matter. He still gave no thought to the possibility that Moreau might grow up to be a professional musician. The boy's enthusiasm for music was doubtless no more than a childhood passion that would soon give way to some altogether different interest, and his devotion to Monsieur Letellier merely indicated an affectionate disposition.

Mr. Gottschalk dreamed that his son would one day succeed to the enterprise he was establishing. It was already on solid ground, and if the good luck of the past two years continued it would be a big business. He had withdrawn from Gottschalk, Reimers & Co., and was an independent broker with an office in the American faubourg, on Camp Street. His clients, daily growing in number, included Europeans with large holdings in New Orleans and several of the richest men in the South, sugar planters in Louisiana and cotton planters in Mississippi. In New Orleans financial circles the name Edward Gottschalk had come to stand for steadiness, foresight, and reliability.

Aimée was too engrossed in the excitement and anxiety of having another baby to exult in expected fashion over the "fame" which had come to the family. The infant, a boy, was born on the very day Célestine became three, December 14. He was named after his father.

On a Sunday evening a few months later Moreau, in the company of his parents, heard his first opera. It was given in the magnificent new St. Charles Theatre, which had been built by the Americans of the American faubourg to offset the Théâtre d'Orléans of the Creoles, as the St. Charles Hotel and Dr. Clapp's Community Church had been erected to offset, respectively, the St. Louis Hotel and the St. Louis Cathedral. The work performed that night was Italian, Bellini's *Il Pirata*; and all the singers were Italian, singing in their own language. It was a gala evening. But the grandeur and splendor which impressed most of the hundreds who were present escaped Moreau. He was so captivated by Bellini's music that he had little idea of the story acted out on the stage. Most of the time he sat back in his seat with drooping head. His parents felt that they had been foolish to bring him.

When the final curtain went down, he showed great impatience to get home. Once there he dashed to the piano and began playing *Il Pirata* melodies. Those he liked especially he repeated over and over. He would have gone on till morning if his father had not sent him to bed. For he had with a single hearing learned by heart all the more striking airs of the opera.

When in Moreau's presence Monsieur Letellier was told of this achievement, he held back all compliments. There was no indication on his face that he was in any way impressed. But when later he was alone for a few moments with Mr. Gottschalk tears came into his eyes as he said, " I'm almost convinced, Monsieur, that the boy has genius."

Henceforth the music master included attendance at opera in his plans for Moreau's education. Before the Italian troupe left the St. Charles Theatre the boy was familiar with Bellini's *Norma*, Rossini's *Semiramide*, and Donizetti's *Lucrezia Borgia*. At the Théâtre d'Orléans he heard *Robert le diable*. " This beautiful creation of Meyerbeer's," he was to say, " colored my whole childhood." He was to retain in his memory the entire score, as he was to retain every note of another great favorite, *Norma*.

Mr. Gottschalk realized that these manifestations of a prodigious memory were more significant than the organ playing at the Cathedral. The image of tears trickling down Monsieur Letellier's sunken cheeks haunted him. If his son was blessed with a gift that might in time make him great, the father preferred—for no reason he could explain—to see him a violinist. So, after consulting with Monsieur Letellier and getting his advice and aid, he went home one evening with the best and most expensive violin obtainable in New Orleans.

Moreau was greatly excited over the novelty. Depending upon his well-trained ear, he tuned it with the piano. Then, to the accompaniment of chords improvised by his mother, he tried out the instrument. Mr. Gottschalk at least recognized that the melody Moreau was struggling to produce was "Hail Columbia." The boy, biting his tongue as he flatted and sharped, fought on to the end. Then, breaking into sobs, he angrily tossed violin and bow on the sofa.

Monsieur Letellier showed no surprise on hearing of this outburst. He merely announced that the next morning at eleven Monsieur Miolan, the new concertmaster of the Théâtre d'Orléans orchestra, would come to give Moreau the first of his violin lessons.

Félix Miolan, a Parisian, was perhaps the most finished violinist who had as yet played in America. He had been trained at the Conservatoire Royal, where his father was professor of the oboe. He was handsome, gay, and very friendly. In his middle twenties, he was still a boy in temperament. Music, he said, was his soul's lifeblood. No one in the Miolan family had ever thought of not being a musician. His brother, Alexandre, was well on the way toward becoming one of the celebrated organists of the nineteenth century. There was a sister, named Marie, at whose christening Félix had stood as godfather. Though she was only two years older than Moreau, she had full control of the exquisite voice God had given her and could sing with the naturalness of a mocking bird. She was to become the great Madame Miolan-Carvalho, rated by certain critics as the most gifted of all French singing actresses.

Moreau was much more interested in Félix than in the violin. The relation between the two quickly became that of good fellows. Indeed, it soon developed that instead of mastering the technic of the bow Moreau was spending entire lesson hours at the piano playing accompaniments for Félix. Monsieur Letellier sensed what was going on and brought to bear his scowling influence. It was difficult to determine which of the two good fellows feared Don Bazile the more. Thereafter Moreau actually made progress in fiddling.

But it was still the sturdy knock on the front door at four in the afternoon which made his heart leap. Don Bazile's lessons, now mainly in piano technic, never ceased to be exciting.

Not even the trials of the summer of 1837 interrupted them.

A great financial panic was sweeping the country and every day Mr. Gottschalk came home from his office with a more worried look on his face. Aimée was fretting over the coming of a new baby, much too soon after the birth of little Edward. Again cannon boomed night and day throughout New Orleans, and again at every street corner vats of burning tar shot up flames. The city was once more suffering a violent epidemic of yellow fever. The Gottschalks believed that they were immune to the disease. But when, in August, it claimed Dr. Joseph Gottschalk, they were terrified lest it strike next in their own household.

The anxiety in the home on the rue des Remparts was not lifted until after October 4, when the new baby was born—another girl, named Clara after the wife of one of the living Gottschalk uncles. Less than ten months separated this new member of the family from her brother Edward. By the time of her birth Mr. Gottschalk knew the panic was not going to force him out of business; moreover, by this time yellow jack had ceased to be a grave threat.

But before 1837 was ended Moreau's parents went through one more upsetting experience—that of moving. After Dr. Gottschalk's death his widow offered his house on the rue Conti for sale and Edward Gottschalk bought it. The location was the most fashionable in the French quarter, near Canal Street and the Levée. Mr. Gottschalk could step from the front door and walk to his office on Camp Street in three minutes. The house, of the prevailing stucco-covered brick, had no galleries. But there was a patio, planted with camellias, Cape jasmines, roses, and an unfamiliar tree, which, according to Sally, was a deadly manchineel, sure to kill anybody who got under its shadow unless he remembered to cross himself. The quarters for the slaves were in a detached building at the back. Here also were the kitchen, carriage house, and stables.

The year 1838 was well begun before Moreau felt at home on the rue Conti. Then, prodded unceasingly by Félix as well as by Don Bazile, he was conscious of little besides music, every day more music.

By the spring of 1839 he could at least play a melody on the violin without feeling he had committed an act of desecration. Monsieur Letellier, who had all along looked upon Miolan's training as a discipline, was at last convinced that the boy had enough of it. When the master came one afternoon to give a piano lesson, he pointed to the violin and said, "Tell your father to sell it or give it away."

So ended Moreau's career as a violinist. Henceforth he as well as Monsieur Letellier was to take it for granted that the piano was his one and only instrument.

Giving up the violin meant that he and Félix no longer saw so much of one another. But the two good fellows remained the best of friends. In the spring, at a concert given in the St. Louis Hotel ballroom by several of the leading artists of the Théâtre d'Orléans, Félix had the boy play the piano accompaniments for his violin numbers.

The evening was a triumph for Moreau. The "little seven-year-old organist" became the "nine-year-old wonder pianist." Again Mr. Gottschalk was very proud; and Aimée, not pregnant this time, gloried in observing the attention directed to Moreau as he walked beside her on their airings.

Among the admirers he won on the night of the concert was Madame Jeanne Boyer, a personage in both the French quarter and the American faubourg. While Monsieur Boyer was respected as owner and director of the academy to which the richest men in the city sent their sons, Madame was recognized as the only proper piano teacher for their daughters. In a position to be highly independent, she gave no lessons outside her mansion on the rue St. Pierre. Her neighbors, making fun of her great size, said she never taught duets because when she and a square piano were in the little downstairs studio there was no room left for more than one girl. The Théâtre d'Orléans artists, whose morals were, to her, always in question, had no respect for her equipment as a musician. But they envied her fees and admired her resourcefulness. She was always on the lookout, they said, for a favor and never failed to find some artist to grant it. When she heard Moreau play Félix Miolan's accompaniments and realized the appeal of the boy's stage presence, she suddenly knew that this prodigy was the one who was going to put new life into her Sunday evening musicales.

These monthly soirées in her home every year from late autumn to late spring were an institution in New Orleans. Social climbers resorted to every sort of means to obtain invitations. The great lady had ways of getting acquainted with the musicians who came to the city, and all of any consequence were to be heard at one time or another in her drawing room. Always present on these occasions were Madame's older pupils, stiff in satin, taffeta, and brocade. With them were their mamans and papas. In a gown of purple or black or gray, with a tiara sparkling among her rich auburn curls, Madame, huge yet graceful, moved regally among her protegées, guarding them from introductions to artists with a reputation for bohemianism.

Moreau first played at Madame Boyer's in the autumn of 1839. Accepted at once as a favorite, he appeared there one month after another, as soloist, in violin and piano duos with Félix, as accompanist for singers, and as pianist in ensembles. Madame's lovely pupils heard the ten-year-old lad race at sight through pieces they had struggled over for years. Those whose hearts he won at Madame Boyer's, as much by his personal charm as by his playing, included musicians of the first rank.

One of these was Mademoiselle Julie Calvé, regarded by the majority of the critics as the most accomplished soprano who had ever appeared on the Théâtre d'Orléans stage. She was a superb actress as well as a magnificent singer, and " Calvé nights " were always sold out days in advance. To the friends who claimed that if she would return to Paris and make a single appearance she could have all Europe at her feet she invariably said, " Paris didn't like me when I was younger, and now I don't like Paris. It's New Orleans that pleases me." When Moreau played, she always sat where she could face him. She was the first to prophesy that his drooping eyelids would one day drive women to distraction.

Another notable musician whom the boy deeply impressed was Eugène Prévost, a new conductor at the Théâtre d'Orléans. He had studied composition at the Conservatoire Royal, had won the Prix de Rome, had seen several of his one-act comic operas produced in France, and was now giving every spare moment to completing a grand opera, based on Victor Hugo's admirable libretto, *La Esmeralda*. New Orleans pleased Monsieur Prévost also, and, except for the period of the Civil War, was to remain his home for the rest of his life. He urged Moreau to develop his talent for improvising, and was no doubt a force in making the boy ambitious to become a composer.

A third highly cultivated musician who frequented Madame Boyer's soirées never heard Moreau play without shedding tears. He was Jean-Baptiste Guiraud, a violinist in the Théâtre d'Orléans orchestra. He too had been a child prodigy, a student of composition in the Conservatoire Royal at thirteen and a winner of the Prix de Rome at fourteen. Destiny denied him Monsieur Prévost's luck: not one of the operas he wrote while in Italy was ever produced. Disappointed and in poverty, he took advantage of the opportunity to come to New Orleans, where he also was to stay. He lived only, it appeared, to realize his dreams of musical distinction in his son Ernest, two years old in 1839. In training this son—who was to be a professor of composition in the Paris Conservatoire and number among his pupils Claude Debussy—the father was to follow the pattern set by Moreau Gottschalk.

Early one afternoon near the end of the year 1840 Monsieur Letellier called on Mr. Gottschalk in his Camp Street office. As usual the music master was brusque and brief. "I've come to tell you, Monsieur," he said, "that Moreau has arrived at that stage where he knows more about piano playing than I or anyone else in New Orleans." He then named the musicians who had heard Moreau play and had learned to know him personally. "It's the opinion of each of them," he said, "that the boy has the genius to rise to the level of the greatest piano virtuosos of our time." He went on to mention the opportunities for musical study in Boston, New York, Havana, and other New World cities and proved to Mr. Gottschalk's satisfaction that if Moreau could not obtain the training necessary for virtuosity in New Orleans he must go to Europe for it. "In Paris he can get it," said the music master, "and in Paris he can be made to feel at home. I, speaking as his teacher, urge that you send him there,

Monsieur Gottschalk, and that you do so as soon as possible. The older he becomes the more difficult it will be for him to learn how to control the delicate muscles the piano virtuoso must bring into action."

That evening Mr. Gottschalk reported to his wife every word Monsieur Letellier had spoken. There was another baby by this time, a daughter named Augusta, born the preceding April 4. Aimée, worn by frequent pregnancies, looked tired and old. As she listened to her husband, tears streamed from her eyes. When he had told all, she said, with difficulty, "Of course we must send him to Paris. But how are we ever going to endure the ordeal of seeing him leave?"

M_r. Gottschalk was far from ready to say with his wife, " Of course we must send him to Paris." Their elder son's leaving home at the age of eleven to go to a foreign city four thousand miles away was a matter that demanded the most serious consideration.

It had long been the custom in New Orleans for Creole gentlemen to send their sons to Europe to be educated. Mr. Gottschalk sought out many fathers who had followed the custom and questioned them at great length. They assured him that there were pensions in Paris where the supervision of a boy's physical, mental, and moral well-being was in all respects expert. Mr. Gottschalk also consulted sons who had recently returned from years of schooling in France. They confirmed the opinions of their fathers and spoke of pensions where students of music were always to be found.

Mr. Gottschalk then had several long talks with Monsieur and Madame Boyer. While they admitted that Moreau was very young, they pointed out that he had the mentality of a highly intelligent youth of eighteen. Nothing, they argued, could be better for strengthening his body than the drill in swordsmanship and horsemanship which the better Parisian pensions sponsored. Both declared that Mr. Gottschalk would be denying himself a privilege granted by destiny to not more than one father out of many millions if he refused to give Moreau the chance for full musical development.

Nevertheless, three months passed before Mr. Gottschalk made up his mind. It was already February when he met Monsieur Letellier on the street one afternoon and said, " I've decided that Moreau is going to Paris." The music master, elated at the news, proposed to arrange a farewell benefit concert for the boy, a big concert. Mr. Gottschalk told him to make it as big as he liked.

That evening Mr. Gottschalk announced his decision to his wife. As he spoke of his letters of inquiry to proprietors of pensions in Paris, she kept repeating, in a trembling voice, "We'll be so proud of him!" But before he finished telling of the preparations that must be completed in order to have Moreau in Paris by autumn she was so overcome by tears that she was unable to listen.

It was like that every time her husband attempted to discuss the subject of Moreau's departure. The boy, practicing five or six hours every day for his benefit concert, dreaming of the ocean voyage and the wonders of Paris, also found it impossible to speak with his mother about leaving.

But her reaction to a sensational event of that spring led her husband to hope that after all she would not make it too difficult for him to follow what he clearly saw as his path of duty. The event was the appearance in New Orleans of the world-renowned dancer Fanny Elssler.

On the evening of March 6, 1841, Mr. Gottschalk, his wife, and Moreau were at the St. Charles Theatre for Fräulein Elssler's New Orleans début. The ballet was *La Sylphide*. At the announcement in France that the beloved dancer was on the eve of an American tour the Paris *Charivari* had said: "We warn these molasses Yankees, these money-making, law-breaking, julep-drinking, negro-selling Yankees, these savages, these trans-Atlantic Arabs, these coarse, ill-mannered, thick-headed, bad-hearted descendants of renegades and rebels, never to think of admiring the charming Fanny on pain of the lasting displeasure and instant resentment of all France." To this name-calling the New Orleans *Picayune* had replied: "Now, we tell these snuff-taking, shoulder-shrugging, frog-eating Frenchmen, these self-conceited Messieurs les Asses-of-de-Jack, these dandy soap-locks, these nondescripts with invisible horns, these long-bearded, these parchment-faced Parisian noodles, that the trans-Atlantic Arabs care about as much for the charming Fanny as they do about the lasting displeasure and instant resentment of all France." The *Picayune* was wrong.

On the evening of March 6, 1841, the charming Fanny was given such an ovation as New Orleans had never before accorded an artist.

In the immense audience, clapping and shouting with an enthusiasm gone wild, no one was more ecstatic than Aimée Gottschalk. As Fräulein Elssler bowed to the applause, time and time again, Aimée did not see the dancer on the stage: she saw Moreau, grown to manhood, as graceful as the charming Fanny and far more beautiful. Within just a few years, his mother was sure, he too would stand on many a stage like this and acknowledge the plaudits of the thousands whom his playing had stirred to frenzy.

At home that night she talked calmly and freely with her husband about Moreau's studying in Paris and insisted that they hurry the arrangements for his departure. Mr. Gottschalk, to sustain her courage, saw to it that she was present at most of Fräulein Elssler's many performances.

Early in April an advertisement appeared in each of the New Orleans newspapers. The heading ran: "Farewell concert for the benefit of Master Moreau Gottschalk, eleven years old, a pupil of Monsieur Letellier of this city, prior to his leaving for France to perfect himself under the great masters."

The date was changed twice to avoid conflict with Fräulein Elssler, who was dancing four or five times a week at either the St. Charles or the Théâtre d'Orléans. But finally, on Friday evening, April 21, at seven o'clock, in the ballroom of the St. Louis Hotel, Moreau's benefit was given.

Monsieur Letellier had indeed arranged a big affair. Besides Moreau, the soloists included Mademoiselle Calvé, Félix Miolan, a tenor, a baritone, an oboist, and a trumpeter—all from the Théâtre d'Orléans, whose orchestra, under the direction of Monsieur Prévost, also took part. Moreau's two independent numbers were specimens of the piano music then fashionable: Madame Farrenc's variations on a cavatina from Donizetti's *Anna Bolena* and Henri Herz's transcription of a chorus from Meyerbeer's *Il Crociata*. Moreau also played with Félix a duo by de Beriot and the accompaniments for the songs sung by the baritone.

The ballroom was filled. The applause, said *L'Abeille*, was equally enthusiastic from the lovers of music who came to enjoy themselves and from the professional musicians who were present to see what the prodigy had to offer. For Moreau there were many bouquets, all of which, to the delight of the audience, he placed with his own hands in the box occupied by his father and mother.

A woman who heard Moreau play that night was to say many years later: "He was very small for an eleven-year-old, and showed that he had never lived the rough-and-tumble life of boys. When he played a slow passage, he seemed to give to each note a portion of his little body, and I found myself fearing that there would be nothing left by the time he got to the end of it. But after each andante there was a presto, which sounded like a hundred happy little feet scampering up and down a broad marble staircase."

The critic of the *Courier de la Louisiane*, after praising highly Moreau's technic and interpretation, wrote: "Young Gottschalk is the first Creole ever to commit himself to a piano virtuoso's career." The critic might have said with accuracy "the first American."

Not even Monsieur Letellier rejoiced over the success of the concert as did Aimée. But with time the excitement waned. Then Fräulein Elssler gave her farewell performance and departed. June came, bringing, as always, the possibility of the return of yellow jack. The spirits in the Gottschalk home dropped low; and one morning, once more in tears, Aimée said to her husband, "To see Moreau leave for Paris will surely kill me." Anticipating this change of attitude, Mr. Gottschalk had made up his mind that he and Monsieur Letellier would work out their plans for Moreau in secret. Aimée was left to weep alone that morning. Then at dinner in the patio that afternoon, when the whole family was gathered at table and the three slaves hovered near, Mr. Gottschalk laid down a law: thereafter in his household, he said, the topic of Moreau's leaving home was not even to be mentioned.

The boy, past twelve now, felt little disappointment. Confident that his father was not going to let him down, he continued dreaming his dreams of Paris and engaged in his usual activities.

Monsieur Letellier still came every afternoon to guide, he said, the playing of a pianist to whom he had taught all he knew. Moreau spent several hours every week playing accompaniments for Félix. On several occasions he substituted for Monsieur Letellier at the Cathedral organ. When he was not occupied with music he was more than likely to be reading. His uncle Gaston Bruslé, who ran a circulating library in connection with his bookshop, could have spoken of the boy's great interest in Ossian, Scott, Châteaubriand, Byron, and Victor Hugo and of his search for every periodical in which there might be a tale by his favorite of favorites, Edgar Allan Poe.

Fate, it seems, was on Moreau's side and had decreed that during this period when he was marking time musically he should profit from the most brilliant musical season New Orleans had ever known, the season which began in the autumn of 1841. A keen rivalry developed between a troupe of Italians singing at the St. Charles Theatre and the regular French company at the Théâtre d'Orléans. The result was that each house presented performances of unprecedented excellence. The Théâtre d'Orléans appears to have come out the winner. In that house in December the music lovers of New Orleans were introduced to a work which for years to come they were to rank above all other operas, Meyerbeer's *Les Huguenots*. At the same house early in 1842 came a musical event never before experienced in New Orleans, the world première of an important opera, Monsieur Prévost's *La Esmeralda*.

But the most memorable event in the musical history of New Orleans that season—the event which stands as a landmark in the story of Moreau Gottschalk's development—was the coming of William Vincent Wallace. He arrived on New Year's Day on a small sailing vessel, which he had boarded at Vera Cruz. He landed with a violin and little else. There was not a person in New Orleans whose name he knew, and not one had ever heard of him.

He spent the night in a cheap hotel in the American faubourg. The next morning he chanced to see in a newspaper the announcement of a concert of sacred music to be given that evening at

Dr. Clapp's church. An hour before the time for the concert to begin he was at the church with his violin. He introduced himself to the choir director, played for him on both the violin and piano, and asked permission to appear in just one short number on each instrument at the end of the scheduled program. The choir director, almost overcome by the stranger's virtuosity whether as pianist or violinist, unhesitatingly granted the request. The audience that night had no notion of leaving after hearing the unexpected artist in two short numbers. Mr. Wallace, now at the piano and now with his violin, was called back again and again, each time to play one of his own compositions. The next day all New Orleans was talking about the magic of " the vagabond Irish music-maker."

Moreau was introduced to him the following Sunday night at Madame Boyer's. The boy expected to see someone resembling one of Ossian's bards. Instead he met a gentleman, correctly groomed. Mr. Wallace played that night three violin pieces he had just composed, with Moreau, reading at sight from manuscript, accompanying him. The visitor next improvised on the piano, developing themes suggested by his audience. He then sang, to his own accompaniment, half a dozen songs for which he had written both words and music. Long before the last one ended, half the group in the drawing room were in tears. This man, thought Moreau, embodied melody. No one like him, the boy was sure, had ever before been heard in America. His music was altogether different from the French and Italian music with which New Orleans was familiar. His tunes captured the listener's heart and held it. As Moreau watched him play and sing, he suddenly recalled the story of the pact between Paganini and the Devil. It appeared that there was also a pact between Mr. Wallace and some supernatural creature. But it could not be a creature out of Hell, reasoned the boy. Years later he was to say, " I actually found myself looking sharp, half expecting to see the tips of two folded white wings protruding below Mr. Wallace's long black coat."

The extraordinary personal history of the Irish musician was already known to most of those present at Madame Boyer's. He was twenty-nine. His father, a bandmaster, taught him how to sing and how to play the piano. At fifteen he was conductor of the orchestra in the leading theatre in Dublin. At eighteen he heard Paganini, and was so affected that he at once began to study the violin. Three years later he played with full orchestra his own violin concerto at a grand music festival in Dublin. That same year he married, and, desirous of adventure, went to Australia with his bride. There, trying to break away from the spell of the violin and piano, he settled on a farm and raised sheep. But the urge to make music was too compelling. To his wife, who refused to leave the farm, he gave his last shilling, and then took to the open sea. By way of Tahiti and other islands of the South Pacific he reached Chile. From there he made his way northward, giving concerts in one Latin American coastal city after another. On the last day of the year 1841 he reached the mouth of the Mississippi. He would not remain long in New Orleans; Dublin was his destination.

Scarcely a week passed during that winter and spring when the visitor did not make three or four public appearances. He played in theatres, ballrooms, lodge halls, and churches, on both the violin and piano, and always his own music. The New Orleans printer who contracted to publish his more popular compositions found it hard to supply the demand for his polkas, schottisches, waltzes, and quadrilles. No one in New Orleans was to be surprised at the immediate and astounding success of his opera *Maritana* when produced at Drury Lane in London in 1845.

Moreau played with him many times, in the Gottschalk home, at Madame Boyer's, at Monsieur Letellier's, in Félix Miolan's studio, and elsewhere. Mr. Wallace spoke of the boy as " the American Franz Liszt." Moreau could not then have dreamed to what extent his own musical ideals were to agree with Mr. Wallace's. A strong friendship sprang up between the man and the boy, a friendship which was to endure through the years.

On May 8 Moreau became thirteen. That afternoon he heard his father speak the words he had anticipated for months. Dinner was over, and the family lingered at table in the patio. Célestine rose to return to her dolls, but her father asked her to wait.

Then, without preliminary, he announced that Moreau would depart for France within seven or eight days. He would be a passenger on the *Taglioni*, a sailing vessel then anchored at the foot of the rue Ste. Anne. The captain, George L. Rogers, a friend of long standing, would have Moreau under his personal supervision until the *Taglioni* reached Le Havre. In Paris the boy would be turned over to Madame Blanche Dussert, who—as Mr. Gottschalk had found out after the most painstaking investigation—was a highly cultivated and most trustworthy widow, the preceptress of sons of gentlemen in a pension on the rue de Clichy. She would attempt to get Moreau admitted as a pupil of the piano in the Conservatoire Royal. Since he was not French, that would be difficult. But if she failed, she would secure the services of some outstanding private teacher of the piano, possibly Fédéric Chopin. Tutors came daily to drill the boys in her pension in Latin, Greek, the modern languages, mathematics, and moral philosophy. She would see that Moreau was provided with the best teachers of fencing and horsemanship. Every detail was settled. Moreau's mother would have at least a week to get his clothes in order.

The announcement threw the household into a state of complete dismay. The children and slaves passed on the news to other children and other slaves, and within two hours the rue Conti seethed with gossip. Certain neighbors insisted that Edward Gottschalk, well aware of his wife's temperament, had been forced to secrecy, that no other course was open to him. Others, especially those who knew that Aimée was again in a "delicate condition," spoke of her husband as "a cruel and monstrous Jew."

The confusion in the Gottschalk home increased with the days. Moreau was torn between excitement over going to Paris and fear that his leaving would actually mean the death of his mother. He was told a hundred times that she would never survive his departure. Propped up in bed, she would say, between spells of weeping, "In sending you away your father will destroy not only me but my unborn child." The new baby was expected in July or August. Célestine, eight and a half, was the only one of the children besides Moreau who was old enough to have any comprehension of the turmoil in the household. Many years later she was to speak of the days preceding Moreau's departure as "agonizing." Without the slaves the equilibrium in the home would have been completely upset. It was Sally who saw that Moreau's clothes were properly packed in the big new trunk ordered by his father.

The day Moreau sailed, May 17, his mother was hysterical. She kept him at her bedside until the last minute, talking of nothing unrelated to religion. She told again and again the stories of Père Antoine, stories the boy had been hearing all his life. She assured him that his music-making was wonderful, but that his future happiness depended upon his alleviating as he could the sufferings of others. Before embracing him for the last time she made him promise that while he was in the Old World he would visit the Holy Land and walk the pathways which the feet of the Blessed Virgin and Jesus had touched.

The *Taglioni* was towed to the mouth of the Mississippi by a steam-powered tug. Moreau took time out from viewing the wonders on the river to write a letter to his father and mother. It was taken ashore at Belize, just before the *Taglioni*, under her own sail, entered the Gulf of Mexico.

The letter stated that the eighteen or twenty first-class passengers appeared to be quite respectable, that Captain Rogers was very kind, and that the piano in the salon had been tuned just as Mr. Gottschalk had requested.

By the time the letter reached the rue Conti, Moreau's mother was out of bed and feeling ever so much better. She was almost reconciled to his leaving. A half-formed decision was bringing comfort—the decision to steer the four children left in her fold and the one soon to be born into Moreau's footsteps. In time the world would talk of the musical Gottschalks as the world now talked of the musical Garcias, the family of the great Madame Malibran.

Moreau kept a journal of his voyage on the *Taglioni*. He wrote of the warm days when the ship was in the Gulf of Mexico and off the east coast of Florida—days which he passed in reading Ossian, Byron, Scott, and Hugo. He told of evenings when the saloon was changed from dining room to drawing room and passengers and ship's officers crowded in to hear him play the piano. He described the sea when it was as calm as Lake Pontchartrain on a still summer afternoon and when it was so rough that the pitching and rolling of the *Taglioni* made him desperately sick. He told of his delight in watching schools of leaping porpoises. He pictured an iceberg in the full glare of the afternoon sun, and wrote of his terror when the pinnacled white mass veered and seemed to be bearing down upon the *Taglioni*. He told of his joy in sighting an island off the coast of Cornwall after weeks at sea, and he gave full particulars about the arrival at Le Havre. His first act upon landing was to mail the journal back to the rue Conti. He was to hear years later that it was read, admired, and knocked about until one of the slave women took it for litter and used it to light a fire.

The second morning after the arrival Moreau and Captain Rogers boarded a diligence for the ride to Paris. Their seats were in the coupé, the choice section of the vehicle. The Captain insisted that Moreau take the place next to a window: he wanted the boy to have the best view possible as he looked for the first time upon the French countryside.

Moreau had read of the hills of Normandy, of the hedges separating the farms, the windbreaks of poplars, the plane trees bordering the highways, the apple orchards, the green islands in

47

the Seine, the thatched farmhouses, the red roofs of the villages and towns, the gray castles, and the hundreds of church spires, each surmounted with a symbol of old Gaul, a crowing cock. But, accustomed as the boy was to the flats and swamps of Louisiana, he had imaged falsely the Norman landscape. It was far more appealing than he had expected; he was never to forget his rapture at his first view of its trim gentle beauty.

The passengers had no time to relax and refresh themselves except during the brief intervals when the diligence stopped for a change of horses. After reaching Rouen the road paralleled the recently constructed embankment upon which crews of workmen were laying railway tracks. " Travel by diligence from Paris to the sea will soon be only an uncomfortable custom to talk about," the passengers agreed. As the day wore on, most of them, including Captain Rogers, complained of fatigue.

But Moreau was as fresh as at the morning start when, late in the afternoon, the diligence made a turn and he saw the Arc de Triomphe de l'Etoile looming in the distance straight ahead. He wished with all his heart to pass through the great arch, which he had seen pictured in newspapers and magazines at the time of its dedication in 1836. But on reaching " this mass of sculptured stone laden with glory," the glory of Napoleon Bonaparte, one of Moreau's heroes, the diligence swerved to the right, made a half circle, and passed through the gates of the Barrière de Neuilly to enter the Avenue des Champs Elysées. That there were those in America who expected the boy one day to conquer with his music the city in which he had at last found himself was far from his thoughts as the diligence advanced slowly toward its destination, the Place de la Concorde. No dream of the future could find a place in his mind as he marveled for the first time at the splendors of Paris.

The driver of the hackney-coach which carried him and Captain Rogers from the Place de la Concorde to the rue de Clichy followed at first a northward course. On reaching the Embarcadère, as the Parisians then called their one railway station, the driver turned east on the rue St. Lazare. After crossing two narrow side streets he turned north again, and from a blue sign painted on the side of a building Moreau saw that he was in the rue de Clichy. This thoroughfare, which he was to traverse thousands of times, was as quiet as a country lane. It mounted so sharply from the rue St. Lazare that the driver had to use a lash on his horses. When the coach halted near the summit of the incline in front of a large detached house on the right, Moreau saw above the door the number 74 and realized that his journey from the rue Conti in New Orleans was ended and that the time had come for Madame Dussert to replace Captain Rogers as his protector.

He found the lady tall, slender, and gray-haired. Her brown eyes, greatly magnified by the lenses of her spectacles, were, as Moreau was to learn, eyes which saw everything. She spoke with precision, as if she wished to remind the world that she was the widow of a noted linguist. Her husband left her neither children nor money, but she showed in appearance and manner that she was capable of making her own way. Though she was not the sort of woman to rouse a boy's affection, Moreau knew the instant he came into her presence that he would trust her as he had trusted his father and Monsieur Letellier.

There was much to tell his parents in the letter begun that night and continued on two successive evenings. After describing the journey from Le Havre, he pictured his room. It was on the floor directly under the servants' attic. Madame Dussert had explained that he must be up high, where his piano practice would not disturb her other pensioners. A small window to the west gave upon a court and was good only for admitting light and air. From the large north window Moreau could look down upon the Barrière de Clichy. Beyond this break in the recently constructed wall of fortifications encircling Paris he could see the whole of the countrylike town of Les Batignolles, made up of pretty villas and green gardens. What pleased him most about the room was the beautiful Pleyel piano his father had promised. No instrument, Moreau wrote, could have a more singing tone and even scale.

The next installment of the letter, written twenty-four hours later, was a record of disappointments. Moreau had assumed that all he needed to be enrolled as a pupil in the Conservatoire was a chance to play before Pierre Zimmermann, the professor who controlled the admission of students of the piano. He had been too self-confident. That morning Madame Dussert accompanied him to the Conservatoire. Though the appointment was for ten o'clock, it was past eleven before Monsieur Zimmermann was ready to see them. Instead of inviting Moreau to play, he asked questions. When he learned that the boy had never before been out of the United States, he threw up his hands as if gravely shocked. "What a folly," he said, "to send him to France! No one who has passed his first thirteen years in the savage atmosphere of America can become a piano virtuoso. The best that country can do in the way of art is to turn out manufacturers of steam engines. My advice to this boy is to go back home and interest himself in mechanics." Madame Dussert, enraged at the insult to Moreau and his native land, led him from the room without another word to the professor. "As for Chopin," Moreau wrote, "he has gone to George Sand's country seat at Nohant, and will not return to Paris until late autumn or early winter."

The final installment of the letter was more cheerful. Moreau and Madame Dussert had called on Charles Hallé, a young pianist with a studio nearby on the rue de Clichy. Hallé, a native of Westphalia, not yet twenty-five, had been in Paris only two years. His playing of German classics at several concerts excited the Parisian critics, who praised with the greatest warmth his technic and musical insight. After hearing Moreau play a single piece, Hallé agreed to teach him. Then, to introduce the sort of music he wished the boy to study, he played Bach and Beethoven for an hour. Moreau, ignorant of such music, found it bewildering. But, he wrote, he had never dreamed that human touch could yield from a piano such tone as Monsieur Hallé produced. Moreau was hurrying his letter, he said, so that he could return to his study of the Bach prelude and fugue he was to play at his first lesson.

He took time to add a few words about his five fellow pensioners. They were the sons of army officers or provincial aristocrats, and they were all older and much bigger than he. At first they had been supercilious, but since hearing him play they were friendly. They already had a nickname for him, Little Millionaire.

It was the middle of September before he got a reply to this letter. The big news from the rue Conti was the birth of the new baby, another girl, on August 2. " We have decided," wrote the mother, " to call her Blanche, after kind wonderful Madame Dussert."

Moreau was already well into the routine he was to follow until the end of 1842. Every weekday, early in the morning, he went to Monsieur Hallé's studio for his piano lesson. Then he hurried back to the pension to read to his Latin tutor a few lines from Caesar. He had no interest in the movements of Caesar's legions; and he anticipated with no pleasure the study of Greek, which he was soon to alternate with Latin. He was not so bored by the second tutor who called every weekday morning—the tutor who corrected his French themes and listened to his interpretation of texts from the great French poets. In preparing lessons for this tutor he found that by concentrating on the sound of the verse he could memorize it as he did music. In this way he got by heart with little effort all of Boileau's *L'Art poétique* and many of the pieces from Hugo's *Les Orientales*. In company with the other boys in the pension he went three afternoons a week to the atelier of Monsieur Grésier on the rue du Faubourg-Mont-martre for practice in fencing. The other weekday afternoons the boys reported to Monsieur Tellier on the rue du Faubourg-Ste.-Marie for instruction in horsemanship.

They were hungry after two hours of fencing or riding. On the way back to the rue de Clichy they passed a tiny shop where the one ware sold was fried potatoes, a portion for a sou handed to the customer on a square of cardboard. Each time they neared the shop Little Millionaire somehow found himself in the lead. His father kept him plentifully supplied with pocket money, and he was rarely forced to deny his fellow pensioners the treat for which they hinted by falling behind. All his life he was to remember the contrasting pictures they made as they went up the sharp incline of the rue de Clichy. Until they came in sight of the pension they slouched like peasants, greedily tossing fried potatoes into their upturned opened mouths. Then, when they knew that Madame Dussert might be watching from one of her upstairs windows, they gulped down what was left of the potatoes, threw the squares of cardboard into the gutter, and walked the rest of the way with the swagger of courtiers.

The weeks moved smoothly—too smoothly, Moreau felt, when after five months under Monsieur Hallé he woke to the realization that he was making little progress toward becoming a piano virtuoso. He had by memory quantities of Bach and half a dozen Beethoven sonatas, but he could have executed any of this music as well before coming to Paris as he could now. Often after hearing Monsieur Hallé play a passage he said, "I'd give anything in the world if I could produce tone like that!" The master invariably replied, "You will," and let the matter go at that. In New Orleans Moreau had been told that what he needed was muscle-building. Monsieur Hallé had never so much as mentioned muscles. His method of teaching was evidently based upon the theory of tireless but blind endeavor.

When Moreau spoke of his dissatisfaction to Madame Dussert, she replied that she must discuss the problem with Monsieur Hallé. A whole month passed. Then one morning when Moreau reported for a lesson Monsieur Hallé informed him that thereafter his piano teacher would be Camille Stamaty and proceeded to spend the hour in speaking of Stamaty's excellence as man and as artist. Monsieur Hallé showed no resentment; and until his departure for England, where he was to make musical history and win knighthood and many other honors, he was to be numbered among Moreau's Parisian supporters.

Musicians referred to Stamaty as the full inheritor of the traditions established by his teacher, Friedrich Kalkbrenner, the virtuoso of whom Chopin said, "He is the giant who throws all other artists into the shade." Kalkbrenner called Stamaty his musical son and Stamaty's pupils his musical grandsons.

Happy over the turn of events which was leading him into this group, Moreau went the next morning, unaccompanied, to the house on the rue St. Honoré where Monsieur Stamaty lived with his widowed mother. A servant showed the boy into a little reception room on the first floor and told him to wait until the master finished a lesson he was giving. Moreau looked at the clock on the mantel and saw that he was five minutes early. As he noted that the timepiece was of Italian manufacture and that the two prints hanging on each side of it were views of Athenian monuments, he recalled what Monsieur Hallé had said of Stamaty's cosmopolitanism. He was Greek on his father's side, French on his mother's, and had passed his early years in Civitavecchia, near Rome. Monsieur Hallé had also spoken of Stamaty's delayed start in music. He was fourteen before he had a piano to practice on. Still at twenty he was good enough, in both playing and composing, to impress Kalkbrenner. The meeting of the two took place just at the time when Kalkbrenner discovered that Chopin, who had recently come to Paris from his native Warsaw, was to decline his offer of three years of free instruction. When the offer was transferred to Stamaty on condition that he give up his clerkship in the Prefecture of the Seine and devote all his time to music, it was readily accepted. So, as Monsieur Hallé explained, the half-Greek rather than the half-Pole became the great Kalkbrenner's acknowledged successor.

Finally the servant returned and showed Moreau into the studio. Monsieur Stamaty was standing in front of one of the two grand pianos which occupied one end of the room. His graying hair, thin body, and pale sunken cheeks made him look much older than thirty-two, his actual age. Whoever saw him never forgot his large gray eyes. They beamed understanding and sympathy, and at once put Moreau at ease. They also beamed the firmness which inspired such confidence as the boy had never placed in Monsieur Hallé. Looking into those eyes, Moreau was ready to believe fully what he had been told about Stamaty's fine temperament as an artist, his mystic devotion as a Roman Catholic, and his free-hearted generosity as a supporter of charities. At that very first meeting he cast a sort of spell over Moreau. The boy recalled his mother's stories of Père Antoine and almost believed that he was in the good friar's presence. He was in the state of mind to follow wherever this new master might lead.

Monsieur Stamaty spent that first lesson hour in introducing to

Moreau the device known as the hand-guide, invented by Kalk-brenner. It was simply a three- or four-foot rod of unresilient iron supported at each end by wooden legs high enough to bring it to the level of the keyboard when set before a piano. The user was supposed to rest his forearms on the rod and then, depending solely upon wrist and finger movement, play the exercises in Kalkbrenner's *Méthode pour apprendre le piano à l'aide du guide-main*. Only in this way, Kalkbrenner insisted, could all the muscles of the hand be brought into full action. Chopin had rebelled at so mechanical a method of practice; but Stamaty insisted that he owed to it the perfecting of his own technic. By the end of that first lesson Moreau promised himself to give the device the opportunity to do what it could for him.

From Monsieur Stamaty's supply of the hand-guides Moreau chose the one with the firmest legs. Though it was heavy and unwieldly, he carried it to the pension. He carried also a copy of Kalkbrenner's *Méthode*. That afternoon in his room he began practicing the exercises which were to tax his power of concentration, patience, and ability to persist for many months.

Without the daily stimulation of Monsieur Stamaty he could never have endured the ordeal. The master, who had himself gone through the grind, anticipated the periods of depression and knew how to direct the boy through them.

He made a special call on Madame Dussert to insist that Moreau miss no opportunity to hear the best music. So at the three great Paris theatres devoted to music—the Grand Opéra, Théâtre Italien, and the Opéra-Comique—Moreau was a frequent attendant, most of the time all alone. He was also seen at concerts at the Salle Pleyel, the Salle Erard, and the Salle Ste. Cécile. After hearing such singers as Rubini and Madame Viardot-Garcia and such pianists as Thalberg and Prudent the boy would return to his hand-guide and forget the pain of the calluses which had formed on his forearms.

An experience one day in Monsieur Stamaty's studio kept him in high working trim for weeks. He met another of the master's pupils, a seven-year-old prodigy named Camille Saint-Saëns. This boy used the hand-guide as if he were amusing himself with a game. Then, when it was removed, he played, with remarkable brilliance, one of his own compositions. Moreau, who in New Orleans had been made to believe that he himself was the most phenomenal of child prodigies, felt completely beaten. But his awareness of defeat was a challenge rather than a cause for depression. As he walked back to the rue de Clichy that day he had never before been so ambitious to excel as a piano virtuoso.

In this long period of shaping his wrist and finger muscles the pursuit which provided the greatest relief was the study of composition. The teacher to whom Stamaty committed this important part of Moreau's musical education was Pierre Maleden, of Limoges. Maleden, about thirty-seven, had spent most of his life either in his native city or in Darmstadt, Germany. Though he had been in Paris for only two years, he had many pupils. Camille Saint-Saëns, who was also entrusted to him for training in harmony and counterpoint, was to say, "The greatest benefit I got from Stamaty was my acquaintance with Maleden."

Moreau was too devoted to Monsieur Stamaty to go that far. But he was to speak many times of his great debt to Maleden. This effectual teacher of composition had worked out his method from hints given by Gottfried Weber of Darmstadt. His basic principle was to be described as follows by Saint-Saëns: "Maleden taught that chords must not be studied in and for themselves— as fifths, sixths, sevenths—but in relation to the pitch of the scale in which they appear. Thus considered, they acquire different characteristics according to the place they occupy, and, as a result, certain things are explained which are, otherwise, inexplicable. Maleden made his system a wonderful tool with which to get to the depths of music—a light for the darkest corners."

Monsieur Maleden was very thin, wore his hair long, spoke French with the nasal accent of Limoges, and was easily excited to anger. All musical Paris talked of the stormy scenes in his studio during lesson periods. More than once when Moreau seemed to be stubborn in accepting some dictum the master, in a rage, grabbed his ear and pressed it with all the strength of his thumb against the marble top of a table.

Yet, in his way, Monsieur Maleden was as inspirational as

Monsieur Stamaty. Under the guidance of the two teachers Moreau moved deeper and deeper into the realm where words fail and musical tones become the only language.

The little he learned of Latin and Greek he picked up during lesson periods. On Madame Dussert's insistence that he add a modern language to his list of studies, he chose Italian; but he made no greater progress with Dante than with Vergil and Homer. He was so absorbed in music that he spent every minute of his study hours in exercising his fingers with the hand-guide or playing the études assigned by Monsieur Stamaty or writing out harmonies for melodies according to the rules laid down by Monsieur Maleden. Though Moreau was very light on his feet and deft in the use of foils, he was bored by fencing. He already knew that in his conception of honor there was no place for the institution of dueling. Through Madame Dussert he appealed to his father; and the agreement to report three times a week to Monsieur Grésier, who had taught swordsmanship to the sons of King Louis-Philippe, was canceled. To Monsieur Tellier, also a teacher of royalty, he continued to report regularly: to look down upon the world from the back of a galloping horse gave the lad an ecstasy somehow related to the ecstasy induced by music.

He had brought from New Orleans a card of introduction to an aged noble lady who was the friend of friends of his mother. She was the Marquise Josephine de Lagrange, prominent at court during the reigns of Louis XVIII and Charles X. After the revolution of 1830 and the accession of Louis-Philippe to the throne the Marquise lived in retirement in her great house on the rue de Grenelle in the conservative Faubourg St. Germain. The first time Moreau called on her he met also her daughter, the Countess de Bourjolly. When he played for the two ladies, they praised him highly. He surely had it within him, they said, to repeat the triumphs of Monsieur Chopin in the salons of the great. They even offered to serve as his patronesses.

When Moreau spoke to Monsieur Stamaty of their generosity, the master merely said, " Their time will come." It did not come until the autumn of 1844, when both Moreau and Camille Saint-

Saëns were preparing for *non-payant* appearances in the spring, each in his own concert. Then, at Stamaty's suggestion, Moreau appealed to the Marquise de Lagrange and the countess de Bour-jolly. A few days later he was invited to play at a soirée given by the elderly Duke de Narbonne. Invitations came later from Baron James de Rothschild, from the patron of the arts Edouard Rodrigue, and from the expatriate Britisher Lord Tudor. Moreau, playing Mendelssohn or Chopin along with transcriptions by Liszt and others, was well received in the salon of each of these personages. Though these soirées were not primarily musical, several admirers remembered his name when his concert was announced.

The cards were sent out early in March, 1845, and every musician in Paris as well as every known patron of music was among the recipients. The card addressed to Monsieur de Beau-chesne, a professor in the Conservatoire, was to be preserved. It reads, in translation: "The young Moreau Gottschalk, of New Orleans, begs Monsieur and Madame Alfred de Beauchesne to do him the honor of attending the musical Séance which he will give in the Salons of Monsieur Pleyel, rue Rochechouart, No. 20, Wednesday, 26 March, at eight o'clock in the evening.— N. B. This invitation is personal, the bearer is asked to present it upon entering." The date "26 March" is crossed out, and "2 April" is written above by hand. At the bottom, also written by hand, appears: "On the part of Monsieur Stamaty."

In organizing the concert the master showed no mercy on Moreau's father's purse. The cards of invitation were expensively engraved. The hall engaged, the Salle Pleyel, with a seating capacity of twelve hundred, was the most luxurious in Paris. Théophile Tilmant, chief conductor at the Théâtre Italien, was employed to choose from his best musicians a small orchestra and to conduct it. Among the assisting artists were the celebrated cellist Auguste Franchomme, a friend of Chopin, and Jean Geraldy, a famous concert baritone. Two other singers of less note, Monsieur Marras and Mademoiselle Bernon, were also employed.

Moreau's main number was Chopin's concerto in E minor. His

two solos unaccompanied by orchestra were Thalberg's transcription of airs from Rossini's *Semiramide* and Liszt's fantasy on Meyerbeer's *Robert le diable.*

The Salle Pleyel was filled. But of the musical great who honored the occasion with their presence only two can be named with certainty. They were Chopin and Kalkbrenner.

When the program ended, Chopin went backstage, took Moreau by the hand, thanked him for choosing his concerto, congratulated him on his interpretation, and prophesied that he would have great success as a virtuoso. The moment of this meeting with Chopin was, Moreau was to say, the biggest of his life.

Kalkbrenner was far too important to go backstage and congratulate the unknown youth from across the seas. Moreau, who knew better than to expect any such attention, followed Monsieur Stamaty's suggestion and, the morning after the concert, called on his "musical grandfather." Kalkbrenner lived in one of the attached houses which surrounded the Square d'Orléans, a small private park off the rue St. Lazare. Because of the number of intellectuals and artists who inhabited this charming hidden corner of Paris, it was known as "the little Athens." Kalkbrenner had as neighbors Chopin, George Sand, Madame Viardot-Garcia, and Pierre Zimmermann. He was getting old, but he had lost none of the conceit that had made him the laughingstock of musicians all over Europe. Moreau found him most cordial. He praised the boy's technic, which he credited wholly to the hand-guide. He then said, "But I don't like the music you played—Chopin, Liszt, Thalberg. They're not classical. You and Stamaty should have chosen *my* music. It *is* classical. And, besides, *everybody* likes it."

The custom of the Paris press was to ignore students' *non-payant* concerts. But in the case of the fifteen-year-old youth from America there was a departure: reviews of the soirée were printed in two of the leading French musical journals. The first appeared in *La Revue et gazette musicale* for April 6. The writer pronounced Moreau a precocious adolescent who had almost reached the stage of virtuosity. The choice of the Chopin concerto—spoken of as "a composition of great difficulty and of little brilliance except in the rondo "—was, thought the reviewer, most unfortunate. The Thalberg and Liszt paraphrases, said he, gave the young American a better chance to exhibit an execution which was "precise, gentle, and elegant." The reviewer concluded: "When age will have provided the young Gottschalk of Louisiana with force, passion, and the ability to make his technic serve his inner sense, he will be as celebrated as any other pianist." The second review appeared in *Le Ménestrel* a week later. Though the writer spelled Moreau's surname incorrectly, he said, without qualification, "The young American played Chopin, Thalberg, and Liszt in a manner which merits for him a first place among our virtuosos."

When reports on the concert reached New Orleans, they were at once communicated to the press. By the time they appeared in the *Picayune, L'Abeille,* and other newspapers they were so exaggerated as to be ridiculous. Yet Moreau's mother, it seems, chose to believe that the concert was what the New Orleans newspapers said it was, a sensationally successful professional début. Her desire to take her five remaining children to Paris and see each of them follow in her eldest's footsteps had become an obsession.

Camille Saint-Saëns' concert, which came a month after Moreau's, led to great changes in the lives of the two boys. The ten-year-old prodigy was received so warmly—especially for his playing of Beethoven's concerto in C minor, with an orchestra again conducted by Tilmant—that Monsieur Stamaty made plans to take him on a concert tour of all Europe. Madame Saint-Saëns was at first sympathetic, but in the end she refused to allow her son to leave Paris. Monsieur Stamaty claimed that she had broken a contract. The prolonged quarrel which ensued affected his health; and then came a great personal sorrow, the death of his mother. A victim of nervous exhaustion, he left for Rome to pass a year or two of retreat in a monastery. Camille was received into the Conservatoire. Moreau, sixteen and a half by now, was unable to bring himself to think of a successor to his venerated Monsieur Stamaty. So he decided that henceforth, as a virtuoso, he would go his way without a teacher.

As a composer, he was less sure of himself. He continued his lessons under Monsieur Maleden, and was greatly encouraged when in the spring of 1846 he found a publisher who agreed to issue one of his piano compositions. Early in the summer it appeared in print, as "Polka de Salon." Though it bore no opus number, Moreau was always to count it as opus 1. The few who heard it must have wondered why the composer had adopted a polka rhythm for such melancholy melodies. In time he was to wonder about that himself.

Shortly after he first held a printed piece of his own in his hands he fell victim to an epidemic of typhoid fever that was sweeping Paris. For days he wavered between life and death. He lost what little flesh he had, shed much of his hair, and sank so low that he recognized no one. Madame Dussert had in mind, she said, every word of the letter she believed she would have to write to announce his death to his parents. But one morning about the middle of July the doctor declared that he had passed the crisis and would live.

A month later Moreau was a convalescent in the wild and beautiful country of the Ardennes, not far from the little city of Sedan. Madame Dussert had left the management of the pension to assistants and had traveled with him from Paris. She stayed by his side until she saw his head again covered with rich brown hair. As strength came back, he did more and more walking. Frequently he crossed paths with singing peasants. One of their tunes, he said, began to beg him for complete musical expression. Fourteen years were to pass before he used the melody as the main theme of a mazurka, "Les Ardennes," published with the date "1846-'60."

The illness, severe as it was, appears to have done him good. Back on the rue de Clichy during the autumn and winter, reporting as before to Madame Dussert's tutors and to Monsieur Maleden, he put on weight so rapidly that he outgrew his clothes. The colds from which he had suffered since coming to France were less frequent and less severe. By the spring of 1847, when he was nearing eighteen, he had leaped into manhood.

He had reached his mature height, about five feet eight inches. Though decidedly slender, he was as full-bodied as he was ever to be. His features were delicate, yet manly. Strangers never took him to be an artist. In carriage, in dress, in manners, and in speech he was an aristocrat. That he had sprung from the banks of the Mississippi and not from some ancient noble estate of France seemed to his conservative Parisian friends inconceivable.

An anticipated event soon burdened him with the responsibilities of manhood. It was the arrival of his mother in Paris. She had with her, as she had long planned, all the children. There were now six instead of five. A "postscript" had been born late in 1846 or right at the beginning of 1847, a boy, named Gaston. Getting off to France was so upsetting that Aimée had not as yet found time to have the infant baptized. Without Célestine, soon to be fourteen, she could never, she said, have lived through the journey. Edward, eleven, and Clara, ten, shifted for themselves. She and Célestine were busy every minute looking after the younger ones—Augusta, seven, Blanche, five, and the baby. The latter part of the voyage was so stormy that everybody almost died from seasickness. How grateful to God she was that she was now in Paris where she could lean upon her eldest as she had leaned for years upon his father!

Moreau was partially responsible for the mass migration. He had, in boyish fashion, believed every word his mother had written about the amazing musical gifts of Célestine, Edward, and Clara; and in his replies he had urged that they be brought to Paris as soon as possible. In one letter he casually proposed that his mother set up a pension, like Madame Dussert's. Her earnings from such a venture, added to the amount he was receiving from his father, would be sufficient, he said, to maintain them all. Then, replying to his mother's recent complaints about her health, he recommended the climate of Paris as the best cure.

Two or three months after Gaston's birth she wrote that she and the children would soon leave for Paris and that she would want a house suitable for use as a pension. Moreau, with Madame Dussert's aid, found a place on the rue des Filles-du-Calvaire.

As soon as his mother and her brood were installed in the roomy old house, he left the rue de Clichy and joined them. To be a member of his own family again after five years as a pensioner, to be free of tutors and of observing rules, was at first delightful. But after a few days Moreau began to see with clear eyes.

Without revealing what he was actually doing, he tested Célestine, Edward, and Clara in solfège, piano technic, and harmony. The examination lasted for a week. In the end Moreau had to admit to himself that not one of them had more than mediocre musical talent. Would they be aware of their deficiencies if they heard Camille Saint-Saëns or another boy prodigy of Moreau's acquaintance, nine-year-old Georges Bizet? Moreau was afraid they probably would not, so deluded they were by their mother's praise.

What of their father? This was the question that weighed most heavily upon Moreau. Obviously, Mr. Gottschalk was now little more than a drudge for his wife and children. All that life held for him was to labor to make the money to maintain a family four thousand miles across the seas. He sold the mansion on the rue Conti and was boarding with a brother until he could erect a cottage on a lot in a cheap section of New Orleans—on Robertson Street, well in the territory which Moreau as a child had known as the savanna. Sally would keep house for him when the cottage was ready. The other two slaves were hired out—to bring in a little more money to send to Paris each month.

Moreau knew what the gossips of New Orleans had been saying since the departure of his mother and her brood. When a gentleman of the French quarter sent his wife and children to Paris to live, his neighbors had just one explanation: he had lost his heart to a beautiful quadroon and wished to be undisturbed in his attentions to her. Moreau, overwhelmed with pity for his father, may well have said to himself, "I hope what these gossips say is true!"

More and more he came to feel that he alone was the cause for the tragic turn his parents' lives had taken. His consciousness of guilt led to sleepless nights—and then, one morning, to a temperature.

That afternoon the fever was so high that it threw him into a state of delirium. His mother, watching at his bedside, noticed that he was clenching and unclenching his fists, to a fast yet well-controlled rhythm. All the while he was working his lips, trying to sing, it appeared. When after a few minutes he seemed to be himself again, he asked for pencil and music paper. His mother brought them, and he began jotting down notes in the shorthand which he alone could read. When he filled half a page, he laid aside the pencil and paper, and, with a smile of relief on his lips, said, "Maybe now I won't hear the drums any more." Then he dropped into a quiet sleep. His mother, without trying to see what was on the paper, put it in his portfolio.

The next afternoon the fever again ran high. But there was no delirium that day. The following afternoon he was much better. The illness was a malarial attack, not a recurrence of the typhoid, as the doctor had at first feared.

Once more on his feet, Moreau felt he must get away and think things out by himself. He was not at ease in his mother's presence. She persisted in treating him with deference. Several times in talking to him her tongue slipped and she called him Mr. Gottschalk, in exactly the tone he had heard her use in addressing his father. Try as he might, he was unable to get his sisters and Edward to relax when he was around. That they were looking to him to replace their father became clearer every day. On an August afternoon two weeks after his recovery he said au revoir to his family and set out for an indefinite stay in the Vosges. He arrived in Epinal on a cool autumnlike morning, the Thursday before the Feast of the Assumption, which fell that year on Sunday.

On the eve of that holy day he sat up all night in his hotel room writing a musical tribute to his mother—two ballades, each of which had come to him in complete form. They are supposedly sung to harp accompaniment by one of Ossian's bards as he points out to a group of kings a field of tombs and reminds them of the vanity of human aspiration. If a spirit of irony prompted Moreau to honor his mother with these lugubrious offerings, he was unaware of it. He was to win the highest critical praise for the two ballades, each of which shows a great advance over the "Polka de Salon."

In the days that followed he thought of composing more pieces, and examined closely the ideas on file in his portfolio. Again and again he ran across the themes he had jotted down when in the delirium. They were melodies he had hummed or whistled all his life—Bras Coupé's call to the dancers of the bamboula on the Place Congo in New Orleans, the cry of the yam vendors of the French quarter, and one of Sally's favorite songs. His mother had explained to him when and how these were committed to paper. He had no recollection whatsoever of the experience, and invariably set the jottings aside as of no value.

He remained in Epinal or the near vicinity until the end of October. He had access to a good piano, and on many a day practiced or played for as much as eight hours. He wrote many letters, especially to his father. He rode horseback, and went on long tramps through the mountains.

All the while he was making decisions. His father must have financial aid, and he was the one to give it. On his return to Paris he would do all in his power to get his mother's pension actually established. At the same time he would seek invitations to play in salons and thus attract as many pupils as possible, such pupils as were able to pay well. It was in this way that Chopin, fifteen years before, had won recognition as a teacher.

Moreau was on the point of setting out for Paris when it occurred to him that he might begin earning money here in eastern France. While in the Ardennes the previous year he made friends with the elderly gentleman who for a quarter of a century had sponsored each season a series of concerts given on Sunday nights in the municipal theatre in Sedan. The gentleman mentioned the appearances there of Franz Liszt and Sigismund Thalberg. So, instead of returning to Paris Moreau went to Sedan. Once there he sought out his friend, who promptly engaged him for a concert in early November. This was in reality Moreau's professional début. The theatre was filled, and his share of the receipts was far more than he had dared to anticipate.

He left Paris in August weak from malaria and burdened with the conviction that he had turned the lives of those dearest to him into a tragedy. He returned in November robust—and confident that he was going to make life a little easier for his father.

With Moreau to urge action and with Madame Dussert to advise, Aimée took up seriously the business of organizing her pension. On Madame Dussert's recommendation she brought in an associate, Madame Henriette Dècle, a lady who had taught in many pensions and who knew how to discipline older children. Soon the following card appeared in such Paris newspapers as were read by the higher classes: "Mesdames Gottschalk et Dècle, pensionat pour jeunes filles, 10, rue des Filles-du-Calvaire."

A girls' boarding school was no place for Moreau—nor for Edward, who by now was twelve. The two moved into lodgings on the rue de Berlin. Moreau soon had Edward looking to him as a brother rather than as a father, and was doing his best to influence the boy to abandon music and turn to the study of law, for which he seemed to have a special aptitude. When Moreau admitted to his mother what he was doing, she raised no objections. She merely exclaimed, her eyes glowing, " Dear Monsieur Lislet studied law here in Paris! "

The presence of a few girls in the Gottschalk-Dècle pension early in December was probably due to certain friends Moreau had won. Since he liked older minds, all his intimate associates were persons of middle age or more. He was often in the company of the piano manufacturer Camille Pleyel, whose memory was packed with personal observations of every important musician of his times, Italian and German as well as French. Monsieur Pleyel's chief rival in business, Pierre Erard, also a man with rich musical recollections, frequently had Moreau at his house for an evening. Since his *non-payant* appearant in 1845 the lad had often gone to concerts or to the opera in the company of Madame Menechet de Barival, distinguished for her writing as well as for her piano playing and composing. Musicians besides Moreau for whom she served as Egeria included Ambroise Thomas. But the friend Moreau respected most at this time, not excepting Monsieur Stamaty and Monsieur Maleden, was Hector Berlioz, in whose makeshift orchestra he had for the past two seasons been employed to play from time to time when a score called for piano. Berlioz advised him regarding his compositions, and was therefore to be referred to as one of his teachers. Friends such as these were listened to when they recommended a pension for girls.

They were heard with even greater respect when they recommended a brilliant young pianist who wished to take a few pupils and was available for salon appearances. Moreau was precise in explaining to his friends that he was not interested in playing in salons such as he had played in when under the protection of the Marquise de Lagrange—salons where the guests liked the music only because it muffled their chatter and made them feel more free to engage in gossip. What he wanted was entrance to the great musical salons where he could make himself known and thus attract pupils who belonged to families of wealth.

After his introduction to the celebrated physician and chemist Mathieu Orfila he knew that such entrée was assured. Monsieur Orfila, born a Spaniard on the island of Minorca, had lived in France from the age of nineteen. Now sixty, he was dean of the faculty of medicine in the university of Paris, physician to King Louis-Philippe, a commander of the Legion of Honor, one of the greatest of living toxicologists, a musical amateur of the highest talent, a born humorist, a monologist of rare skill, and a man of the noblest character. The medical students in Paris claimed that in experimenting with poisons he tried them out on himself, and so his nickname came to be " King Mithridates of Pontus Redivivus." Because of his interest in music the students spoke of his house on the rue de l'Odéon as " Orpheus' Heaven."

Moreau played there—Bach, Mendelssohn, and Chopin—on at least half a dozen evenings in January and February, 1848. Among the musicians who appeared with him was Jacques Offenbach, a cellist nearing thirty who had not yet thought of trying his skill at writing operettas.

Moreau was always prepared for a surprise in Monsieur Orfila's salon. Once, when he was in the middle of a Chopin waltz, he happened to look in the direction of the entrance. Standing in the doorway, unattended, was one of Louis-Philippe's sons: not even for a prince of the blood royal was Monsieur Orfila willing to break his rule of admitting no one to his salon when music was being played. On another evening the host and hostess had their guests roaring with laughter by rendering in true professional style a duo bouffant from one of Rossini's operas. On still another occasion the honored dean entertained his guests with a monologue of his own creation, a burlesque account of his observations while supposedly under the influence of a poison that gave his body all the appearances of death and left his mind clear. He showed his high estimate of Moreau when he gave him a standing invitation to the famous Thursday breakfasts at which he received the great men of science of the day.

It was he who saw that Moreau was asked to play in the salon of the Countess de las Mercedes Merlin, known to Parisians simply as Madame Merlin. She lived on the rue de Berlin, in a mansion facing the house where Moreau had his lodgings. Even if she had not been an excellent amateur singer and a great patroness of musicians, he would have been interested in her. For she was also a native of the New World, the daughter of a Spanish grandee who served his government in Cuba. She rated the Germans above all other musicians, and encouraged Moreau's ambition to make the music of Johann Sebastian Bach better known to Parisians. In playing at her soirées, at which there were often as many as four hundred guests, he frequently confined himself wholly to Bach.

Monsieur Orfila spoke of Moreau's interpretations of Bach to Narcisse-Achille de Salvandy, the Minister of Education in the royal government and, by virtue of his portfolio, the state supervisor of the fine arts. Monsieur de Salvandy found it to his advantage as a politician to present only the best artists at the soirées held monthly in his old-fashioned house on the rue Cassette in the Faubourg St. Germain and to require them to play such music as was educational in character. So it is certain that when Moreau's name was proposed to him he had the young American pianist very carefully investigated. The reports were evidently favorable. For early in January, 1848, Moreau received an invitation to play a sufficient number of selections from Bach to fill eight or ten minutes at the next soirée to be given by the Minister of Education.

For Moreau the day this invitation came was a lucky day. He had, indeed, experienced nothing but luck since his return from the Vosges. His mother's pension, it seemed, was going to be a success. He had as many pupils as he could take care of, required as he was to hurry from one house to another in all parts of Paris to give the lessons.

On the evening of February 16, 1848, in the Salle Pleyel, he enjoyed a privilege he had anticipated since his departure from New Orleans—the privilege of hearing Frédéric Chopin in a public appearance. Not since February, 1842, five months before Moreau's arrival in Paris, had Chopin given a concert. The scene had been this same Salle Pleyel. Of that occasion Liszt had said, " It was a concert à la mode." It was the same on this February evening in 1848. Candlelight, flowers, perfume, the elegance of an audience of gentlemen and ladies, and music—such music, all of it written by Chopin himself except for the selections sung by a soprano and a tenor and a Mozart trio played by Chopin, the violinist Delphin Alard, and the cellist Auguste Franchomme. As Moreau reveled in the evening, perhaps in the company of Madame Menechet de Barival, his great thought was that he wanted his own concerts to be just like this.

No, he had not yet composed such music as he wished to play. And since his return from the Vosges he had been so busy practicing for salon appearances and looking for pupils that he had not once picked up a piece of music paper. But he was gradually ordering his life to make time for writing. Chopin's magic awoke his finest dreams and had him floating with his aspiration for a full week.

Then came the fatal day of February 24, 1848, and with it the beginning of the rush of world-shaking events which crushed the immediate hopes of every musician in Paris. It was the day when Louis-Philippe and his Queen stole from a back door of the Tuileries and, disguised as "Mr. and Mrs. Smith," began their flight to England. It was the day the poet-politician Alphonse de Lamartine, acting in his capacity as majority leader in the National Assembly, proclaimed the Second French Republic. It was the day that inaugurated the year of revolution which was to leave few countries in the world unaffected. Music-minded Paris at once became politics-minded. Scheduled concerts and private musical soirées were canceled. Chopin—with Kalkbrenner, Hallé, Berlioz, Madame Viardot-Garcia, and many other artists personally known to Moreau Gottschalk—went to London. The French capital, which had been a musical paradise since Moreau's arrival six years before, was now, like many another capital on the Continent, a musical desert.

Well-to-do families left Paris for the country. Moreau lost most of his pupils and saw his mother's pension depleted. June came and found him still hoping that the revolution would follow a bloodless course. Then, with the troops of the Republic and the armed bourgeoisie on one side and factory workers and the unemployed on the other, street fighting broke out. Within a few days it reached such a stage of violence that a contemporary described it as " the most fierce, obstinate, and bloody battle of modern times."

On the advice of Monsieur Orfila, Moreau got his mother, sisters, and brothers to Clermont-de-l'Oise, a village forty miles north of Paris, the seat of a state-maintained insane asylum. The head physician at this institution, a close friend of Monsieur Orfila, was notified that the Gottschalks were coming, and on their arrival he had lodgings in the village ready for them. But with the two pianos Moreau had insisted upon bringing the rooms were too crowded for comfort. So an apartment was fitted up for Moreau and one of the pianos in the staff house of the asylum—a building outside the great walls which shut in the patients.

It was a beautiful retreat, situated in the heart of a forest. From each of his windows Moreau could reach out and touch the limbs of trees.

He hardly had time to begin wondering why the head physician, a stranger, was so kind and how he could show his appreciation when that gentleman casually mentioned his faith in the efficacy of music in treating certain types of insanity. Sly Monsieur Orfila!

On the instant, Moreau grasped all that had been back of the great man's insistence that he come to Clermont-de-l'Oise.

The very next morning he played to a group of about fifty patients. Thereafter he played daily—some days to as many as four groups. He also tested the voices of certain patients, and with those who knew a little about singing he organized a choir.

The head physician and his assistants treated the musician as a member of the medical staff. Every day at one o'clock they all had dinner together, and Moreau took advantage of the opportunity to hear the opinions of experts on a problem which had for years fascinated him, the problem of how the human mind functions. He was given a variety of opinions, most of them facetious.

One day he asked what mental power was brought into action when a man accomplished a feat without being aware of what he was doing. Several of the doctors ventured answers, illustrating them with fantastic yarns. Then Moreau told of his own experience in filling half a page of paper with his musical shorthand when he was in delirium from a fever and of having afterwards no recollection of the act.

"Did you find any value in what you wrote?" asked the head physician, suddenly becoming serious.

"No," said Moreau. "That is, I don't think so. Just some Negro tunes which have been a part of me all my life."

"They're perhaps more a part of you than you've ever thought," said the doctor. "It might be to your advantage to study their musical possibilities."

Moreau attached little importance to the doctor's suggestion. Even so, back in his apartment that afternoon he opened his portfolio and turned to the page on which he had written when in the delirium. The shorthand was very rough. But Bras Coupé's "Dansez bamboula!" was clear. Also easily readable was the yam vendor's cry,

> Quand patate la cuite,
> Na va mange li!
> Na va mange li!

And there was no mistaking Sally's song. Then, as Moreau gazed at the paper, he found signs and marks he had not noticed before —indications for keys, for dynamics, and especially for rhythms. Soon it dawned upon him that what he had taken to be three unrelated themes were in reality well integrated and that he held in his hands the sketch for a composition in all respects a unit. It was music such as he had never played, but it seemed to him to possess power and charm. When he tried it out on the piano, he liked it still more. There could, he decided, be only one title for the piece—" Bamboula: Danse des nègres."

Again at his writing table with a clean piece of music paper before him, he put down the D flat bass octaves which represent the drum beats actually or mentally heard from the beginning of the piece to the end. The task of getting the whole on paper in finished form occupied a week of steady application.

Before the task was done, another of Sally's songs was haunting him day and night. It was the spiritual into which the Louisiana Negroes had converted the old English dance tune " Skip-tum-lu, my Darling." He heard it in the key of E flat minor—a melody so tender and arresting that it would stand, he was sure, any number of repetitions. So he decided to develop it with variations. But to give novelty to the piece as a whole he took a hint from Bach and wrote a wholly original prelude, a little work which critics were to consider one of the most magical of his creations. While writing this and devising the variations for the spiritual, he felt, he was to say, that he was once more a tiny boy in Sally's lap looking deep into the savanna that spread out in the distance. Therefore the title he chose for this second of his Negro compositions was " La Savanne: Ballade créole."

When he played the new pieces for his mother and the children, they shouted, danced, sang, laughed, cried, and recalled, all at the same time, reminiscences of New Orleans. But when he asked his mother how she thought Paris would react to such music, she said, " Why, it's ' nigger stuff ' son. Paris would shame you for playing it." Though he reminded her that Chopin had won the hearts of Parisians with " Polish stuff " and that Glinka had created a furor in France with " Russian stuff," she persisted in saying, "You should look upon these new compositions as just fun for us."

The doctors at the hospital did not agree with her. None of them were musicians, but they knew enough about the effect of music to forbid Moreau to play the new pieces for the asylum patients. The Negro rhythms and melodies stirred up things deep in their own minds. "God only knows," said the head physician, "what effect they might have upon the mentally unbalanced."

As the weeks passed, Moreau's faith in his new music grew stronger. His great desire was to get back to Paris and try out "Bamboula" and "La Savanne" in a salon. But it was October before Monsieur Orfila wrote that it would be safe for him and his mother to return with the children.

They found the city calm, and apparently as populous as ever. Though France was still in a state of revolution, those who had fled the capital in droves were returning in droves. Soon Moreau, again with Edward on the rue de Berlin, was traveling from one quarter to another to give piano lessons; and three or four of his mother's pensioners were back.

The first salon hearing of the new music came early in November at one of Madame Merlin's soirées. "La Savanne" was played first, and the guests applauded it warmly. Then they listened to "Bamboula" and went wild. It was ten minutes before they quieted down sufficiently to pay attention while Moreau—speaking for the first time in his life to such a large group but showing no trace of stage fright—explained in detail the intent back of each composition and the origin of the themes. Then, after requesting that there be no applause during the brief interval separating the two pieces, he repeated them, with "La Savanne" again coming first. This time the guests were twice as excited as they had been before. The hour grew very late, but they refused to go home until they heard "Bamboula" once more.

They were at least four hundred in number, and the next day each of them—patting his feet as he hummed the themes—raved to a dozen other persons about the amazing music of America and young Gottschalk's magical interpretation of it. Before the week was ended Moreau played the new pieces at Monsieur and

Madame Orfila's first soirée of the season, and another group of enthusiastic admirers began spreading his fame. Soon invitations to play the American music in salons were pouring in in such numbers that to most of them Moreau had to say no.

But when a card came from the renowned journalist Emile de Girardin and his equally renowned wife, known in literature as Delphine Gay, Moreau sent an immediate acceptance. Because of the far-reaching influence Monsieur de Girardin wielded through his newspaper *La Presse*, he had been called since the beginning of the revolution "the first power of France." The invitation he dispatched to young Gottschalk early in December, 1848, was what a command from King Louis-Philippe would have been a year earlier.

The soirée was given just before Christmas. Moreau was to remember every minute of it, and years later was to write of it as if it had occurred the evening before.

Shortly after ten o'clock he arrived at the de Girardin mansion, which was located on the rue de Chaillot. The great house, almost new, had been designed on the model of a pagan temple. The guidebooks of the time listed it among the splendid architectural oddities of modern Paris.

Moreau upon entering the huge salon saw that it was rectangular in shape. At each end and on one side stretched a marble colonnade, forming a series of shadowed recesses. On the other side were the arched entrances and, in the space between, an immense fireplace, now in full blaze. A seven-foot grand piano partially screened the recess directly opposite the fireplace. It was here that Moreau found himself after he had been greeted by Monsieur and Madame de Girardin.

Sitting on a couch in the recess, "fully occupying it with his majestic corpulence," was the famed basso Luigi Labrache, whom Moreau had met in other salons. He had served as a pallbearer at Beethoven's funeral, had given singing lessons to Queen Victoria, had married his daughter off to Sigismund Thalberg, was numbered among the closest friends of Chopin and George Sand, and for years had been one of Rossini's few intimates. Moreau was to call him "the fattest man and the finest spirit the world of our time has known." At sight of the American he rose, "pressed him to his great bosom throbbing with kindness," and then presented him to the other artists of the evening.

Moreau had heard them all countless times in the Théâtre Italien, but he had never before been in their company. One was the baritone Georgio Ronconi. Another was Giulia Grisi, the soprano, who, according to Paris, "possessed the lost arms of the Venus of Milo," and, according to Heinrich Heine, was "the singing flower of beauty." The third was one of the most magnificent tenors of all time, Giuseppe Mario.

Also in the recess were two others to whom Moreau was presented, the Prince de la Moskova, Marshal Ney's son, and Prince Poniatowski, a composer. It was difficult to believe that the former, a dilettante interested in resurrecting the music of the Middle Ages, was the offspring of a military genius. He and Poniatowski merely bowed to Moreau. The two were absorbed in an argument over the comparative merits of the musicians of the north of Europe and the musicians of the south. While Moskova was all for the Germans, Poniatowski was loud in his defense of the Italians. Signor Labrache, in a voice which had the chandeliers swinging, undertook to drown out their quarreling with one of his humorous tales.

But Moreau was too interested in looking out upon the great salon to pay attention to what was going on in his immediate circle. The simplicity of his evening attire was right, he told himself. It was appropriately American in an assemblage where most of the gentlemen were resplendent with medals, ribbons, and decorations of all sorts. He had never before played in such a formal salon, and he should, he supposed, be nervous. But he felt no more tension than he felt when he was to play for his mother. As he searched for recognizable faces, he held his left hand over his eyes to shut off the glare of the lights. It was getting late, and he expected at any moment to hear footmen knock on the floor with their staffs for silence. Then the music would begin.

Monsieur de Girardin moved from one group of guests to another. It seemed to Moreau that wherever he turned his eyes he saw the bulky journalist bowing to kiss a lady's hand. There was good reason for the smile of triumph on his face. For months he had brought to bear the full force of his power to make Prince Louis Napoleon the first president of the Second French Republic, and now all the signs prophesied his success.

Moreau, who knew little about the ways of French politicians, was greatly surprised when he saw one of Monsieur de Girardin's chief opponents, Alphonse de Lamartine, standing before the fireplace conversing in animated fashion with the Princess de Beauveau. If the election for the presidency had taken place in July, he would now be in the chair which seemed destined for Louis Napoleon. But there was nothing in his mien to indicate that he was a man whose great hour had come and passed. Nor could Moreau see in him the poet who had created the *Méditations* and *Jocelyn*. He appeared to be lost in his vanity. All France talked of his shapely hands and feet, and there could be no doubt that he was now standing so as to show them off to advantage. The hero-worshiping young American began to feel the cold touch of disillusionment.

It was a relief to turn and see the great domed forehead of Victor Hugo, who sat at a little table all by himself near the tail of the piano. There was no foolish vanity in this poetic presence. Victor Hugo seemed to be looking into the future. He was turning over in his mind, Moreau was sure, the ideas that would be woven into a bitter poem to add to his *Contemplations*.

Across the room, also alone at a little table, sat Théophile Gautier, appearing to Moreau not at all as the author of *Mademoiselle de Maupin* but as the painter he had aspired to be before turning to letters. He had pencil and paper, and was absorbed in drawing personages scattered here and there about the salon.

Two whom he had drawn were Madame de Girardin and Jerome Bonaparte. They were sitting on a sofa at Moreau's left, near enough for the American to overhear what they were saying. Delphine Gay was George Sand's one rival among the women writers of France. Moreau belonged to the group which championed Madame de Girardin as the greater. In his judgment the vulgar realistic George Sand was incapable of the loftiness of Delphine Gay's recent drama, *Cléopatre*. Jerome Bonaparte expressed his displeasure at Rachel's delivery of a certain speech in that play and asked Madame de Girardin how she had intended it to be recited. As she repeated the lines in a low voice, Moreau watched the expression on the face of the onetime King of Westphalia. He was nearing seventy, but he looked no more than forty. It struck Moreau that the familiar pictures of Napoleon might easily be mistaken for portraits of this man who was now listening to Madame de Girardin. He could not have changed much since that distant time when as a young adventurer in America he won the heart and hand of Elizabeth Patterson, the daughter of a Baltimore merchant. Would he have retained his youth so remarkably if he had refused to yield to the Emperor's command to cast aside his bride and had lived his life as a simple citizen of Baltimore?

As this question occurred to Moreau, he noticed that Madame de Girardin had suddenly become silent. Then he looked toward the doorway and saw the actress under criticism. Accompanying Rachel was the Parisian Beau Brummel of the time, the Count d'Orsay. She had come direct from the Comédie Française, and Moreau knew that at the end of her performance she had appeared before the curtain to deliver, in this period of revolution, "La Marseillaise." Moreau in his imagination could hear her, neither speaking nor singing, but pouring into her rendition "the something that rouses terror."

She was scarcely seated, on the sofa beside Madame de Girardin, when the awaited knocks were sounded. Slowly the talking and laughter subsided, and slowly Monsieur de Lamartine, who remained standing before the fireplace, adjusted his feet and hands so that the ladies could admire them. Then, when Ronconi and his accompanist were at the piano on the point of opening the musical program, a commotion was heard in one of the doorways.

As all eyes turned in that direction, they saw Alexandre Dumas bluster in, pushing forward his little eight-year-old daughter. "Messieurs and Mesdames," the romancer shouted, "I introduce to you my latest masterpiece!" Even Monsieur de Lamartine applauded the child, as she gracefully acknowledged her noisy reception by making curtsies in all directions.

When the laughter aroused by this characteristic prank on the part of Dumas was hushed, Ronconi sang. He was followed by Grisi and Mario, who gave two or three duets. Then Labrache sang an air from Rossini's *Otello* and Leporello's " Catalog " from Mozart's *Don Giovanni*.

Though Moreau realized that it was now up to him to hold his own with four of the most celebrated of living artists, he was completely self-possessed as Monsieur de Girardin took his arm and led him to the piano. In a neat speech the journalist paid tribute to the artists who had sung, saying that they were too well known in Paris to be introduced to an assemblage of Parisians. But, he added, there was still another entertainer for the evening, a young American amateur pianist unknown to most of those present, Moreau Gottschalk, of Louisiana. He would play two compositions of his own—compositions based on the music native to his province.

Bowing to the slight applause, Moreau saw that there was no servant at hand to raise the wing of the piano. So he raised it himself. Then, standing before the keyboard, removing his gloves as he talked, he explained very briefly the origin of each of the numbers he was to play. Seated finally at the instrument, he forgot all about the famous faces turned upon him and gave himself wholly to " La Savanne " and " Bamboula."

Monsieur de Girardin's guests were not such as music can drive wild. Nevertheless they clapped and shouted " Bis! " until Moreau repeated " Bamboula."

As he rose from the piano to acknowledge the applause this time, he saw that no one was sitting and that the whole salon was in movement. He had no notion of what was going on until he felt Signor Labrache's arm around his shoulder and heard the basso say, " Come, my young friend. You and I will go to the supper room with the princes and the dukes. If we were in London, we would be told to go to the mezzanine and eat with the servants. But, thank God, we're not in London."

Moreau, observing the interest which everybody was manifesting in food, wondered if, after all, the French were more considerate of art than the English. He doubted whether a single one of all these guests would recall his name the next morning. In time he was to learn that he had made a memorable impression upon at least two—Théophile Gautier and Victor Hugo.

A few days after the soirée Moreau received a very kind note of thanks from Monsieur and Madame de Girardin. He knew that the four singers had each received a high fee. But while they were artists, he, as Monsieur de Girardin had been careful to point out in introducing him, was an amateur. The pittances paid to him for playing in Berlioz' orchestra and the purse handed him after his appearance in Sedan constituted all he had earned for exhibiting the virtuosity he had spent his life to develop. He made up his mind that before long he too would rank as an artist and receive an artist's rewards.

On his return to Paris after the Sedan concert he had tried without success to interest a number of publishers in his completed compositions—the two ballades written at Epinal, a concert étude, a concert waltz, and several mazurkas. For weeks now these same publishers had been besieging him in their efforts to gain the rights to print "Bamboula," "La Savanne," and any other American music he might write. He showed wisdom when early in January, 1849, he signed a contract granting to the brothers Léon and Marie Escudier all rights to be his exclusive publishers. In their list of composers appeared such names as Berlioz and Giuseppe Verdi. The journal they issued, *La France musicale*, had a much larger circulation than any other French journal devoted to music. They were in the best position to bring Moreau to the attention of the wide public whether as composer or virtuoso.

No more than three or four days after the signing of the contract they sounded, said Moreau, the publicity trumpets for his professional Paris début. As the weeks passed the trumpets grew louder and louder.

The concert came on the evening of Tuesday, April 17, 1849, in the Salle Pleyel. Once more the air in the familiar hall was perfume-laden from the profusion of flowers. The twelve hundred seats, priced at ten francs and five francs, had all been sold by the end of the previous week. The audience was as aristocratic and elegant as the audience which had welcomed Chopin the year before.

In a wall seat on the right, four or five rows from the front, sat Moreau's mother, happily weeping from the time her son appeared on the stage until he made his final bow. On a hassock placed in the seat next to her sat Gaston, not yet three years old. "He must have in his heart the memory of this event," said Aimée. Stringing out in the row came, in order, Célestine, Blanche, Clara, Augusta, and Edward—a younger child and then an older.

In the row directly behind sat the girls who made up the Gottschalk-Dècle pension. Madame Dècle, who had them in charge, did not need to watch so closely to keep them from flirting with boys in the audience. Moreau often played for them, and they were all in love with him; whenever he was visible they saw no other man.

Madame Dussert and her present pensioners were together in another part of the hall. Near them were the tutors who had tried to teach Moreau Latin, Greek, and Italian. Scattered here and there were a few of his old fellow pensioners, men of the world now. They recalled no doubt how they used to inveigle Little Millionaire into buying fried potatoes.

Monsieur Stamaty and Monsieur Maleden were up front. Fourteen-year-old Camille Saint-Saëns and eleven-year-old Georges Bizet were in the audience. In company with the latter was his Conservatoire teacher, Antoine Marmontel, who had recently become one of Moreau's intimate friends. Madame Menechet de Barival was in her box. Among the scores of established artists who had heard of the American's magic and were on hand to decide for themselves was Sigismund Thalberg, the universally recognized king of pianists since the retirement of Franz Liszt.

Monsieur and Madame Orfila, Madame Merlin, Monsieur de Salvandy, and hundreds of their salon guests who had become admirers of the American were present to wish him Godspeed at the start of his professional career.

Moreau was heard first in Georges Onslow's septet for piano, flute, oboe, clarinet, horn, bassoon, and contrabassoon, the assisting artists all being from the orchestra of the Théâtre Italien. A baritone from the Grand Opéra followed with an aria from Weber's *Oberon* and songs by Schubert and Reber. Moreau then closed the first half of the program with the adagio and finale of Beethoven's *Sonata Appassionata.* The second half was opened by Henri Seligman, first cellist in the orchestra of the Opéra-Comique, who played his own fantasy on themes from Bellini's *Norma.* A soprano from the Théâtre Italien then sang two arias from Donizetti's *La Favorita.* Moreau ended the concert with a group of his own compositions. First came a mazurka, just published and sent gratis by the Escudiers to all subscribers to *La France musicale.* Next in order was " La Savanne," in print for less than a month and already in a second edition. Then came Moreau's tribute to his mother, announced for immediate publication as "Ossian: deux ballades." The last number in the group was " Bamboula," published early in the year and, in spite of its technical difficulties, already bought by thousands. It served as the grand climax of the evening. As on every occasion Moreau had played it to an audience, its repetition was demanded.

The musical critiques in the leading Paris newspapers gave special space to the concert, and none of them contained unfavorable comment. The authors welcomed the young American to France. " He is the one new foreign pianist courageous enough to venture into revolution-torn Paris this season," wrote Adolphe Adam in *Le Constitutionnel,* evidently ignorant of the fact that Moreau had been in France almost seven years. The critics without exception complimented him on his pleasing stage presence. They spoke of his thorough understanding of the music of Beethoven and Onslow and praised his brilliant technic. In commenting on his own compositions they used such adjectives as *sparkling, dramatic, noble,* and *electrifying.* All agreed in placing the American in the "poetic school" of which Chopin had been long considered the great representative.

Of more delight to Moreau than the praise of the critics was an unexpected honor that came as an aftermath of the successful concert—an honor due, he was to learn, to the influence of his friend Monsieur Marmontel. It was the inclusion of "Bamboula" among the modern works to be played in the annual concours for students of the piano at the Conservatoire and an invitation to Moreau to serve as one of the judges. The jury also included the Conservatoire professors of the piano, headed by Monsieur Zimmermann. When the day for the concours arrived, late in June, Moreau had the satisfaction of sitting as an equal on the platform with the man who just seven years before refused to hear him play because he came from America and advised him to go back to his native country and interest himself in the mechanics of steam engines.

The preceding summer the revolution almost depopulated Paris. This summer the inhabitants fled a danger still more terrifying, an epidemic of Asiatic cholera. From the time the first case was reported, Moreau's mother was—quite understandably—in a state of panic. Again her eldest saw to it that she and the children were transferred to the country. He then left for Le Havre, expecting to go on to London. But once in the seaport he decided to remain in France. After lingering with friends in Le Havre for almost a month he joined his mother—in time for her to nurse him through a recurrence of malarial fever.

One of the victims of the cholera that summer was his "musical grandfather," Friedrich Kalkbrenner. Then when Moreau got back to Paris, the middle of October, all his musical friends were talking about poor Chopin, dying in an apartment on the Place Vendôme—dying of *her*, the faithless George Sand, Moreau was to believe. On October 17 Chopin's end came.

Moreau attended the splendid funeral in the Church of the Madeleine on October 30. He heard Mozart's *Requiem* superbly rendered by a group of distinguished soloists and the full choir and orchestra of the Conservatoire. He joined the throng of musicians who followed the coffin to the Cemetery of Père Lachaise. As he walked with the long procession which moved slowly eastward by way of the boulevards, he no doubt kept thinking of the numerous critics who were saying that he more than any other young pianist of the time showed the promise of becoming Chopin's successor. One of these critics was Monsieur Marmontel, who said, " Chopin himself expressed his sympathy for Gottschalk; it pleased him to recognize in the delicate nature of this younger man an organization tender and sensitive, a sister to his own." Moreau naturally felt complimented to hear himself compared with Chopin. But in his progress as a musician he had already arrived at the conclusion that no true artist is ever the successor to anyone.

Though he and Monsieur Pleyel were still the best of friends, he had recently signed an agreement to use in public the piano manufactured by the Erard Company. This firm and the Escudiers were keeping his name before the public. " Gottschalk de la Louisiane " they labeled him, and Parisians in greater numbers every day spoke of him as such. Many among his close acquaintances forgot what his Christian name was. Even his own sisters were referring to him as Gottschalk. Though not yet twenty-one, he was in all respects a professional, an artist with a name.

If he learned a single lesson from Monsieur Stamaty, it was that the artist must never fail his public. The Escudiers engaged him to play Weber's *Concertstück* with full orchestra at a grand concert in the Théâtre Italien the last Sunday evening in November. That afternoon he visited the pension on the rue des Filles-du-Calvaire and carried Gaston a new set of blocks. While stretched out on the floor showing the child how to build log cabins he stuck a splinter in the first finger of his right hand, the finger he used most in bringing out a melody. That evening he left a bloody piano on the stage of the Théâtre Italien. But not even the most intent listener suspected anything wrong. The critics praised the performance as technically flawless.

In an early number of *La France musicale* for 1850 the Escudiers ran a half-page advertisement of his new American composition,

" Le Bananier: Chanson des nègres." Gottschalk had finished it shortly after his return to Paris in October, and had played it with the greatest success in salons. Those who had heard it were calling it " a pendant to ' Bamboula.' "

The only likeness between the two pieces is that both had their origin in Negro folk music. In treating the tune which forms the basis of "Le Bananier" Gottschalk took hints from Bach. The first of the two strains which make up the song, keyed in C minor, has a musette accompaniment. In the second strain the melody is supported contrapuntally by two other voices. With the song thus fixed in the hearer's mind, Gottschalk proceeded to give it an original development.

His opportunity to present it in a public performance came near the end of January when he appeared as an assisting artist in a concert given in the Salle Erard by the famous violinist, Henri Max-Meyer. Gottschalk played in the opening number, a Mozart quintette. He was not on the stage again until next to the last number, which was given over wholly to him. He played first one of his mazurkas, then " La Savanne," and finally " Le Bananier." News of the effect in salons of this " pendant of ' Bamboula ' " had got abroad. It was the composition on the program most eagerly awaited. " As the young American played the Negro melody," said one critic, " it seemed that black pearls were dropped from the air to bounce upon the keyboard in a wild yet ordered dance." The hearers, stirred to a state of frenzy, demanded two repetitions. Then it was a full five minutes before the hall was quiet enough for Monsieur Max-Meyer to end the scheduled program with Paganini's " Le Carnaval de Venise." As soon as he played the last note, the audience began to shout for the American. It was not Gottschalk's concert, and he refused to return to the stage alone. The embarrassing situation was solved when he and Max-Meyer both came back and, using music, played a duo they had never rehearsed, a fantasy on motifs from Rossini's *William Tell*.

Gottschalk was to say that in his opinion the most abominable of musical abominations were, first, pieces of the genre of " The Maiden's Prayer " and, second, transcriptions from operas. But the latter had been made so fashionable by Liszt, Herz, and Thalberg that it was unwise for any young virtuoso to exclude them from his programs. In such language, at any rate, the Escudiers and Monsieur Erard argued. Consequently Gottschalk abandoned his publicly announced intention of using a Bach prelude and fugue to open his own approaching concert and hastily got ready for that purpose a transcription for two pianos of the overture to Méhul's *La Chasse du jeune Henri*. The Escudiers had it in print when the day for the concert arrived, Wednesday, February 27.

At the second piano that evening was one of the most famous of French virtuosos of the time, Alexandre Goria. The other instrumentalist who assisted was the cellist Jacques Offenbach, then conductor of the orchestra at the Comédie Française. A soprano, contralto, and baritone also took part. In playing his own original compositions Gottschalk began with the ballades inspired by Ossian and followed them with " Le Bananier." Then, forming a second group, came " La Savanne " and " Bamboula." Gottschalk ended the program with the two final movements of Weber's sonata in C. So great was the excitement that the managers of the Salle Erard, where the concert was given, called in the police to keep the ovations within the bounds of order.

" Were we not right," asked *La Musique* in a review of the concert, " when we spoke a year ago of the talent of Gottschalk? We said: ' A great artist has made himself heard. There is novelty in his compositions and in his manner of playing them. Within a short while he will be among the most brilliant stars of the modern school of piano playing.' Since that prophecy was made Gottschalk has advanced with the pace of a giant. His successes during the past year in both salon and concert hall have won the admiration of both public and artists. The great musicians heard him last Wednesday night, some for the first time. These last had been wondering whether all the praise for the American was not for a charlatan. They are now his most enthusiastic admirers. They say that he copies no other composer and no other performer, that his originality, in form and in spirit, will leave its mark on the art of the piano. His concert was decisive—and triumphal."

Neither this review nor a number of others equally rich in praise could have meant much to Gottschalk. He had been working too hard all winter, and the morning after the concert awoke with a high fever. For more than two weeks he was very ill. His mother came to the rue de Berlin, and once more watched at his bedside. Several afternoons his temperature ran so high that even she despaired of his life. Bulletins on his condition appeared in certain newspapers every two or three days.

In the mornings, when his fever was low and he was rational, he persisted in saying that he would fill all the engagements for which he was under contract. It turned out that he was right. At the end of March he was strong enough to play two of his own mazurkas and a composition by Goria at the farewell concert given in the Salle Ste. Cécile by the great Henriette Sontag, who, after many years of retirement, had returned to the stage and had sung during the winter at the Théâtre Italien. Early in April he played at a benefit for the blind. A few days later he appeared with a galaxy of artists at a grand benefit for the poor in the Salle Herz. Among his auditors that evening was the Prince-President, Louis Napoleon. Then on April 21 he played his medley from *La Chasse du jeune Henri*, again with Goria, at Offenbach's concert in the Salle Pleyel.

The cellist—still unaware of his genius for composing light opera—was not a virtuoso of the first rank. He depended upon his assisting artists to make his concerts attractive. On this occasion, because of Gottschalk and Goria, he drew an immense audience. But he almost spoiled the evening by the bad playing of his own arrangment for cello of Gottschalk's " Le Bananier." " How could a man as practical as Offenbach," asked one critic, " have dared such a desecration when Gottschalk himself could have easily played the piece? "

Artists other than Offenbach were meeting with great success in interpreting the American's music. Goria played " Le Bananier " at the Sontag farewell and repeated it in a dozen other concerts. Alfred Jaell introduced the same composition to audiences in Brussels and London along with a mazurka which Gottschalk had dedicated to him, " La Moissoneuse." Two other mazurkas were in the repertoire of Joseph Wieniawski, who was touring Germany and Russia with his brother Henri, the violinist. Emile Prudent introduced "Le Bananier" to Central Europe. Each of these pianists was writing to Gottschalk urging him to produce more from which they might choose.

By May 8, when he became twenty-one, he had made up his mind to do what they were asking. When he thought of how slight his body of published work was he felt ashamed—and frightened. But within five months, he estimated, this situation would be remedied. For he expected to have ready by November an American concerto to play at a *La France musicale* concert. He expected also to have in press by then four or five more "pendants to 'Bamboula.'" His head was full of ideas for all these works; and he had in prospect ideal surroundings in which to do the labor, a rambling old house on the Lake of Neuchâtel in Switzerland, near the town of Grandson. The Parisian friends who owned the place offered to turn over to him an entire wing. His seclusion would be perfect. He might, while en route to Switzerland, give a concert or two in Lyons. But once beyond the French border he would forget that he was a virtuoso. Because of the great popularity of "Le Bananier," the latest allotment of royalty paid to him by the Escudiers was surprisingly large. It was quite likely that on his return to Paris he would be in a position to turn over all his pupils—except possibly the very best ones—to other teachers.

Among these very best pupils was André Moser, a Swiss. The summer of 1850 he was back in his home in Geneva. As soon as he heard that his music master was in Grandson he went to see him.

Gottschalk had a tale of mishaps to relate. He was delayed in getting away from Paris. Because he carried neither an American passport nor a French card of identity he was arrested in Dijon and held in custody until he got access to his baggage and produced a sufficient number of letters to convince the police that he was Gottschalk. The experience humiliated him so deeply that he abandoned his plans for a concert or two in Lyons. In Les Rousses, near the Swiss border, the missing papers were again demanded. Again he was arrested, and the ordeal of Dijon was repeated. Then when he finally reached Switzerland he fell victim to a malarial attack. For sixteen days he lay ill in Le Sentier. He had traveled by railway train or diligence from Paris to Le Sentier, but for the rest of the journey to Grandson he was carried in a litter. The month with his friends in their picturesque old house, where from his north window he had an excellent view of the famous fortress of Grandson, had restored his strength. He was ready now to give himself up wholly to his American concerto.

But young Moser had brought along a letter—an invitation to Gottschalk to play on the evening of Wednesday, August 7, with an orchestra that gave weekly concerts in the Municipal Casino of Geneva during the summer season. The managers of the orchestra, said the letter, would leave Monsieur Gottschalk free to choose his concerto and would be happy if he would agree also to appear on the program in a number of independent selections. The proposed fee, which covered the rehearsals for the concerto, was twice the amount Gottschalk had received for his last concert in Paris and ten times as much as he had ever been paid as an assisting artist. Forgetting his American concerto, he exclaimed, " No virtuoso could say no to this! "

So André Moser went back home carrying two letters from Gottschalk. One was an acceptance of the invitation from the managers of the Geneva orchestra, and the other, to be posted in Geneva, was a plea to Monsieur Erard to dispatch at once the best concert piano available in his Paris warerooms.

Gottschalk was in Geneva, playing in salons and making the acquaintance of local musicians, when the piano arrived. It was built by Erard for the Paris Exhibition of 1849, and was the longest grand piano any manufacturer had ever attempted.

Seated in pride before the magnificent instrument on the evening of August 7 in the concert hall of the Geneva Casino, Gottschalk played, with fine orchestral support, Weber's *Concertstück*. Later, closing the first half of the program, he played Goria's fantasy on themes from Bellini's *Sonnambula* and—for the first time without a second piano—his own paraphrase of the overture to *La Chasse du jeune Henri*. Finally, as next to the last number for the evening, he gave " La Savanne," " La Moissoneuse," and " Le Bananier." He played as much as he would have played if the concert had been his own and not the orchestra's, and he was received with great warmth.

But the evening was Weber's.

On looking out into the auditorium from the wings before the beginning of the concert Gottschalk noticed that the seats in the front row, still unoccupied, were equipped with special cushions of a rich red velvet. An orchestra player standing beside him explained that this row was reserved for the Grand Duchess Anna of Russia and her entourage, that she always passed the summer on her estate near Geneva, and that she rarely missed a concert when anything from Weber was being played. At his first appearance on the stage Gottschalk noticed that the front row was filled. But absorbed as he was in the music he forgot that royalty was among his auditors. Now, as he waited alone in his dressing room while the orchestra was playing the last number on the program, an attendant came in and handed him a card. The name it bore, " the Baron de Vauthier," was to him entirely strange. Seeing the puzzled look on his face, the attendant said, " The chamberlain to Her Imperial Highness, Monsieur. He's at the door." " Show him in," replied Gottschalk.

A moment later he and a very old man stood face to face, and their eyes showed that a strong sympathy had begun to well in the heart of each. " All the time you were playing," said the Baron, still holding both of Gottschalk's hands, " you were talking to me about Weber, one of the best friends I ever had." Then, in a shaky voice and with tears in his eyes, he told how he had heard the *Concertstück* the first time it was ever played before an audience—at the Royal Residence in Dresden with Weber himself at the piano. " You played it more perfectly than he," said the Baron. " You mustn't expect me to say that you played it better."

The Grand Duchess, he explained, was fatigued and had not remained for the last number on the program. She had sent her congratulations to the American on the great success of his début in Geneva and had requested the Baron to see the young man in comfort to wherever he was staying. Gottschalk rode to his hotel that night in the most splendid equipage he had ever entered. But he was unmindful of the luxury. He was absorbed in the Baron's reminiscences of Weber.

Thereafter Gottschalk and his new-found friend saw one another daily. They either went for a drive or stayed at Gottschalk's hotel and talked. The Baron, who had been in the household of the Grand Duchess Anna for almost half a century, had seen the great of his time come and go. The Grand Duchess was German, born a princess of the house of Saxe-Coburg-Gotha. She was a sister of Queen Victoria's mother and of King Leopold I of Belgium, and an aunt of the reigning Duke of Saxe-Coburg-Gotha and his brother, the British Prince Consort. When she was still under sixteen she was married to the Grand Duke Constantine of Russia, the eccentric son of a mad father, Czar Paul.

The marriage took place in 1796, shortly after the death of Catherine the Great, who had arranged it. After enduring her husband's monstrous behavior for three years, Anna fled from Russia and came back to Coburg. But the powers that direct the destiny of a princess forced her into a reconciliation with Constantine, and she returned to St. Petersburg. Though more abused than before, she held out until 1801, when Czar Paul was assassinated and his eldest son, who was childless, ascended the throne as Alexander I. Constantine was next in the line of succession, and Anna saw before her the possibility of being one day the Empress of Russia. Nevertheless, she again fled from St. Petersburg. This time Russia made no overtures for her return. For, claimed Constantine, " She was aided in her flight by the man who has become her lover." Genevese gossips had long insisted that the man was the Baron de Vauthier. Gottschalk, forming his conclusions partially from hints dropped by the Baron, was almost convinced that they were right. Anyway, with his predilection for the romantic, he liked to believe that his aged friend and the abused Grand Duchess had found a way to enjoy for almost fifty years the peace of true love.

Just one week after his Geneva début Gottschalk met the Grand Duchess at her château. The occasion was a garden fête in honor of two of her guests, the Queen of Sardinia and the Duchess of Saxe-Weimar. Gottschalk found the Grand Duchess a charming old lady with a great curiosity about America. She had been reading the newspaper reports of Jenny Lind's approaching tour of the United States and was very inquisitive in regard to her manager, Mr. Barnum. She had got it into her head that he was a great American statesman, a president or something else very important.

The Baron had given Gottschalk a few lessons in court etiquette. But the young American forgot all about what was expected of him when he was once in the presence of the friendly Grand Duchess. Then when he was presented to Queen Adelaide of Sardinia he was deep in an argument with her over the comparative merits of Broadwood and Erard pianos before he had time to think of the formalities. The Queen apparently never came in contact with a musician without letting him know at once that she considered the English instrument superior to all others. Gottschalk of course was obliged to defend the piano for which he was now a public representative.

He was invited to the fête as a friend of the Grand Duchess's chamberlain, not as an artist who was expected to perform. But a piano—neither a Broadwood nor an Erard—was at hand, on a little platform under the trees; and, with his hearers around him, seated in chairs or on the grass, Gottschalk played such music as he loved to play—Bach, Weber, Mendelssohn, Chopin, and his own Ossianic and American pieces.

When the Baron called at his hotel the next day, he brought from the Grand Duchess a memento of appreciation for his playing at the fête. It was a jewel case of gold encrusted with silver; on the lid was a cameo ringed with diamonds.

Within less than a week Gottschalk was again at the château, this time for an intimate luncheon in a small dining room. The entertainment was so informal that it was bohemian. The royal ladies in whose honor the garden fête had been given were as merry as young girls. When Gottschalk sat down at the piano which had been brought into the room he noticed that a low screen stood between him and the Grand Duchess's chair. It was impossible for him to see more than her head and shoulders; but, glancing at her from time to time as he played, he could tell that she was busy with her hands, as if sewing or knitting. The mystery was not solved until he finished his American pieces. Then, shouting "Bravo!" with everybody else in the room, she held up a crown of oak leaves and roses. The Duchess of Saxe-Weimar took it, ran to Gottschalk, and, standing behind him, placed it upon his head.

The Geneva newspapers reported Gottschalk's appearance with the orchestra very favorably. But the opinion of the critics was of far less weight in building up public interest in the American than was the increasing talk about the attentions of the Grand Duchess Anna and the Baron de Vauthier.

At his second appearance in the Casino, on August 21, the demand for seats was so great that two hundred chairs were placed on the stage. Still it was estimated that as many were turned away as succeeded in gaining entrance. On this evening the concert was nominally as well as actually Gottschalk's. The orchestra supplied only the six musicians who appeared with the American in Onslow's septet for piano and wood winds. André Moser played the second piano in two transcriptions, both by Gottschalk—*La Chasse du jeune Henri* and *William Tell*, the latter arranged the preceding week and presented as a tribute to Switzerland. Gottschalk alone gave the rest of the program, playing Beethoven, Weber, and his own music. He had never before been on the stage from the beginning of a program to the end.

In reporting this concert, the Geneva critics were extravagantly laudatory. Among them was Julius Eichberg, in time to migrate to America and, as a violinist, make musical history in Boston. He and all the others began their critiques by calling attention to the presence of the Grand Duchess and her suite in the front row. The lengthy tributes to Gottschalk made it evident that the Swiss interest in him had become an excitement.

Soon it was a furor, not unlike the mass hysteria over Jenny Lind raging in New York at the same time. Gottschalk could scarcely relax after one concert before the day arrived for another —not only in Geneva but in Lausanne, Yverdon, Vevay, Neuchâtel, and at Aix in Savoy. Wherever he appeared the house was packed. The flowers tossed at him, it was said, were sufficient to carpet every hall in which he played. The audiences were merciless in demanding encores. At the conclusion of a concert in Lausanne Gottschalk played " Le Bananier " five times! With the audience in a mad uproar for a sixth hearing of the piece, he stole out by a stage entrance and, as he said, " left the lunatics to yell to the desert."

Gold was pouring into his pockets—as much for a single concert as he earned for a whole month of teaching. Moreover, the demand for his music in the Swiss shops was so great that the Escudiers could not supply it. Such popularity, he reasoned, could be only temporary. He must take advantage of it while it lasted.

His moral support during these exciting days was the Baron de Vauthier, who had known for half a century how to live with fame. Under the advice of the kind old man, Gottschalk learned that he must not be seen on the streets, that he must make no attempt to answer the letters which were pouring in, and that he must leave unread the tributes—in verse as well as prose— which were filling columns in the newspapers. Frequently he drove with the Baron to the Grand Duchess's château, where he always found the restfulness he craved.

Now that he ran the risk of being mobbed by fanatic admirers if he ventured outside his hotel on foot, he found that he had a little time for composing. But he was in no state of mind to attempt anything as serious as his American concerto. He turned rather to the simple task of rewriting his first published composition, "Polka de Salon." With the melancholy melodies given a more fitting development and with the piece renamed "Danse ossianique," he dedicated it to the Grand Duchess Anna and sent it to the Escudiers for immediate publication. It was also in gratitude to the Grand Duchess that he wrote at this time his fantasy on "God Save the Queen," a melody which all Europe in the year 1850 associated with the most illustrious member of the house of Saxe-Coburg-Gotha, Victoria of England.

October passed, and the calls for concerts were still coming in. But after a concert in Geneva on the evening of November 6, when the furor over Gottschalk was more frenzied than ever before, he was not again to be seen on the shores of Lake Leman. He disappeared—and in doing so created a great public mystery. The Grand Duchess Anna, the Baron de Vauthier, André Moser, and others in Gottschalk's immediate circle of intimates, including his friends in Grandson, listened to the fantastic rumors which flooded Switzerland, smiled, and said nothing. The whereabouts of society's idol was still a subject of the wildest conjecture and gossip when five weeks later the newspapers of Geneva quietly announced that on the evening of December 17 Gottschalk would give his farewell Swiss concert in Yverdon and that all the proceeds would go to the Grandson hospital, a wing of which was to be named in his honor.

The character of the rumors which raged in Switzerland during the five weeks following Gottschalk's mysterious disappearance was reflected in an article published in *Le Siècle* of Paris over the signature of the eminent musician and critic, Oscar Commetant. "Jenny Lind has been surpassed," wrote Monsieur Commetant. "At least she has never been carried off bodily. It is precisely this which has happened to Gottschalk. After his November 6 concert in Geneva, where he was showered with flowers, an attractive Swiss Amazon waited at the stage door of the Casino for him to come out. When finally he appeared she threw a mantle over his head, took him in her arms, and carried him off. His frail and delicate body made his capture easy. Thus it was that the young American pianist precipitately left Geneva after having been the delight of the elegant Genevese society."

Gottschalk had no comment to make on Monsieur Commetant's published story. He read it at a time when he was still in the greatest bewilderment over all that had happened to him in Switzerland. He had discovered there that he possessed tremendous powers. The problems which had given him sleepless nights—such as his concern over family finances and his dissatisfaction over the time consumed by teaching—were now as nothing. He still had no notion as to how he was going to adjust himself to the revolution in his life when he got back to Paris in time to celebrate New Year's, 1851, with his mother, sisters, and brothers in the pension on the rue des Filles-du-Calvaire.

The reunion made him feel that he must see his father. While in Switzerland he dispatched letters to New Orleans regularly, reporting in full his fantastic triumphs. Now he wrote begging his father for a visit.

Back with Edward on the rue de Berlin, he lived as simply as he had always lived. His pursuits were what they had been the year before, except that there was no more traveling from one quarter of Paris to another to give lessons. The few specially talented pupils whom he still taught came to the studio into which he had converted one of his rooms.

At a soirée at Monsieur Orfila's early in January he introduced " Le Mancenillier," a Negro composition which he had completed during his " mystery month " in Switzerland. Though he called the new piece a serenade, it is in form and spirit a ballade, an outgrowth no doubt of his memory of hearing Sally's songs and tales about the poisonous manchineel tree of the West Indies. The work was at once accepted as " a brilliant pendant to ' La Savanne.' "

One evening in Monsieur Marmontel's studio, where the guests were all musicians, Gottschalk heard Georges Bizet, well past twelve now, imitate his playing of " La Moissoneuse," " Le Bananier," and " Bamboula." The boy's amazing expertness in recreating nuances made Gottschalk feel that he himself was at the piano. He had never felt so in hearing Prudent, Goria, and Jaell play his music.

He was sure that the boy was a genius, and spoke to the Escudiers about him. The outcome was that young Bizet was engaged to appear at the February *La France musicale* concert in the Théâtre Italien. He was the only pianist on the program, and was allowed to choose the pieces he wished to play. The first he named was Gottschalk's "La Moissoneuse."

At odd moments during February Gottschalk devoted himself to arranging the orchestral score of Weber's *Concertstück* for string quartet. He was superstitious about this work, which had led to his triumphs in Switzerland; and he wished to present it to Paris in a new form at his first spring concert, already announced for March 20.

The hall he chose was the Salle Bonne-Nouvelle, opened only a few weeks earlier with a concert given by Emile Prudent. It had at once become fashionable. Moreover the seating capacity exceeded that of any older concert hall in Paris.

It was filled to capacity on the evening of March 20, and was the scene, agreed the newspapers, of " flowers, elegance, and enthusiasm." The Weber *Concertstück*, presented as a quintet, was received with great applause. With the first violinist, Constant Hermann, Gottschalk played the andante and allegro from Beethoven's *Kreutzer Sonata*. Two singers assisted, a soprano and baritone, both from the Grand Opéra. Gottschalk's solos, all of his own composition, included two works new to Paris, the fantasy on " God Save the Queen " and " Danse des ombres." The latter, which belongs among his Ossianic pieces, was another product of his " mystery month " in Switzerland. Of the eight pieces listed on the program he had to repeat five. He was also forced to yield to shouts for two unlisted favorites, " Bamboula " and " Le Bananier."

At the beginning of March one of the factory buildings of the Pleyel company was burned to the ground, and the hundreds of employees thus deprived of the chance to work were by now destitute. Monsieur Pleyel several times talked with Gottschalk about their misery; and the American, with the altruism that marked his activities more and more strongly, announced, the week of his March 20 concert, that he would give a benefit for the unemployed workers. He deliberately set the date forward to April 21, hoping that his father, who had written that he was sailing from New Orleans March 18, would reach Paris in time to be present.

He was not disappointed. Mr. Gottschalk, gray-haired and wrinkled now, but with eyes as bright as Moreau had always known them, sat with his family in a front row of the Salle Pleyel on the evening of April 21. Every seat in the hall, priced at twenty francs each, was sold two weeks in advance. A full three hundred paid ten francs each for the privilege of standing. If the hall had been twice as large, said the newspapers, it could not have accommodated all who tried to buy tickets.

Gottschalk's loyal admirers from the aristocracy were among his hearers. But it was not an evening of flowers, perfume, and fashion. It was political as well as artistic. Supporters of the Prince-President's policy of winning the good will of the Parisian proletariat were there is great numbers. Gottschalk played that night to men and women who had never before heard a piano virtuoso. He deliberately made the program popular. His assistants were two singers, both of whom sang only well-known opera arias. His own numbers were made up of transcriptions from operas and of such of his pieces as one heard whistled on the streets. The climax of the evening came when, after the playing of " Bamboula," a worker, in worker's smock, walked up to the stage and presented Gottschalk with an enormous bouquet, a token of thanks from those to whom the entire proceeds of the concert were to go. To his vast audience that night Gottschalk symbolized the French ideal of the democratic American.

The next afternoon, in the little private salon of the pension on the rue des Filles-du-Calvaire, Mr. Gottschalk sat with a pile of the day's newspapers on the table at his side. In one he read, " The benefit concert at the Salle Pleyel last evening turned out to be such a triumph for Gottschalk as no pianist except Franz Liszt has ever before experienced in Paris." Such superlatives of praise characterized the report in each of the newspapers, and in not one was there a hint of unfavorable criticism. Moreau, seeing his father's interest, placed in his hands a set of clippings which he had accumulated in the past six weeks.

The first which Mr. Gottschalk read was from the pen of Pier-Angelo Fiorentino, music critic of the conservative *Le Constitutionnel*. It was lengthy, and laudatory from beginning to end. The passage which most impressed the father was as follows: "Monsieur Gottschalk is very young. In mien he is modest, dignified, and reserved. In his outward manner as in his talent there is much of the grace and melancholy of Chopin. The compositions of Monsieur Gottschalk have great distinction, originality, and charm. They are in general short; they never tax a hearer's patience. Many of the little masterpieces which he has created have become widely popular. His execution is of a finish, a brilliance, a preciseness, a velocity, and a spirit altogether astonishing. At the moment when he seems to be caressing a melody, producing tones which are faintly audible, he suddenly draws from the keys a hurricane of sound, overwhelming his audience by his unanticipated power. But it is not by contrasts skillfully managed, not by sudden shifts from the gentle to the stormy, that he succeeds in electrifying his hearers. His talent is of a character more elevated and more serious. It is his inspiration, alive and abundant, the reflection of a poetic sense, innate and deeply felt, which enables him to win such applause and such triumphs. One must say to this charming artist what Gretry said to Nicolo: 'You're on the right road. See that you stay there.'"

Mr. Gottschalk next picked up a clipping from Le Charivari and found his eyes fixed upon the following sentences from Taxile Delord's critique on Moreau's March 20 concert: "The most intelligent and most inspired orchestra in the world would find it difficult to improve upon Gottschalk's presentation of Weber's Concertstück as a quintet. It would be equally difficult to give to the piano score of Beethoven's great sonata in A more warmth and force than the American gives."

From Théophile Gautier in La Presse the father read: "Monsieur Gottschalk is worthy to stand beside Liszt, Prudent, and Thalberg, not because he is their imitator, but because he is himself. The novelty which marks him as a significant artist is due to the fact that, after forming his talent by solid studies, he has allowed his fancy to wander freely in the savannas of his native country. He has recreated for us the colors and perfumes of America. I have admired him unreservedly since the first time I heard him."

Mr. Gottschalk next came upon two clippings from *L'Evéne-ment*. The first, he found, was a long article on the future of French art. In the section on music there was an allusion which read: "Gottschalk, the young bard come from America." The author of the article was Victor Hugo. The second of the clippings from *L'Evénement* was by Madame Menechet de Barival. It showed, Mr. Gottschalk saw, that she, like Hugo, was impressed by the poetry in Moreau. At the end of her critique she said: "When Monsieur Gottschalk is at the keyboard he is the medium through which the most tender emotions and the most exquisite sentiments find the expression denied them in words."

Mr. Gottschalk next picked up a clipping from *Le Journal des débats* for April 3. It showed that it had been much read, and he did not wonder why when he saw that the writer was Hector Berlioz. It was lengthy, giving first a generalized discussion of the art of piano playing and its rapid development in recent years.

Then came: "Monsieur Gottschalk is one of the few now living who possess all the different elements which make a pianist of sovereign power. He is an accomplished musician. He knows the limit beyond which the liberties taken with rhythm lead only to disorder and confusion, and this liberty he never transcends. His grace in bringing out sweet melodies is perfect. Still when the demand is for velocity, passion, and brilliance he meets it with an effect which astonishes and dazzles. The childlike simplicity of his smiling caprices, the charming ease with which he renders simple things, seems to belong to a second personality, distinct from that which characterizes his thundering energies.

"The success of Monsieur Gottschalk when he is playing to a civilized audience is great. It makes one happy to observe how his hearers are transported. At the concert which he gave last month in the Salle Bonne-Nouvelle, most of his pieces had to be repeated. I must say that Monsieur Gottschalk on that evening merited a eulogy superior to the eulogies I have already given him: he executed in the most masterly manner the piano part of Beethoven's sonata in A for piano and violin, Monsieur Hermann with his unrivaled talent playing the dangerous violin part.

Neither in style nor form does this work approach in any way what is accepted as piano music. It is impossible to surpass Monsieur Gottschalk's playing of the andante, to give more relief to the multitudinous arabesques of the variations, and to direct with finer effect the last section of the finale without letting it lose its vertiginous ardor.

"Monsieur Gottschalk has brought from his native America many curious songs, borrowed from the Creoles and Negroes. He has drawn from them themes for the most delicious compositions. Everybody in Europe is now acquainted with 'Bamboula,' 'Le Bananier,' 'Le Mancenillier,' 'La Savanne,' and twenty other ingenious fantasies in which tropical melodies lull most acceptably the ears of a Europe always eager for novelty. The highly merited celebrity he has attained will make it possible for him to recross the Atlantic with the certainty of being received as a prophet in his own country."

Mr. Gottschalk had to wait until another day to continue reading the clippings. Since his arrival in Paris he had been almost constantly in Moreau's company. The other members of the family realized that he wished to spend his time in this way, and did not interfere. This evening, though only twenty-four hours had passed since the taxing benefit for the Pleyel workers, Moreau appeared as assisting artist in two concerts, first in the Salle Ste. Cécile and then in the Salle Erard. His father heard him in both.

The next week he heard him play on two different evenings in the immense Théâtre Italien at the concerts given by the eminent Belgian violinist Charles de Bériot. Then Mr. Gottschalk was at the Salle Herz on May 12 when his son appeared with another celebrated violinist from Brussels, Henri Vieuxtemps.

With the playing of Vieuxtemps, Mr. Gottschalk was familiar. In the spring of 1844 the Belgian and Ole Bull each gave a series of concerts in New Orleans at the same time. The Americans favored the Norwegian, and the French were all for the Belgian. A typical New Orleans battle ensued, and though seven years had passed it was still, said Mr. Gottschalk, an undecided contest.

If in coming to Europe he hoped to take back to America his wife and children, he met with disappointment. Clara and Augusta, his wife urged, had Moreau's talent and ambition. It would be a crime, she argued, to deprive them of the advantages of Paris. Then there were Blanche and Gaston. "No one can tell yet what they will do," said Aimée. She was determined to hold on to the pension, and must, she insisted, have Célestine to help her and Madame Dècle run it.

But the husband did win at least one concession: it was agreed that Edward should go back to New Orleans with him. The boy, already fifteen and a half, was probably as talented in music as either Clara or Augusta. But his mother, possessed of the fancy that he would one day be another Monsieur Lislet, was easily persuaded that he should study law in the country where he was to win his fame.

At the family conclaves everyone took it for granted that in matters financial the father and eldest son stood as one—two providers working as a unit. So the problem of supplying the money for Aimée's great plans for her daughters and little Gaston was not even mentioned.

But it was the chief topic of conversation when Moreau and his father were alone together. Mr. Gottschalk believed that his son had riches within his grasp. He had been present at Jenny Lind's début at the St. Charles Theatre in New Orleans on February 10. He had seen the best seats auctioned, a number of them receiving bids for as high as two hundred dollars each. Within a year or two the Swedish singer would come back to Europe with such a fortune as a Parisian musician of the highest rank could not accumulate in a lifetime. Moreau's Swiss experiences had proved that what Jenny Lind was doing in America he could also do. "And the backing of a vulgar P. T. Barnum is not necessary," Mr. Gottschalk insisted.

Moreau did not need to be urged to try his luck in his native country. When the European newspapers began to report Jenny Lind's American tour he made up his mind to find out how the United States would receive him. But before leaving Europe he must, he told his father, try out Spain. His friend Goria met with great success there until he became involved in politics and was forced by the government to leave. Moreau would be more circumspect. If he could find a way to win the favor of the royal family, he would see his Swiss triumphs repeated.

The Gottschalk farewells took place at the pension on a morning near the end of May. That afternoon Mr. Gottschalk, Moreau, and Edward arrived at Bourges, the end of the railway line to the southwest. The next day the three set out for Bordeaux by diligence. There Mr. Gottschalk and Edward embarked for America. Moreau's last words to them were, " I'll meet you both in New York in just one year."

$\mathcal{T}$ hough the local newspapers hailed him as the peer of Liszt, Gottschalk gave perfunctory performances at his concerts that summer in Bordeaux, Tarbes, Bayonne, and Biarritz. He was devoting his best energy to the task of mastering the Spanish language. The teacher who accompanied him from place to place was an impoverished Castilian gentleman, aristocratic enough to be familiar with the etiquette demanded at the Spanish court. Gottschalk recognized the man's value and engaged him to serve as his secretary during the Spanish tour. The two reached Bilbao on an afternoon in early October.

Gottschalk knew that without the patronage of the Grand Duchess Anna he would never have achieved his Swiss successes. His aim now was to gain the protection of the highest personage in Spain, the young Queen Isabella. He assumed that she had at least seen his name. For he had dedicated " Bamboula " to her, had sent her the special copy printed by the Escudiers for the purpose, and had received from one of the royal secretaries a note expressing Her Majesty's appreciation. Now he was trying to devise a way to approach her directly.

He had heard no other reigning monarch of Europe so much talked about. In 1846, when she was sixteen, she was married to Prince Francisco d'Assisi de Bourbon. On the same day, her sister, a year younger than she and heir presumptive to the crown, was married to the Duke of Montpensier, a son of King Louis-Philippe of France. An attempt by the Spanish and French governments to cover the fact that Louis-Philippe maneuvered the Queen's marriage as well as her sister's proved futile. It was widely known, moreover, that the husband he chose for the Queen was incapable of fatherhood. His scheme was obvious: while he had not dared threaten the displeasure of the great European powers by making his son the Spanish prince consort, he had arranged matters so that the line of succession to the Spanish throne would fall to his son's heirs. But by 1851 history had proved that in precipitating the "affair of the Spanish marriages" Louis-Philippe committed one of his gravest blunders. His maneuver brought his country to the brink of war with Great Britain and added to the unpopularity which resulted in his downfall. In the meantime Isabella circumvented her unhappy situation by resorting to adultery. Her husband, whom the Spaniards spoke of in public as "the King" and in private as "Fanny," was obliged to play the part of father to children sired by her lovers. A daughter, who died in infancy, was born in 1850. Another baby, as Gottschalk knew, was expected any day now. He realized that he was trying to win the Queen's favor at an awkward period.

In adopting a course of immorality Isabella had before her the example of her mother, the Dowager Queen Cristina. In 1844, when the daughter still venerated virtue, she, as Queen, forced her mother to marry the handsome guardsman who had been her paramour for eight or ten years. Titled the Duke of Rinzares, decorated with the Order of the Golden Fleece, and accorded the honors due a grandee of Spain, the guardsman, in spite of lapsing occasionally into the manners and speech of the barracks, had come to be a figure of considerable influence at court. He was able at least, it was said, to keep Cristina from talking too much when Isabella decided to discard a lover, perhaps an opera singer or an actor, and take a new one, perhaps a general.

The Duke of Rinzares was the personage to whom Gottschalk appealed in seeking a royal command. Near the end of October, after he had been installed in a hotel in Madrid for a week, he called on the Duke and presented letters of introduction. He left the Duke's palace full of hope.

But days passed, and nothing came of the Duke's encouragement. A letter which Gottschalk wrote to his father on the morning of November 17 shows how depressed he had become. "The Queen," he declared, "has not yet decided to allow me to

play before her. The nobility are reserved towards me. I've heard
that the Queen, on being told that I'm an American, exclaimed
that she'd never patronize an artist from the United States.
Whether the rumor is true or not, it has been spread abroad,
and the courtiers dislike to show me too marked a degree of
courtesy for fear of irritating Her Majesty."

Gottschalk himself went out and posted this letter. He had
been back in his apartment only a few minutes when an emissary
from the Duke of Rinzares arrived to announce that Her Majesty
the Queen wished to hear him play at the royal palace that very
evening. The audience, the emissary explained, would consist
only of the Queen, the King, the Queen Dowager, and the Duke
of Rinzares.

Gottschalk spent a busy day. His secretary drilled him in how
to bow in the Spanish manner and how to walk backwards. At
Gottschalk's request the King's private pianist called at the hotel
that afternoon, and for three hours the two musicians rehearsed
the duo they were to play for Her Majesty. Then Gottschalk
had to make sure that he was rightly appareled for a court
appearance.

He was ready at nine that evening when the King's pianist
came to escort him to the royal palace. Within fifteen minutes
they were at the foot of the grand staircase. At the top of the
ascent they were stopped by sentries who required them to give
their names. Then they walked down a long splendid gallery
guarded by halberdiers cloaked in mantles. At the end of the
gallery they were led into the antechamber where they were
relieved of their hats and greatcoats. Then a young nobleman,
his breast covered with medals and ribbons, led them into a
salon where five or six officers of state, in court costume, were
evidently awaiting Her Majesty's orders. Gottschalk and his
companion had to pass the length of still another great gallery
before they were shown into the immense square apartment where
they saw standing in readiness the two pianos upon which they
were to play.

Gottschalk, dazzled by the brilliance of the lighting in the
room, for a moment felt frightened. Then a young man, dressed

in evening attire as simple as his own, came up to him and said, in a French which showed only a hint of an accent, "Ah, Monsieur Gottschalk! How happy I am to receive an artist of your genius! It's the good fortune of Spain to have within her borders a musician whose great reputation is based upon such sure ground." At the first sound of the high-pitched voice, which Gottschalk had heard caricatured in many a Parisian salon before the outbreak of the revolution of 1848, he knew that the speaker was the King. Then the Queen Dowager, stout and middle-aged, yet dignified and courteous, welcomed Gottschalk with the simplicity with which his mother might have greeted a strange young man. The Duke of Rinzares was equally cordial. The American remembered that he must remain standing; and, to his relief, the King stood also. Gottschalk was to say of him in a letter to his father, " Speak of him as the world will, I have never met a more amiable, polished, nor kind gentleman, nor one who knows better how to utter words that sink into the heart of an artist." The American soon heard a rustle of silk, and the King said, "Monsieur Gottschalk, it is the Queen." Attendants raised the tapestry over the rear door, and Her Majesty entered.

Gottschalk was almost too stupefied to remember his secretary's instructions on how to bow. It was as if a mountain of dark blue brocade embroidered in gold had walked into the room. He had seen the Queen's portrait often enough to know that she was very stout, and he was not surprised to observe that the robe she wore had been designed to conceal her pregnancy. It was her tallness for which he was not prepared. She appeared to him more a goddess than a queen. But the gracious smile with which she acknowledged his bow restored his composure. He saw that after all she was just a young woman with rich brown hair, warm dark eyes, and a smooth beautiful complexion.

As soon as she was seated, she said, in Spanish, "Whenever you are ready, Señor, I shall be happy to have you perform."

The two pianists played the duo they had practiced that afternoon, Gottschalk's recently finished fantasy on themes from Verdi's *I Lombardi*. The opera had been produced in Paris under the title *Jerusalem*, and it was as such that Gottschalk was always to know his paraphrase. When he came to the finale, he noticed that the Queen had moved to the divan to his left and was watching his hands very intently. The King was standing to his right, leaning against an arm of the sofa on which the Dowager Queen and the Duke were seated.

Compliments followed the playing of the duo. Then the King asked for " Le Bananier," one of his great favorites, he said. Gottschalk played the piece, and then his " Danse ossianique " and " La Moissoneuse." When the latter was finished, the King said, " That is real music, Monsieur. It's poetry. But I must tell you that it's too good for the taste of Spain. The only pianists the Spanish admire are those who perform keyboard acrobatic feats."

By this time Gottschalk felt very much at home. The talk was free, and when he found difficulty in expressing an idea in Spanish the King made it clear.

Finally the Queen said something to Gottschalk which he failed to understand. The King immediately saw the look of embarrassment on his face and said, " She wishes to hear the composition you dedicated to her. We've been greatly pleased with it, and never miss an opportunity to hear it played." Gottschalk begged indulgence, explaining that he had not practiced the piece in weeks. " Say you so! " exclaimed the King. " Then you *must* play it. For I wish to see how you can interpret a piece of music badly." Gottschalk's rendition of " Bamboula " soon had the Dowager Queen on her feet, and before the piece was ended she and the Duke were dancing a Spanish dance to the Negro rhythm. When Gottschalk looked up from the piano after the thundering coda he saw astonishment on the face of every one in the room and knew that the Queen had her heart in the " Bravo! " she shouted.

The Dowager Queen, addressing Fanny as if he were a ten-year-old girl, said, " This evening's entertainment should encourage you to practice the piano more assiduously."

" Alas, Madame," Fanny replied, " my piano will remain closed all day tomorrow. I shall not have the courage to touch it for some time, I fear."

The King, certainly without his awareness, carried his hospitality a bit too far for the comfort of the American when he stood at the door waving farewell until the musicians were out of sight, thus making it necessary for them to walk backwards the full length of the first of the galleries they had to pass through to get out of the palace.

Gottschalk did not sleep that night until he wrote to his father retracting what he had said in the letter posted that morning. He was confident, he affirmed, that he had won the Queen's favor and that his conquest of Spain was assured.

There was just one worry on his mind, too trivial, he thought, to mention to his father. It was the attitude of the King's pianist. The man had behaved like a gentleman on the way to and from the royal palace. But in playing the *Jerusalem* fantasy he had fumbled three times and Gottschalk was sure he had done so deliberately. The man was close to the King and would have to be watched.

Actually, Gottschalk had won more royal favor than he had thought. The very next evening he was a guest at an intimate ball given by the Queen Dowager. When he arrived at the great ballroom in her palace, she was seated with the Queen on a canopied dais. Royalty looked on while the guests made merry. Gottschalk fell half in love with a beautiful young countess, and danced five or six polkas with her. The King and the Duke of Rinzares walked about the room, addressing a word to this one and that. When they came to Gottschalk, they repeated the compliments they had spoken the previous evening. "All eyes," Gottschalk wrote to his father, "were fixed upon me, and my triumph over those who had treated me coldly was complete." The court physician—on hand in case the Queen should suddenly be in labor—told Gottschalk that the Queen Dowager was speaking of him as a greater virtuoso than Liszt.

Early in December the Queen was delivered of a daughter, the princess who replaced the Duchess of Montpensier as heir to the throne. The public, joyous over this event and eager for entertainment, welcomed warmly the announcement that Gottschalk, under royal patronage, would give three concerts in the Teatro del Circe in Madrid before the end of 1851. Though the prices were twice as high as patrons of concerts in Madrid were accustomed to pay, the tickets were all sold within a single day. Each of the concerts turned out to be the scene of the wildest Spanish enthusiasm.

In January, Gottschalk went to Valladolid to give more concerts. He was preceded by letters from Isabella to the high public officials of Old Castile—letters demanding that Señor Gottschalk be accorded all the honors due a distinguished representative of a foreign country.

On the evening before his first concert in Valladolid he was the guest of honor at a banquet given by the Governor of Old Castile, a grandee whose wife was the Infanta Josefa, one of the King's sisters. The banquet was attended only by gentlemen. There were many toasts—to music, to the United States, to the onetime Spanish province of Louisiana, and to the pianist himself. In responding Gottschalk spoke in Spanish, and several times amusingly confused his idioms. When the sweets were served, he noticed that the cake placed before him was different from the pastry served to the others. The Governor explained that the special cake was a modest tribute to the honored American from the Infanta Josefa, who, following a recipe transmitted to her family by a Moor of the fourteenth century, had made it with her own hands.

Gottschalk had the chance to thank her in person for her tribute the next evening. He had made his last bow at his sensationally successful Valladolid début when he was told that the Governor and Her Royal Highness were waiting for him in the private reception room of the theatre. He found the Infanta Josefa young and attractive, and as kind and as profuse in compliments as her brother, the King.

Before the end of January, Gottschalk played to two more audiences which filled every inch of space in the Valladolid theatre. When he was not rehearsing with his assisting artists for these appearances, he was possibly at the Governor's palace, where Josefa and her husband received him with the greatest hospitality. He had announced a fourth concert for February 5.

But February 3 intervened, reminding him afresh of the power and strange ways of Fate.

Early that morning he heard the tragic news from Madrid— news which sent all Spaniards flocking to churches to pray for the life of their sovereign. On the day preceding, Candlemas Day, Queen Isabella, carrying in her arms her infant daughter, went to the Church of Atoca for the ceremony of Purification. When she walked into the porch of the sanctuary, where the whole court was assembled, Martin Merino, an aged priest with republican ideas, rushed upon her, pushed her infant from her breast, and, aiming at her heart, struck twice with a dagger. As yet the surgeons were unable to determine whether she had a chance to survive.

That afternoon, driving with his secretary in a hired carriage, Gottschalk went to the Governor's palace to leave a card expressing his sorrow over the catastrophe and his sympathy for the royal family. The only person he saw at the palace besides the servants was the King's pianist, whom he had invited to Valladolid to assist in his last concert. The man was outwardly polite, but Gottschalk was now certain that at heart he was envious and resentful. Deep in the fellow's mind, the American felt, was the question, " What are *you* doing here? "

Gottschalk hurried out, re-entered the carriage with his secretary, and told the driver to return to the hotel. But before the horses picked up speed, Gottschalk heard his name called. He ordered the driver to stop, and when he opened the door of the carriage and looked back he saw the King's pianist running towards him. Gottschalk, half out of the carriage, was supporting himself by holding to the jamb of the doorway with his left hand. When the man came near, an insane look of triumph suddenly spread over his face, and, with the quickness of a tiger, he dashed forward, grabbed the carriage door, and, with all his force, slammed it shut on the American's fingers.

Gottschalk fainted from the pain, and his secretary, staunching the flow of blood as best he could, hurried him to the nearest hospital. The doctor who dressed the wound frankly admitted to Gottschalk that his little finger might have to be amputated.

When he asked how the injury occurred and the secretary spoke up to tell the truth, Gottschalk, acting on a quick impulse, interrupted and said that he himself was wholly responsible, that he had absent-mindedly closed a carriage door on his hand.

Queen Isabella and Gottschalk had both fallen victim to violence within the same twenty-four-hour period. Just a week after the attacks made upon them, again on the same day, the Queen learned that she would live and Gottschalk learned that with patient care and gentle exercise the fingers of his left hand would by the end of three months be again strong and pliable.

As this heartening assurance sank into his consciousness, he felt convinced that in telling his doctor a lie about the cause of his injury he had acted with wisdom. He was in Spain to make money out of making music. He still had excellent chances, and he did not wish to see them jeopardized. His name, he felt, must for the time being be associated in the Spanish mind with music and music alone.

If he had obeyed his inner warning to have nothing to do with the King's pianist as he had obeyed the impulse to lie to the doctor, he would never, he told himself, have invited the man to play with him in Valladolid. He had done so for no other reason than to exhibit friendliness. But the man was too great a knave to be accorded gentlemanly treatment. He was not likely, Gottschalk reasoned, to strike again. However deeply he might have ingratiated himself in the favor of the girlish King, he was sensible enough to know that if the Queen were informed of his assault on the American artist who was giving concerts in Spain under her patronage he would face a long imprisonment, possibly even death by garroting. Still Gottschalk and his secretary were having the fellow watched. They had learned that he had fled from Madrid and was now in a small town on the Portuguese border.

Gottschalk's lie to the doctor was immediately picked up by the newspapers and repeated throughout Spain. Letters of commiseration were arriving daily. Among them was a kind message from the royal palace in Madrid, written by a secretary on behalf of both the Queen, who was still confined to her bed, and the

King. Gottschalk was to see that the newspapers printed also bulletins on the progress of his recovery and reports on his plans to return soon to the concert stage.

From the moment the news of Gottschalk's misfortune spread abroad the Governor showed every consideration. The American, shut in his hotel room with his left hand in a sling, was given every day or two the opportunity to enjoy a new specimen of the Infanta Josefa's artistry as a pastry cook.

Gottschalk had discovered at his concerts in Madrid and Valladolid that the Spaniards, as the King claimed, expected a pianist to perform musical acrobatics. Now, with nothing to do except plan for his coming concerts, he threw himself into composing what he called a symphony for ten pianos, " El Sitio de Zaragoza," in reality a medley of popular Spanish tunes connected by stormy bravura passages. He also began work on a show-off number for his individual use, a paraphrase of Paganini's " The Carnival of Venice." Within a few days he had many sheets of music paper filled with notes.

As soon as he was permitted to leave his room, he relaxed from his composing by taking long walks. One afternoon, on a picturesque market place in the old quarter of Valladolid, he crossed paths with a street urchin, half naked and cold.

The waif was evidently running wild, sleeping wherever he could find a shelter from the rain or snow. His food, he said, was a small loaf of bread every day, bought with the bit of money he earned by molding and peddling little clay figures. " A fellow artist! " exclaimed Gottschalk, as he recognized among the boy's wares a mule, a goat, and a dog. The child said that the only name he had was Ramon and that he was seven years old. Gottschalk saw that he was undoubtedly Andalusian. But the urchin could remember neither the name of the town he had come from nor how long he had been on the road. He just knew that he was running away, getting farther and farther all the time from his father, who was forever beating him. He had a brother much older than he, but there were no sisters and no mother.

The little clay figures and the soft brown eyes begging for

kindness and protection were too much for Gottschalk. He took the child to his hotel, had him fed and bathed, and then kept him wrapped in a blanket while his secretary went out and bought clothes. But Gottschalk, finding that the ready-made suits fitted badly, had a tailor come in and measure the boy for several Andalusian costumes, in rich colors, elaborately embroidered. "At the end of a few weeks," Gottschalk was to write, "the boy was transformed, thanks to the clothes I ordered made for him and thanks also to that happy thoughtlessness of childhood which forgets the troubles of the evening and conceals with a golden veil the darkness of the morrow."

Gottschalk was too absorbed in his composing to think seriously about what he was doing in taking the waif in. If he considered the consequences at all, he decided to let the consequences take care of themselves.

His finger healed as the doctor had said it would. By the end of May he was ready for the Madrid concerts which the newspapers announced.

He arrived in the capital on the afternoon of June 2 in company with his secretary and Ramon. The latter had with him a bull which, at his protector's suggestion, he had molded for Her Majesty. Gottschalk saw to it at once that the boy's story reached the Queen's ears. As he expected, he was summoned two or three days later to bring the child to the royal palace.

Ramon himself carried the precious bull, wrapped by his own hands in a piece of red silk and tied with a gold cord. "I presided gravely at the ceremony of presentation," Gottschalk was to say. When Her Majesty unwrapped the bull and set it on a little table, Gottschalk was sure that she was "dazzled less by its contour than by the originality of its pose." But she knew that it represented beauty to Ramon, and when she put her big warm hands on his head he was so overcome with joy that he cried. Ever afterwards, said Gottschalk, Ramon was to fancy his little bull standing with the many other pieces of statuary he had seen in the magnificent royal palace.

Madrid, said the newspapers, had never before experienced anything like the public excitement created by the series of concerts given by the American in June and July in the vast Teatro del Principe. The heat of summer seemed to increase rather than lessen the enthusiasm. "El Sitio de Zaragoza," performed by ten pianists with Gottschalk leading and playing the many interpolated cadenzas, met with so favorable a reception at the first concert that it was repeated at each of the others. No one seemed to think of it as noise rather than music. One critic went so far as to say, "In composing this work an American has unveiled the true heart of the Spanish people." At every concert flowers were tossed upon the stage until they formed great mounds. The audiences consumed so much time in applauding that a program was rarely finished until long past midnight.

Honors were heaped upon Gottschalk. The Queen made him a Cavalier of the Order of Isabella the Catholic. The Spanish Academy of Arts made him an honorary member. He was the guest of the government at state banquets. He was called upon to review regimental parades. Military bands serenaded him with his own music. He was the distinguished guest at several bull fights. A favorite toreador, Don José Redondo, presented him with a sword which had been used by one of the great heroes of the arena, Francisco Montes.

Outside as well as inside Madrid the people ignored the heat whenever there was a Gottschalk concert to attend. In every city in which he played in August and September he was greeted by enormous audiences. At Cordoba he gave a long series of concerts, and was engaged in another at Seville when October arrived. Under the direct patronage of the Queen as he was, he appeared in no city without giving at least one concert for the benefit of charity.

By the middle of October he was in San Lucar, the seat of the Duke and Duchess of Montpensier. At his first concert he was presented to Their Royal Highnesses, and the next day was received at their palace. In the son of Louis-Philippe and the sister of Queen Isabella he at last found in Spain a royal couple whom he could respect as well as like. The Duchess had adopted the Duke's democratic ways. The two treated the American as if he were an equal. They made him feel free to call at the palace

THE YOUNG GOTTSCHALK IDEALIZED IN CRAYON

TITLE PAGE OF THE FIRST EDITION
OF AN EARLY GOTTSCHALK COMPOSITION

A PAGE FROM GOTTSCHALK'S WORK BOOK

GOTTSCHALK IN 1853

ADA CLARE

VOL. 6.

NO. 146.

Saturday, October 11, 1862.

LOUIS M. GOTTSCHALK,
PRINCE OF PIANO-FORTE.

GOTTSCHALK AS SEEN BY AN AMERICAN CARTOONIST

GOTTSCHALK IN 1862

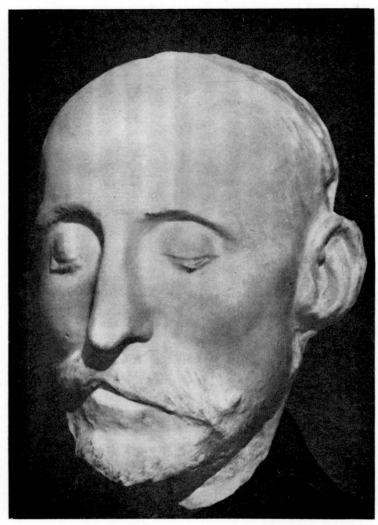

GOTTSCHALK'S DEATH MASK

at any time—to indulge in delightful conversation in French and to play Bach, Chopin, and other music he loved but dared not present at his concerts. Within a few days he was enjoying so much his association with the Duke and Duchess that he halted his tour and made plans to stay in San Lucar for a month or two.

He knew that the Queen feared and despised her sister and brother-in-law, and had their every movement watched. But he never guessed the strange workings of Her Majesty's uneasy mind until the morning toward the end of November when a dignitary of the royal police called on him at his hotel. The official handed him a paper; and at a glance the American saw that it was an order, with no reasons stated, for his immediate departure from Spain.

Gottschalk's secretary leaped to the conclusion that the King's pianist had again struck, and this time with cunning. But Gottschalk had another theory. The sudden withdrawal of the Queen's favor could be due only, he was sure, to her suspicions over his friendship with the Duke and Duchess of Montpensier.

He was never to talk much about his dismissal from Spain, nor to deny any of the fantastic reasons advanced by rumor. It was to be said that certain love letters between him and the Queen had been intercepted and that her cabinet forced her to send him out of the country. It was to be claimed that the Infanta Josefa had favored him with her body as well as with her pastry and that her husband, the Governor of Old Castile, was responsible for his expulsion. It was to be said in newspapers all over the world that the Queen, madly in love with him, issued the order for his ejection upon hearing that he was involved in an amorous affair with one of her ladies in waiting, the Countess of Montijo, soon to be the Empress Eugénie of France.

Gottschalk had no regrets about leaving Spain. He had accomplished the purpose of his tour: his pockets were overflowing with Spanish gold. He was tired—very tired—of the pianistic acrobatics demanded by his Spanish audiences. And it was long past time to redeem his promise to meet his father and Edward in New York.

On the very day he received the order of dismissal he called on the Duke and Duchess and said his adieus, guarding every word he spoke lest he give a hint that his sudden departure was not of his own will. Back at the hotel, he assigned a last task to his secretary, the task of seeing Monsieur Erard's pianos, ten all together, shipped back to France.

He still had Ramon on his hands. What could he do with the boy?

If there were any doubts in Gottschalk's mind as to how he should answer this question, they vanished when he found out, by chance, that the boy's father, an Andalusian gipsy, was a convicted murderer, in prison awaiting execution by garroting. Determined that the lovable youngster would never know more about his past than he had known the day he was found in Valladolid, Gottschalk adopted him.

The American and his Spanish foster son sailed from Cadiz on November 26. Three days later their ship docked in Marseilles. They reached Paris on December 1, in time to witness the excitement that marked the death of the Second French Republic and the birth of the Second Empire.

For three weeks Gottschalk stayed on the rue des Filles-du-Calvaire with his mother. When his sisters asked why in the world he had done such a thing as adopt a boy, he invariably answered with the question, " Could I see him go back to the streets to freeze and starve? " Then he would add, " Anyway he has his uses. You see how he and Gaston have taken to one another."

Gottschalk had no time to make calls. So, to bid hail and farewell to his friends, he gave a private recital in the Salle Pleyel. He was to say that he never played so well as he did that night, when he restricted himself to the music he loved best and knew that between him and each of his auditors there was full sympathy.

When he said goodbye to his mother, she exclaimed, " We'll never meet again, my son! " He tried to assure her that she was speaking nonsense. Yet within his heart of hearts there was the vague feeling that she was speaking the truth. Once more she made him promise that one day he would visit the Holy Land.

Gaston was bereft when he saw his playmate, gay in a brilliant new Andalusian costume, set out with Moreau. The journey to Le Havre was made by rail, and Gottschalk was scarcely aware that he was passing through the country which had so charmed him on his arrival in France ten and a half years before. It was December 24, 1852, when he and Ramon boarded the steamship *Humboldt* for the voyage to New York.

When Gottschalk looked out his porthole the next morning, he saw that the *Humboldt* was entering the harbor of Cowes. All day long the ship remained tied up at a wharf, taking on cargo. In the afternoon Gottschalk went ashore for a walk. It was cold, and within a few minutes his greatcoat was wet with mist. Though the one day of his life which he spent in England was Christmas, it was cheerless and most uncomfortable.

The next morning he was awakened by the sun shining in his eyes, and when he looked out he saw that the ship was on the open sea. Until New Year's the weather remained good. But that day the *Humboldt* ran into the heavy westerly gales and rough seas which continued to belabor her until the morning of January 10, when she steamed into New York Bay.

It was a mild sunny Monday. But Gottschalk and Ramon were so weakened by ten days of seasickness that they were not in the mood to pay attention to the unseasonable promise of spring. As the ship entered the mouth of the North River, some-one pointed out Castle Garden, situated on a tiny island off the southern tip of Manhattan. Gottschalk knew he had heard of the building before, but he was too befogged at the moment to recall that it was the scene of Jenny Lind's New York triumphs.

The sight of his father and Edward waiting for him at the pier drew him out of his daze, and when half a dozen reporters rushed to him with questions he was ready with quick answers. Because he spoke English with a French accent and led by the hand a small boy obviously foreign, the representatives of the press as much as told him that he lied when he said he was an American.

In letters to his father written after his departure from Spain he had insisted that the man of all men to manage his American début was William Vincent Wallace, in New York since 1851 in company with his new wife, a professional pianist, and his sister, an opera and concert soprano. Gottschalk had also addressed several appeals direct to Mr. Wallace, but had left Europe too soon to receive answers. Now, in a hansom cab with his father and brother driving to the Irving House, he learned that the Irishman, touched over the trust placed in him, had made all arrangements for the début.

There were to be two concerts. While the first, to come on Friday, February 11, would be small and intimate, the second, announced for the Thursday following, was to be in all respects grand.

The man employed by Mr. Wallace to direct the publicity had already proved himself an expert advertiser. The current number of *Graham's Magazine* carried a long biographical article on Gottschalk. The same article in pamphlet form, advertised as a compendium of facts regarding a great American pioneer, was on sale in bookstores throughout New York, and a French version was to appear serially in *Le Courier des Etats-Unis* in February. Another biographical article, more carefully written, was to be published in the February issue of the *Musical Review*. Since the end of December every newspaper in New York had been running brief items on Gottschalk. Much had been made of the arrival of the two immense Pleyel grands for use on his first American tour.

He was scarcely settled with his father, brother, and Ramon in a suite at the Irving House when Mr. Wallace called. There was an hour of jolly talk. Then the Irish manager presented Gottschalk with a list of the private homes in which he was to play in the course of the next three weeks.

In these salon appearances, as well as on the occasion of a recital at the Irving House for representatives of the press, Gottschalk avoided the music announced for his concerts and confined himself mainly to Spanish dances culled from " El Sitio de

Zaragoza," Chopin mazurkas and waltzes, and several new compositions by Mr. Wallace.

In this year 1853 only three pianists with European reputations comparable to Gottschalk's had played in New York. The début of each was either vulgar or flat. The first to come, Leopold von Meyer, made his bow to New York on October 20, 1845, at a variety entertainment at the Park Theatre. The ten or twelve minutes allotted to him was just enough for two numbers, an opera paraphrase and an Oriental march, both his own creations. Preceding him on the program was a one-act farce, and following him came "a dancing of the polka by the Misses Vallée." Henri Herz made his American début just a year later at a church, the Tabernacle, and devoted himself entirely to opera fantasies of his own composition. Maurice Strakosch, a refugee from revolution-torn Europe, first played in New York, also at the Tabernacle, on June 22, 1848. It was an extremely hot evening, and only a few of the pews were occupied.

Mr. Wallace had planned to make Gottschalk's début novel, dignified, and persuasive. He showed that he was a manager with foresight.

The first of the two concerts—presented, as billed, on Friday evening, February 11—was in every way modest. The place was Niblo's Saloon, a concert hall adjacent to the great theatre used mainly for opera, Niblo's Garden. Mr. Wallace had fixed the hour at seven-thirty so that patrons could if they liked leave immediately after the conclusion of the concert, pass down a corridor, and reach their seats in the theatre in time to hear Madame Sontag in her first big aria in *La Sonnambula*. If Gottschalk that evening missed the elegance of the aristocrats who thronged to his concerts in Paris, he at least found the flowers and the perfume. He found also every seat in the hall occupied.

The program required just a little more than an hour. Appearing with Gottschalk in his *Jerusalem* fantasy and in a recently composed concert waltz for two pianos was Richard Hoffman, an English virtuoso who had toured in America with Jenny Lind and had decided to make New York his permanent home. Two of Gottschalk's four independent numbers were opera paraphrases, his own arrangement of the overture to *La Chasse du jeune Henri* and Liszt's *Lucia* transcription. Both were played during the first half of the program. In the second half Gottschalk gave first "La Moissoneuse," "Danse ossianique," and "Le Bananier," all listed on the program under the heading "Poetic Caprices." He ended the evening with his arrangement of "The Carnival of Venice." Among the assisting artists besides Mr. Hoffman was the soprano Rosa de Vries, the one woman singer in New York that season who was able to hold public favor in competing with Madame Sontag and Madame Alboni. The three others who took part in the program were the flutist John A. Kyle, the baritone John Frazier, and the accompanist George F. Bristow.

The audience applauded warmly; Gottschalk even heard—for the first time in his experience in giving concerts—some whistling. But there was no insistence upon encores. Never before had Gottschalk played "Le Bananier" in public without being required to repeat it. He felt, he said, that his hearers wanted to express their appreciation with the enthusiasm of Europeans but that for some reason they did not dare.

Though the reviews the next day were all highly favorable, Gottschalk was not sure about the success of his first appearance until the next Thursday evening, when he faced his second New York audience. This time his hearers were numbered by the thousands. "A mere pianist," the *Times* was to report the next morning "has filled the great Niblo's Garden from pit to ceiling."

Mr. Wallace chose a night when there was no performance of opera and engaged the full opera orchestra, he himself serving as conductor. Gottschalk was to say that in his first number, Weber's *Concertstück*, he had never had more sympathetic orchestral support. He again played the *Jerusalem* paraphrase, with Mr. Hoffman again at the second piano. Gottschalk ended the first half of the program with "Bamboula." In the second half he played "La Savanne" and "Le Bananier" as a group and "The Carnival of Venice" as an independent number. The two soloists who shared the evening were Madame de Vries and another opera singer much liked in New York, the basso Luigi Rocco.

It seemed to Gottschalk this time that the New Yorkers had come out of their shells. "The flattering demonstration of favor," as one newspaper called the applause, made him feel that Americans were almost as receptive as Spaniards. He had to repeat both "Bamboula" and "Le Bananier."

The critics agreed that the two concerts constituting the American début were a great triumph for the Louisianian. All emphasized his virtuosity. In writing of his work as a composer most of them chose the *Jerusalem* fantasy and "The Carnival of Venice" for extended praise. Not one of them pointed out anything of special interest to Americans in the original music. They wrote of Gottschalk as they might have written of Liszt, or Thalberg, or Prudent.

In planning the two concerts Mr. Wallace gave little thought to expense. On the final reckoning, Gottschalk discovered that his American début had cost him $2,400.

While the bills were still coming in, P. T. Barnum called on Gottschalk at the Irving House and offered him $20,000 a year clear of all expenses for a two- or three-years' tour of the entire United States. The young man was tempted. But his father argued that, in the first place, the figure was much too low and, in the second place, any association with the vulgar Barnum would in the end prove hurtful if not disastrous. Moreau—as he had done all his life—yielded to his father's opinion.

On the last day of February, Mr. Gottschalk and Edward boarded a steamer for the return to New Orleans. Ramon was with them. Before leaving Louisiana Mr. Gottschalk had made arrangements to place the boy in the care of a trusted couple whom he had known for many years. Ramon was to go to a school where he could learn both French and English. In recent months he had showed no interest in molding figures out of clay. If the interest returned and he manifested real talent, he was to be sent where he could be trained to be a sculptor. If he showed an inclination for some other pursuit, he was to be prepared for that. All his expenses until he reached manhood were to be defrayed by his foster father.

By the hour the New Orleans boat sailed Gottschalk was on

the way to Philadelphia. His ultimate destination was also New Orleans. But he arranged to travel by train, stagecoach, and river steamer and give concerts on the way. In his company was Hermann Feitlinger, the baritone whom he had employed as an assisting artist. The third member of the party was the pianist who played the singer's accompaniments and took care of Gottschalk's Pleyels.

Madame de Vries and Mr. Hoffman as well as Mr. Feitlinger appeared with Gottschalk in two concerts in Philadelphia, on March 1 and 3. News of the packed Niblo's Garden on the evening of February 17 had stirred the interest of Philadelphians, and they tried to outdo New Yorkers in welcoming "the King of Pianists," as the newspapers labeled Gottschalk.

In the second concert in the Pennsylvania city "the King" included among his solos a number listed on the program as "Fragment from the Symphony 'The Battle of Bunker Hill.'" The piece was in reality a part of "El Sitio de Zaragoza" with the Spanish melodies replaced by "Yankee Doodle," "Hail Columbia," "The Star-Spangled Banner," and two songs which had recently sunk into the heart of America, "Oh, Susanna" and "Old Folks at Home," both the work of a Pennsylvanian just three years older than Gottschalk, Stephen Collins Foster. The playing of the piece was an experiment: Gottschalk wished to see the effect upon Americans of their own national music. He found that it stirred the Philadelphians as he had not believed an American audience could be stirred. He noted at the same time that his Negro music had only interested them. He renamed the medley "National Glory" and decided to use it frequently in future concerts.

Before he left Philadelphia he met a cousin whom he had heard about all his life, Leonard Myers, two years his senior. Whether the relationship was on Moreau's father's or mother's side and just how close it was he was never to say. Leonard had grown up in Bucks County, Pennsylvania, and was now an ambitious young Philadelphia lawyer with a wife and two or three children. He and Moreau liked one another at their very first meeting, and their friendship was to grow with the years.

Gottschalk, Mr. Feitlinger, and the accompanist traveled by train and stagecoach to Pittsburgh. There they boarded the river steamer which took them down the Ohio. Gottschalk for a reason unknown passed by music-loving Cincinnati. But he could not think of omitting Louisville, where a number of leading men of business were his father's clients. The Louisville newspapers advertised him as " the King of Pianists, a Son of the South."

He reached the Kentucky city March 16, in time to play at small gatherings in the homes of two or three of his father's friends before the date set for his first concert, Saturday evening, March 19. That Saturday was a day of anxiety: the Pleyels had not arrived. The best piano available stood up under a tuning, but when eight o'clock came and Gottschalk saw that he would have to use it he was in terror lest the pyrotechnics of " National Glory " make it collapse. It survived the ordeal. But the stamping, whistling, and " hog-call shouting " which followed roused a still greater fear in Gottschalk—the fear that frail wooden Mozart Hall would fall down. Like the piano, the building remained intact; and on Monday evening it withstood another stormy demonstration when Gottschalk, using one of the Pleyels this time, had to stop " National Glory " at the section made up of " Old Folks at Home " and repeat the Foster air three times. He left Louisville the evening of March 22 with a clear profit of more than a thousand dollars in his pockets.

He and his associates journeyed southward on the *Belle Key*, listed as one of the most luxurious of the " floating palaces " in the Louisville-New Orleans service. Gottschalk found the steamer anything but luxurious. The gentlemen's cabin was a dormitory, with each pair of berths, an upper and a lower, shut off by curtains. The only furniture for a passenger's private use was a berth, a low stool, and a wash basin. The water in which one washed his face was taken from the river, perhaps where a barrel of garbage had just been dumped. In the daytime the gentlemen's cabin was converted into the dining saloon. Everybody ate at two or three long tables. Gottschalk noticed that several planters had brought along slaves to wait on them at meals and prepare special dishes to supplement the boat fare. He himself had no fresh food except for the few times when the boat stopped at plantation landings and took on supplies of eggs and butter.

He was horrified when he went down to the lowest deck and saw the hordes of blacks destined for the New Orleans slave market. While in Spain he had read Mrs. Stowe's recently published *Uncle Tom's Cabin*. As he looked upon the dejected wretches, he felt that pages from that book were being brought to life before his eyes. His route was the one usually followed by artists traveling from New York to New Orleans, and it was their custom to give charity concerts aboard ship before arriving at their destination. Gottschalk forestalled a request for such a concert on the *Belle Key* by calling on the captain and asking permission to play daily for the Negro slaves below deck. The officer looked at him as if he had lost his mind, and then said, sullenly, "You should know, sir, that that can't be done."

With all her faults, the *Belle Key* was fast. She was wharfed in New Orleans the night of March 30, a full eight hours in advance of her announced arrival. Gottschalk saw not a single familiar face on the pier. So, in company with his two associates, he took a cab for the St. Charles Hotel, where, he knew, his father had engaged a suite in advance.

When he was at last alone in his room, on an upper floor, he put out the light and, still fully dressed, went and stood at the big open window. It was a warm spring night, still and cloudless. He had not thought for a long time of the apparent nearness of the stars in the Louisiana heavens. Across the street, directly before him, was the St. Charles Theatre, where he had heard his first opera and had seen Fanny Elssler dance. A short distance beyond was the roof of the Camp Street building in which his father had had an office for almost twenty years. Then came the Levée and the river, both unchanged. As he breathed in the spring air, he caught the odor of magnolia blossoms. Then the St. Louis Cathedral clock, with a ring so familiar that it seemed he had never been where he could not hear it, began to sound the hour. He counted the strokes, as he had done when he was a boy of three. It was midnight. But he was so full of the feeling of being at home again that he could not think of sleep.

He went downstairs and set out for his father's cottage on Robertson Street. Soon he was on the rue des Remparts, walking slowly past the house where he was born and where he had begun the study of music. When he came to the Place Congo, he turned westward across the square and saw from the well-pressed earth that it was still the scene of the dancing of the bamboula. So far he was in recognizable surroundings. But the territory he now entered was altogether strange. What he had known as a savanna had been transformed into a residential district as compact as the French quarter. He had to search for Robertson Street and then for his father's house.

Mr. Gottschalk and Edward had gone to bed at ten o'clock with the expectation of rising early so they could be at the pier to greet Moreau when the *Belle Key* arrived. His knocking roused them both at the same time. Though only a month had passed since the three were together in New York, this reunion in New Orleans was a special event. So, with brandy and cigars for the two men and a bowl of fruit for the boy, they settled down for a night of talk.

Sally, awakened by the voices in the front part of the house, got up, threw a wrapper over her night dress, and, in bare feet, came in to investigate. At sight of Moreau she stopped in her tracks, crossed herself, and, after staring at him for a full half minute, broke into her throaty laugh. The next instant she had him in her arms and was kissing each cheek. Then she drew back, and, laughing her laugh again, dashed off to the kitchen to make a big pot of strong black New Orleans coffee.

After breakfast the next morning Mr. Gottschalk went to his office and Moreau and Edward set out to make calls. Moreau found his grandmother Bruslé still young in mind, though she was now well past eighty. She could never, she said, forgive Aimée for leaving New Orleans and taking all her children with her. There was a call on Uncle Gaston, who now sold sheet music as well as books and stationery. From him Moreau learned that all his music in stock in New Orleans stores had been sold within two days after the newspapers announced his return. Moreau and Edward next visited Ramon. The boy showed, to his foster father's satisfaction, that he was already happily adjusted to his new home.

At the St. Charles Hotel at ten o'clock Moreau kept an appointment with Monsieur Letellier, who was doing for his début in New Orleans what Mr. Wallace had done for the début in New York. Business was business, and Don Bazile kept his emotions in check as he welcomed the pupil who had far more than fulfilled his highest hopes. But the few who witnessed the meeting could not fail to observe that Moreau was the great pride of the music master's life.

With many conferences that day, and with no sleep the night before, Gottschalk was ready for bed at nine o'clock that evening. But before he had anything like the sleep he needed he was awakened by an orchestra playing his " Le Mancenillier." When he went to his front window and looked into the street, he saw that he was being honored with a serenade. After listening to the playing of three or four of his pieces he sent an attendant down to invite the musicians, about twenty all together, up to his room. When they came he found that they were members of the orchestra of the St. Charles Theatre and that among them were several of his old friends. It was his turn to show his appreciation of their tribute. So, garbed in a dressing gown, he sat at one of his Pleyels and gave them a recital which lasted for an hour.

On Saturday, April 2, the New Orleans newspapers carried the first announcement of the début, to take place the following Wednesday evening in Odd Fellows' Hall on Camp Street, all seats reserved at two dollars each, evening dress obligatory. On Monday, April 4, the day the tickets went on sale, each of the important newspapers carried on the first page a picture of Gottschalk, a lengthy biographical article, and the opinions of the critics who had heard him play at a rehearsal on Saturday. On Tuesday the newspapers reported that all tickets for the début had been sold within eight hours and that none had got into the hands of speculators. Also in the newspapers that Tuesday were accounts of the " welcome home " banquet given to Gottschalk on Monday in the hall of the Perfect Union Lodge on the rue des Remparts. In the Wednesday morning newspapers appeared the program for the début.

Flowers were delivered to Odd Fellows' Hall all that day. "That evening," said one who was present, "the place was more a blossoming garden than a concert saloon." Fifteen hundred of the élite of New Orleans glittered that night. Gottschalk had never seen at the Salle Pleyel an audience more splendid in appearance.

A young German pianist who had recently settled in New Orleans, Hermann Paulsackel, assisted in the opening number, the *Jerusalem* fantasy. Then came two singers, Mr. Feitlinger and a soprano from the Théâtre d'Orléans, Madame Widemann. Gottschalk closed the first half of the program with "National Glory."

A demonstration of approval, New Orleans style, followed. In order to get off the stage after making his first bows Gottschalk had to walk on roses and Cape jasmines. When he came back to acknowledge the applause a second time, he was leading his father. As soon as the uproar was silenced, Mr. Gottschalk, speaking in English, addressed the audience as if it were made up wholly of old friends and close neighbors. In concluding he said: "Without your sympathy, encouragement, and support Moreau could never have accomplished what he has accomplished. I speak for him as well as for myself when I say that I thank you all with all my heart." Then he added, "Moreau also has a word for you."

The occasion had Moreau pretty well overcome. But he did succeed in saying, in French, that the number he had just rendered was his profession of allegiance to the United States and that he hoped he was more eloquent in playing the piano than in talking in public.

He opened the second half of the program with his *La Chasse du jeune Henri* paraphrase. Later he played as a group "Danse ossianique" and "Le Bananier." He had to repeat the latter twice. As he had done in each of his American appearances, he closed the program with "The Carnival of Venice."

But his fashionable auditors had no notion of going home. They demanded "Bamboula" and "La Savanne," and at Moreau's suggestion sang with him as he played the familiar melodies in each. Then they must have "Le Bananier" once more so that they could sing it too. When Moreau was ready to sit down at the piano the final time, he said, "I'm going to play just one more piece, one you've never heard. It's an Aragonese jota, written while I was in Spain. When it is published it will bear the dedication, 'To my old friend and master, Monsieur Letellier.'"

The consensus of newspaper comment on the début was summarized by the critic of the New Orleans *Crescent*: "Expectation is at an end, and reality fills up the measure of our fondest dream. Triumph crowns the long years of devoted application, and the child of genius now reaps the rich rewards of his patient toil. We may in honest pride boast that our native city, our own dear New Orleans, has furnished a bright new star to the galaxy of the world's great artists."

Except for a hurried trip to Mobile to give a single concert on April 21, Gottschalk remained in his native city precisely six weeks after the début. He gave five more concerts in Odd Fellows' Hall, the last being a grand charity benefit at which he received from a committee of citizens headed by the mayor a medal of California gold bearing on one side his portrait and on the other side the inscription "à L. M. Gottschalk, ses compatriotes de la Nouvelle-Orléans, 11 mai, 1853." He gave three concerts at the Théâtre d'Orléans, playing with orchestra under Monsieur Prévost's direction Weber's *Concertstück*, Chopin's concerto in E minor, and Prudent's "Le Bois." He also gave a concert for the workers of New Orleans in the hall of the Mechanics' Institute at fifty cents for admission, no seats reserved. In addition to these ten soirées of his own, he made six public appearances as assistant to other artists.

On days when there were neither concerts nor rehearsals he visited old friends. He saw much of Monsieur Prévost, who preached to him the necessity of returning to Europe if he did not wish to stagnate as a composer. On one of the evenings he spent at Madame Boyer's he heard a New Orleans girl, Rose

Kennedy, play "Bamboula." She brought out the rhythms with such precision and force that everybody in the room, including even stout Madame Boyer, "had to get up and dance." Gottschalk vowed that she played the piece twice as well as he did himself. On all his visits to musicians Monsieur Letellier was his companion. "Don Bazile just follows Moreau around," said New Orleans.

An event planned for some evening during his sojourn in his native city took place on April 14 in the Théâtre d'Orléans. It was the première of the one-act opera *Le Roi David*, the work of the fifteen-year-old son of one of Gottschalk's old supporters, Jean-Baptiste Guiraud. In 1849, the boy composer, Ernest Guiraud, had gone to Paris for a two-years' stay. Gottschalk, who was always held up to him as an example of what one brought up in New Orleans could accomplish, encouraged him in every way, aroused Monsieur Marmontel's interest in him, and introduced him to one of the best friends he was ever to have, Georges Bizet. At the first performance of *Le Roi David* Gottschalk sat in a box where he could not be seen. He rejoiced as he witnessed such an ovation for Ernest as he himself had been accorded the night of his début. "The young Guiraud undoubtedly has genius," he said in the letter in which he described the première to Monsieur Marmontel. His last words to Ernest were, "Return to Paris as soon as you can, just as I'm going to do."

At two o'clock on the afternoon of May 18, in company with his father and brother, he embarked in secret on the river steamer *Magnolia*. The newspapers had announced his departure on this vessel, which was to sail for Natchez at five o'clock. He felt that he lacked the physical strength to respond to another "demonstration of favor" from the New Orleans public. Long before five o'clock his admirers were at the pier in hundreds. When they saw Mr. Gottschalk and Edward come down the gangplank, they realized that their idol had eluded them. He could hear them shouting "Vive Gottschalk!" as the steamer backed out into the Mississippi.

Mr. Feitlinger and the accompanist were with him on the *Magnolia*. Also with him was the impresario who had agreed to serve as his manager the coming year. He was the elderly William F. Brough, a onetime popular concert and opera baritone.

As the four journeyed up the Mississippi and Ohio, Gottschalk made many more hundreds of dollars to add to his bank accounts in New York and New Orleans. He played to two packed houses in Natchez, all seats reserved, price two dollars, the ushers identified by the pink rosettes on their left lapels. He had at least a good house at the one concert given in Memphis, admission one dollar, no seats reserved. He again played to two wildly enthusiastic audiences in Mozart Hall in Louisville. His single concert in Cincinnati was, said the *Enquirer*, "fashionably attended."

He would have remained in Cincinnati for more concerts if he had not run into competition with the troupe headed by Maurice Strakosch and his wife, the contralto Amalia Patti-Strakosch. Cleveland, where Gottschalk's friend Alfred Jaell was appearing with the small orchestra known as the Germania Society, presented the same problem. So in traveling northward by train from Cincinnati Gottschalk went direct to Buffalo. There, on June 20, he, Feitlinger, and the accompanist made their last joint appearance.

While Mr. Brough was busy in New York that summer planning Gottschalk's fall and winter season, Gottschalk himself was traveling with one of his Pleyels, giving recitals at the fashionable resorts. He played at Trenton Falls and at Saratoga. He then went to Cape May, at the invitation of his cousin Leonard Myers, who was summering there with his family. For two weeks Gottschalk played daily in the Congress Hotel, and also found time to write a tribute to Leonard, a concert polka entitled "Forest Glade," the earliest of his American publications.

He kept himself occupied while in Cape May in order to relieve his uneasiness. A yellow-fever epidemic of a violence never before known was raging in New Orleans. The mortality rate was higher than it had been in 1833 from yellow jack and the Asiatic cholera combined. Gottschalk believed that his father was immune to yellow fever. His concern was over Edward.

Late in the summer, in Newport, he played at a benefit for the New Orleans yellow-fever sufferers. Alfred Jaell was his associate. Each confined himself almost wholly to playing pieces written by the other.

October arrived, and the letters Gottschalk received from his father and brother became optimistic. The death rate had dropped greatly. "After a week of cool weather," Mr. Gottschalk wrote, "New Orleans will be relieved from the most severe plague ever suffered by any city in the New World."

Gottschalk's hopes were high when he reached New York and saw Mr. Brough's schedule for the fall and winter. There were dates running through January, 1854, for concerts in New York, Boston, Philadelphia, Baltimore, Washington, and several smaller Eastern cities. In February and March there were to be five or six weeks in Havana and then a series of farewell concerts in New Orleans.

Gottschalk had made up his mind to go back to Paris in April. He was sure that by that time he would be rich enough to devote himself exclusively to composition for two or three years.

He began the new season with a concert in Niblo's Saloon the evening of Thursday, October 13. The competition in New York at that time was great. Madame Sontag, who had lured Alfred Jaell into her troupe, was on the scene for a series of farewell concerts. A company made up of Ole Bull, Maurice Strakosch, and the ten-year-old girl wonder soprano, Adelina Patti, was also on the scene. A competitor still more formidable, the French conductor Louis Antoine Jullien, was drawing thousands to Castle Garden every night to hear the hundred-piece orchestra he had brought from London. Yet there was a sufficient number of New Yorkers interested in Gottschalk to pay two dollars each for the privilege of filling Niblo's Saloon the evening of October 13.

In choosing the three assisting artists Mr. Brough and Gottschalk had looked for youth and charming stage presence as well as for talent. The one singer, the coloratura soprano Henriette Behrend, had been enticed from Monsieur Jullien's corps of soloists. The pianist employed to play with Gottschalk in duos and to accompany Mademoiselle Behrend was Jan Pychowski, who had studied his instrument in his native Prague. The third assistant, the Welshman Aptomas, alias Thomas Thomas, represented a type of music little known in America in 1853, that of the harp. His appearance with Gottschalk the evening of October 13 was his American début.

Except for "National Glory," renamed "American Reminiscences," Gottschalk played nothing which he had not played in his previous New York concerts. But the critics had so much praise for his gifts as composer and adapter, for his transcendent virtuosity, and for his electrifying personality that they failed to

135

notice his want of variety. They commented at length on the pleasing balance of the concert. "Only Gottschalk, with his unerring sense of art," wrote one, "would have had the happy thought of including a harpist in the ensemble of performers."

A morning or two after this auspicious beginning of the new season Gottschalk and his troupe took the train for Boston, where they were billed for a concert the following Tuesday, October 18. Mr. Brough, the only one in the party who understood the New England temperament, warned the others that they were facing a test which might prove difficult. Gottschalk laughed at such misgivings.

He refused to take seriously the adverse criticism which a Boston musical review, *Dwight's Journal*, had heaped upon him since his return to the United States. The editor, John Sullivan Dwight, a Unitarian minister who had developed an interest in music while a member of the celebrated Brook Farm Community, was saying that Gottschalk could not be a musician of importance because he received his training in frivolous pleasure-loving France and not in staid philosophical Germany. Mr. Dwight was also saying that the distinction of being the first American to become a piano virtuoso of the top rank belonged not to Gottschalk but to a Boston youth now meeting triumphs in Germany and England, William Mason, the son of Dr. Lowell Mason, the venerated composer of "Nearer, My God, to Thee" and "From Greenland's Icy Mountains." But Mr. Dwight was naïve enough to reveal the real reason for his conclusions: he missed no opportunity to remind his readers, most of whom shared his extreme abolitionist views, that Gottschalk was a Southerner. He even went so far as to hint that the praise lavished upon the Louisianian by his French critics was bought by his wealthy slave-holding father. To Gottschalk it was incomprehensible that any section of the United States, especially one with New England's reputation for intellectuality, could put trust in charges which were so obviously the outgrowth of ignorance and prejudice.

But when he confronted his audience in Music Hall on the evening of October 18 he was disillusioned: Mr. Dwight, he learned, was a power in New England. Though the price of admission was only a dollar, most of the seats were unoccupied. The three or four hundred persons who were present had no smiles for him as he bowed to their feeble applause. Looking into the frowning faces, he shuddered at the thought of the trying two hours which lay ahead of him and his associates.

They did as well as they could with the same program which had delighted New York the week before. Mr. Aptomas—possibly because the audience thought he was a good Methodist, since he was Welsh—came closest to a warm welcome. "The Bostonians," Gottschalk was to say, "listened to my playing of 'Le Bananier' as if they were hearing a sermon preached by the Devil." It was an evening without encores. The faces were as sour when Gottschalk ended the program with "The Carnival of Venice" as when he and Mr. Pychowski opened it with the *Jerusalem* fantasy.

Gottschalk was greatly surprised the next day to find that the majority of the critics agreed in placing his virtuosity above that of any other pianist who had played in Boston. But the same critics pronounced his program an insult to the intelligence of New England, spoke of his compositions as trivial, and intimated their dislike of him as a man. It was easy to see that each of them had been swayed by Dwight's propaganda.

Both Gottschalk and Mr. Brough were angry rather than depressed. A second concert was billed for Friday evening, and they were determined to make it fit Boston standards. So in the newspapers for Thursday appeared notices that the price for the second of Gottschalk's soirées in Music Hall would be fifty cents. Then in the newspapers for Friday morning came the announcement that Gottschalk's numbers for the concert that evening would be two of his ballades inspired by Ossian, Liszt's *Lucia* paraphrase, Onslow's sonata for two pianos with Mr. Pychowski assisting, and Beethoven's *Kreutzer Sonata* with a Bostonian, Emile Suck, as violinist.

Only Gottschalk and Mr. Brough knew that there would be a slight change from the printed program. For one of the Ossianic ballades a Beethoven bagatelle was to be substituted. If Mr. Dwight and his disciples failed to recognize it and attributed it to

Gottschalk, they would have a hard time living down their embarrassment when the truth was made known.

Gottschalk, optimistic over the evening to come and boyishly jubilant over the trick he was to play on Mr. Dwight, was in high spirits that Friday morning. He spent the hours until twelve o'clock at Music Hall rehearsing with Mr. Suck and Mr. Pychowski; and, as he commented on the playing of this passage and that, his wit bubbled.

But Fate had decreed that his memory of Boston be black.

At three that afternoon, when he was alone in his hotel room, an attendant came up with a telegram. It was from New Orleans, and contained the bare announcement that Mr. Gottschalk had fallen victim to yellow fever and that the doctors had given up hope of his surviving. After reading the message Gottschalk calmly said to the attendant, " Go and tell Mr. Brough that I must see him at once."

When the manager came, a minute or two later, Gottschalk looked up at him with a face completely ashen and, handing him the telegram, said, " Boston must know nothing of this before tomorrow. We will give the concert just as we have planned it."

But, probably through the telegraph agency, the news leaked out. That night at Music Hall just before the hour for the concert to begin ushers kept coming backstage to report that the house— filled to capacity, with the admission at only fifty cents—was buzzing with rumors. Certain persons were saying that Gottschalk had heard that morning of the murder of his mother in Paris. Others were saying he had been notified of the suicide of his father in New Orleans. Still others were whispering that his mistress had suddenly fallen dead in New York. He and Mr. Brough decided that the only way to stop the absurd talk and get the audience calm enough to listen to music was to make public the truth. So the manager appeared on the stage and announced the news which came from New Orleans at three that afternoon.

Gottschalk manifested that night the power of the self-discipline which the true virtuoso must command. He shut out anxiety and grief, gave himself wholly to music, and played as well as he had ever played. The violinist, almost overcome by stage fright, made the rendition of the *Kreutzer Sonata* an agonizing ordeal. Gottschalk had to push, lead, and support the man in every conceivable way in order to keep him from breaking down altogether. When the time came for the second Ossianic ballade, Gottschalk substituted the Beethoven bagatelle without the slightest indication that he was departing from the printed program.

He was on a train bound for New York the next morning when he read the Boston newspapers. This time his critics—two of whom he had seen in company with Mr. Dwight the night before —mingled pity, mild praise, and mean innuendoes. But not one of them had detected that in a certain number on the program Gottschalk was playing Beethoven when he was supposed to be playing Gottschalk.

There was at least this victory to bring a bit of cheer as Gottschalk started on the long sad journey to New Orleans. He had also the hope that the doctors were mistaken and that he would find his father alive.

On reaching New York, where he got information on travel schedules unavailable in Boston, he took passage on the steamer *Black Warrior*, due to sail for Mobile at five that afternoon. He knew that a boat sailed every day from Mobile to Milneburg on Lake Pontchartrain. Just before boarding the *Black Warrior* he sent Edward a telegram giving the route he was to take.

When he arrived in Mobile, eight or ten days later, there were letters waiting for him. As he opened the first, his eyes fell upon a clipping from the *Picayune* for Tuesday, October 25. It read: "Died on Sunday morning the 23rd inst., at eleven o'clock, in his home on Robertson Street, Edward Gottschalk, aged fifty-eight, for many years a resident of this city." The end came after Moreau embarked. For two days his father agonized in that last phase of a fatal attack of yellow fever, the phase known as the black vomit.

The letters told of the funeral. But they were to be lost, and neither Moreau nor anyone else left a record of the place where Edward Gottschalk was buried. The only known documentary statement as to his death was filed by one Jean Bosmot on November 4, 1853, in the office of the New Orleans Board of Health.

By that day Moreau was installed on Robertson Street with his brother. Capable old Sally was taking care of the cottage just as she had always done. She was no longer the property of any one individual. Her late master died without a will, and nothing could be done about settling his estate until papers came from Paris granting someone complete power of attorney.

It was January before Moreau received the legal authorization to act as the sole representative of his mother, sisters, and brothers. He had already found out, from his paternal uncles and the lawyer they retained, that his father's debts far exceeded the assets. He had known that his father's financial situation was precarious, but he had never imagined to what extent.

His first act as administrator of the estate was to inform the creditors that all their claims when properly authenticated would be honored. He was sure that his father had expected this of him, and he never thought of doing anything else.

His savings came far short of the amount required to cover the debts. Still he manumitted the three slaves. Then he agreed to pay to Sally a pension for the rest of her life. The two younger women were already supporting themselves in homes where they would be allowed to remain. Though he was not an abolitionist of Mr. Dwight's type, he hated slavery too much to be himself a slaveholder.

He shouldered his various responsibilities without a word of protest. He wrote to his mother that she would continue to receive two hundred dollars a month as heretofore and that he had instructed his French publishers, the Escudiers, to pay over to her all royalties accruing from the sale of his music in Europe. It never occurred to him to shirk the duties he had assumed on becoming Ramon's foster father. And he insisted upon supporting Edward, who had given up law and was ambitious to go back to France and become a Parisian journalist.

Gottschalk's dream of returning to France to devote himself exclusively to composition for several years belonged to a buried past. He had to have money. That meant that he must give concerts where they would be most lucrative—here in the New World.

He earned almost a thousand dollars to turn over to his father's creditors by giving two concerts in New Orleans before competition—again with Madame Sontag, Alfred Jaell, Ole Bull, Maurice Strakosch, and Monsieur Jullien—made it impossible to give more. The first took place in the hall of the Mechanics' Institute on February 1 and the second in Odd Fellows' Hall two evenings later. In each he featured his work for ten pianos, with American airs replacing Spanish airs and the title changed from "El Sitio de Zaragoza" to "The Battle of Bunker Hill." Among the nine assisting pianists was his brother Edward. At these concerts Gottschalk introduced to the public the most enduring of his Negro compositions, "The Banjo."

A week after the second concert he and Edward had the cottage on Robertson Street sold and everything packed to leave for Cuba. The *Picayune* of February 12 reported: "Moreau Gottschalk, the pianist, Louisiana's own accomplished artist, has called upon us to take leave, being on the eve of his departure for Havana, whither he goes not only for the benefit of his somewhat impaired health, but also for the pursuit of his profession. May his laurels be ever green and abundant."

After a year of going back and forth in the United States, Gottschalk declared in letters to his French friends that if his native
country was to develop a civilization conducive to the flowering
of the art of music she must not only silence her intolerant Mr.
Dwights but eliminate her multitudinous vulgarians, whom he
called " shopkeepers of temporary prosperity." These men were
to be identified, he said, by their flashy clothes, the diamond pins
in their cravats, the heavy gold rings on their watch chains, the
obscene stories they told at bedtime in the men's cabin on a river
steamer, and their pride in being ill-mannered, coarse, and
offensive.

On his trip on the steamer *Shotwell* from Memphis to Louisville
the preceding summer he had run afoul of fifteen or twenty of
these " shopkeepers." At a recital one evening for the benefit
of a Louisville hospital they kept up their conversations throughout the playing of the first number, and when he calmly asked
them either to remain quiet during the next number or retire
they raised such a row that the captain of the boat intervened.
After that they showed Gottschalk how rude they could be. At
table they alluded to him as " the professor," bowed to the ladies
just as he bowed, and mimicked his French accent.

On the voyage from New Orleans to Cuba in February, 1854, in
company with Edward, he again ran into a crowd of these " shopkeepers," most of whom were bound for California by way of
Havana and Aspinwall. For a reason unknown to him, they took
offense at two elderly Italians on board. Both, though simply
dressed, were obviously aristocrats. Nevertheless the American
boors made them suffer many indignities.

Gottschalk, wishing to show the two foreigners that an American could be a gentleman, introduced himself to them. He soon learned that both were counts and that each was receiving the income from a domain probably twice as extensive as any great Mississippi Valley cotton plantation. After this first interview he put down in the notebook in which he had begun to record his impressions: " O, you miserable wealth-worshiping shopkeepers! How you would change your dance before the two Italians if you knew their identity! "

He later got their extraordinary story. They were philosophers, traveling for the sake of philosophy. Fifteen years before, in Spain, they met by chance and discovered that they had a common aim in life, the aim of finding out by direct contact the varying modes of behavior among civilized peoples. Since then they had never been separated. Each was taking notes, and on their return to Italy the one who was more gifted in writing was to make a book out of their joint observations.

Gottschalk asked them what they thought of behavior in America. Their answer was, " The Americans are strong healthy children, full of promise." Then Gottschalk asked them how long they thought it would be before the Americans grew up sufficiently to understand and further such an art as music. " Perhaps two centuries," they agreed.

As soon as Gottschalk and Edward landed in Havana they went in search of a music store with a private room equipped with a good piano. They finally found what they wanted in the shop belonging to the brothers Edelmann. Here Gottschalk spent his first evening in Cuba playing Italian music for the two philosophers, with whom he had by this time become well acquainted. He was trying, he said, to repay them partially for the many things they had taught him. " But for the American roughs," he wrote in his notebook that night, " I might never have met two of the most interesting gentlemen I have ever known." The next morning they sailed for Mexico, and he was never again to hear of them.

He and Edward had expected tropical warmth in Cuba, and were dressed in linen. Their first night on the island, when they had only their hand luggage, an icy wind from the north swept down. The next day they went about shivering until they found permanent quarters in a pension, had their trunks brought from the customhouse, and got out their woolen clothes.

Gottschalk was scarcely installed in the pension when he went to bed with a cold and fever. After a day or two he was suffering from a severe dysentery. The younger of the Edelmann brothers, Carlos, an excellent amateur pianist, was present the night Gottschalk played for the two philosophers. He was entranced by the virtuosity of the artist from the United States, and was now seeing that he had the best medical care and was made as comfortable as possible.

Gottschalk was not too sick to sign an agreement granting to the Edelmann brothers the management of his Havana concerts. On the last day of February, when he was out of bed and hard at work on four new compositions, they announced in the newspapers that he would make his début within a fortnight.

In building up public interest they arranged to have the important Havana musicians call on Gottschalk. Among them was the nineteen-year-old pianist and composer, Nicolas Ruiz Espadero, destined to be numbered among the foremost Cuban men of music. He and Gottschalk immediately entered into a friendship that was to be most fruitful in the life of each.

The début concert, a modest affair, was given as announced on the evening of March 13 in the assembly hall of a school building. The assisting artists were a soprano, a violinist, and a guitarist, all local musicians. Gottschalk's opening piece was " La Savanne," which one Havanese critic called " a beautiful pastoral poem sung on the piano." Two compositions recently completed but never to be published, a development with variations of " Old Folks at Home " and a fantasy on themes from *Lucia*, made up his second number. In closing the program he played first " The Carnival of Venice " and then a third recently completed work, a brilliant and extremely difficult impromptu based on the Cuban Negro dance known as the cocoyé.

The public interest the début aroused was sufficient to induce the Edelmanns to present Gottschalk in a grand concert in the

Teatro de Villanueva on Tuesday evening, March 29. In addition to the two Pleyels, which had accompanied him in all his wanderings since his departure from France, eight other pianos were needed for this occasion. The program was opened with a four-piano fantasy on *William Tell*, the players besides Gottschalk being young Señor Espadero, his teacher Señor Aristi, and a visiting pianist, Luiz Desvernine. Among Gottschalk's four or five solos was the fourth of his new pieces, " Souvenir de la Louisiane," never to be published. Then, as a triumphant finale, came Gottschalk and nine other pianists in " El Sitio de Zaragoza " in the original Spanish version. Edward was once more included in the ensemble.

The use of so many pianos at one time proved as exciting a novelty in Cuba as in Spain. The program was repeated eight days later, and this time the vast Teatro Tacón was required to meet the demand for seats.

Gottschalk won his triumph not a day too soon. Early in April the musical interest in Havana centered in the return of a native Cuban, the boy violinist Paul Julien, who had won prize after prize at the Paris Conservatoire and had played with great success in both Europe and the United States. Gottschalk left the field to the newcomer, saw Edward off for Paris, and made arrangements to set out with his Pleyels and, acting as his own impresario, give such concerts as he could in the Cuban provinces.

He played at Matanzas and Cardenas. From the latter city he went to Guïnes, where he gave another concert or two. The proceeds from these provincial appearances could not have amounted to much. For when Gottschalk was once more in Havana he was so greatly in need of money that he advertised his Pleyels for sale.

He received no acceptable offers, and the instruments were still with him when he turned up in Cienfuegos early in July. He made friends with the English and French consuls stationed in this small city, and at their instigation the governor of the province gave a grand ball in his honor. At the conclusion of the dancing Gottschalk played half a dozen numbers, including " Adiós a Cuba," another composition which was to remain in manuscript. He followed up this introduction to the élite with two concerts to be remembered as sensational events in Cienfuegos. "If only I could stir such excitement in a city forty times larger!" said Gottschalk.

He loved warm weather. But the heat of the Cuban summer proved too extreme for him. He succumbed to malaria, and, at a doctor's orders, spent a month in idleness on a plantation near the village of Caimoto, ten miles from Cienfuegos. He was too weak to take walks. "During the hours of daylight I read quantities of books and smoked quantities of the best cigars in the world," he was to say. In the evening he would lie on his bed and count the many different sounds he could hear. Finally the soft singing of the plantation slaves in a guarded compound a short distance away would put him to sleep.

The stronger he became in body the more worried he was in mind. This illness was a calamity. Practically all the money he had made in Cuba had gone to those who depended upon him for support. His father's creditors were sending bills, demanding payments, threatening suits.

He was a well man again when, at the end of August, he arrived in Santiago. But the heat in this hottest of all cities in the West Indies made him feel worse than when he was running a high temperature. He did not dare venture from his hotel except early in the morning and at night. Shut within the four walls of his room, on his bed under mosquito netting, turning from this position to that to find a cooler spot, he spent hours every day asking himself the one question, "What can I do to make money?"

He had captured Paris with "Bamboula." Stephen Collins Foster had captured all America with "Old Folks at Home." Did he, Gottschalk, have it within him to write something that might capture the whole world? The more he pondered this question the more convinced he was that the basic elements in such a composition must be sentimentality and religious trust—as in "The Maiden's Prayer."

He had called this work by Miss Bardazewska the most abominable of musical abominations, and he was to continue to condemn the sort of music it represents. Still, in his desperation, he yielded to the temptation to try to create a counterpart to it. He looked upon the piece he turned out as a last hope. So " The Last Hope " he named it.

As soon as it was copied, he sent it to a music publishing house in New York—Firth, Pond & Co. Several months passed before he received their answer, an offer of $50 on condition that he surrender to them all rights to the work. By that time he had given several successful concerts in Santiago, Puerto Principe, and Remedios. He was more affluent, and felt more optimistic over future concerts. So he accepted the offer of Firth, Pond & Co., thinking that that would be the last of " The Last Hope."

But in the concert he gave in Odd Fellows' Hall in New Orleans on the following March 13, just three weeks from the day he left Cuba, he needed a piece to stand as a contrast to his latest Negro dance, " María la O." Since " The Last Hope " seemed appropriate enough, he included it on the program.

A New Orleans woman who heard the first public performance of the piece wrote of it as follows: " Gottschalk played it without notes, as he plays everything. His head was slightly bowed, and I'm sure his eyes were closed. He was praying a prayer of gratitude, giving back to God a measure of the music with which God had endowed him in such great abundance. I was crying so when he came to the end that I felt ashamed of myself. Then after I looked about and saw that nearly everbody else was crying also, I felt better."

Among the non-weepers were the newspaper critics. To them the big event of the evening was the playing of " María la O." According to a program note, this piece had its origin in the singing and shouting Gottschalk heard one evening as he wandered in the woods near Santiago and came upon a band of reveling Negroes. The critics without exception pronounced it more mature and stronger than " Bamboula." Yet Americans outside of New Orleans were so little interested in Gottschalk's Negro music that " María la O " was never printed.

He repeated it—this time in combination with another Negro composition new to New Orleans, the impromptu on the cocoyé—

in a second soirée in Odd Fellows' Hall. The third and final concert in his 1855 season in his home city was a grand affair, given in the Théâtre d'Orléans with the assistance of the entire opera company. On this occasion he played only old favorites.

During his three months in New Orleans that spring Gottschalk missed no opportunity to gather in dollars. He was an assisting artist in three or four concerts, he was the " featured entertainer " at a "commercial fair" held in the St. Charles Hotel, he played on two different occasions in Mobile, he gave lessons, and he at last sold his much-traveled Pleyels. His creditors must have felt that he was doing his best for them.

But they must have been troubled when they read in the newspapers of a balloon ascension he made with a balloonist who was then amusing New Orleans with daily flights. Gottschalk's answer to those who questioned his foolhardiness in risking his life in this fashion was, " I just wanted to feel the ecstasy of seeing the earth drop down and spread out below me." He was to commemorate the experience years later in a composition entitled " Extase."

At the end of May he left by steamer for New York, and by the middle of June was in Trenton Falls. Here he spent several weeks, writing mazurkas and waltzes and giving recitals for the tourists who stopped over while on their way to and from Niagara. His next place of sojourn that summer was Saratoga. At the end of August he was in Newport.

Back in New York in September, in a furnished room on Ninth Street just east of Broadway, he was once more laid low with malarial fever. He was penniless as well as sick: his last dollars had gone to his mother. The warm-hearted young doctor who was attending him lent him money and told him he would never get well if he continued to fret over his mistake in not accepting P. T. Barnum's offer of $20,000 a year.

Then two letters came.

The first was from Jonas Chickering—a man of Boston, of all places. It listed the advantages to Gottschalk if he would agree to use exclusively in his American concerts the Chickering piano, and with it there was a check for $100. In former times Gottschalk would have returned the money in indignation. But he was now too poor to be proud. He wrote a cordial letter to Mr. Chickering, thanking him for the advance payment and assuring him that he would feel honored to join the company of artists whom the admirable Chickering piano was serving.

The second letter was from William Hall, a New York gentleman of many activities—high officer in the state militia, assemblyman in the state legislature, owner of a Broadway music store, impresario on occasion, and music publisher. His communication was an offer to sponsor Gottschalk in a series of intimate concerts in Dodworth's Hall in New York the coming season and to consider for publication any music he might have in manuscript. Gottschalk replied that he was ready to sign a contract for the Dodworth's Hall appearances and that he was sending by messenger the manuscripts of several pieces he had played in Cuba and New Orleans the previous season.

Two weeks later Mr. Hall, who had contracted to pay royalties on all Gottschalk music sold, called on Firth, Pond & Co. to obtain from them the rights to "The Last Hope." Since the publishers had disposed of only a few copies of the piece, they were very happy to sell at the figure at which they had bought, $50.

Then came a third letter, bearing the signature "Ada Clare, alias Ada McElhenny." Gottschalk recognized the address as that of a theatrical boardinghouse in his neighborhood. The writer briefly expressed her regret over reading of his illness in the newspapers and then said, "If you feel that a visit from an old friend might cheer you up, I should be very happy to call."

The summer of 1853—when Ada McElhenney was an extremely self-conscious girl of eighteen, belatedly emerging from adolescence —Gottschalk had been a fellow guest with her and her family at a hotel in one of the resorts where he stayed, probably Saratoga. The family consisted of her grandfather, Hugh Wilson, a wealthy planter from Charleston, South Carolina, her brother Eugene, two years older than she, and her sister, Susannah, a year or two younger. Gottschalk found in Mr. Wilson a gentleman with a mind, and spent many hours in his company. Having tea with him and his grandchildren every afternoon at five became a sort of ritual.

Mr. Wilson, like most Carolinians, was interested in genealogy, and Gottschalk picked up considerable information on Ada's family history. Her paternal grandfather, the Reverend James McElhenney, was a forceful figure among the Presbyterians of the South from 1790 to the year of his death, 1815. In the winter he preached for a parish on St. John's Island, near Charleston, and in the summer for a parish in upcountry Pendleton District. For a summer home he built Fort Hill, which about ten years after his death became the country seat of John C. Calhoun. Ada's father had already attained a place among the most able lawyers of Charleston when, in the prime of life, his career was cut short by death. One of his half sisters married into the Calhoun family. Another half sister married into the family of General Andrew Pickens, aided her husband in his election to the governorship of South Carolina, and bore him a son who was to rise to the same honor. Ada's one full paternal aunt married the brother of the statesman and orator Robert Young Hayne, and became the mother of Paul Hamilton Hayne, a young poet who was showing great promise. Mr. Wilson—who had been the guardian of Ada and her brother and sister since their mother's death in 1847—had no need to speak of his own family heritage. Gottschalk had admired his aristocratic mien before meeting him.

With all the troubles on Gottschalk's mind since the summer of 1853, he had pretty well forgotten Mr. Wilson and the McElhenneys. But as he caught the delicate perfume of Ada's stationery and studied her fine penmanship, memories began to stir. He could picture her going about the hotel public rooms with her nose buried in a book, usually the poems of Byron or Mrs. Hemans. He recalled that her brother and sister usually addressed her as Tommy—for tomboy, they explained. He could see again the wonder on her face as she heard him tell her grandfather of meeting Jerome Bonaparte. He could also see her, ill at ease in an evening gown, at his hotel recitals. She always sat near the tail of the piano and gazed at him as if entranced while he played.

He immediately answered her letter. He had, he wrote, recovered from his illness and would call at her house the next afternoon and hoped to find her at home.

Through his doctor and others he learned that day, to his surprise, that Ada Clare was not unknown to the theatrical and literary worlds. She made her stage début in a small rôle in Charles T. P. Ware's production of *The Hunchback* early in the autumn of 1854. At that time critics complained of her thin voice, and had not spoken highly of her acting in her appearances since then. As a writer, she fared better. Her love lyrics, published from time to time in the New York *Atlas* the preceding spring, were much discussed; certain critics went so far as to claim that in Ada Clare America at last had a woman poet with genius.

When Gottschalk called at her boardinghouse the next after-noon, he was shown into a little private sitting room on the first floor. After waiting for only a minute or two he saw one of the most beautiful blondes he had ever beheld walk in, a big smile lighting her face. That this attractive woman could be the Charleston girl he had known two years before seemed impossible. But she assured him that she was indeed Ada McElhenney.

He remembered her as plump, eating quantities of cake at tea. Now she was slender and petite. Nothing could be more feminine than her light-auburn hair. But she had cut it short and wore it parted on the left side: evidently she had not abandoned altogether her hoyden taste. Gottschalk saw that she had also retained her boyish habit of tossing her head, thus shaking a forelock out of place. Her complexion, once rough and freckled, was a smooth delicate ivory. Gottschalk wondered why he had never noticed the loveliness of her pansy blue eyes. Perhaps when he had known her they lacked the expression of melancholy, of world-weariness, which now made them so appealing. Her little tip-tilted nose seemed comic the first time he saw it; now it was indescribably pretty. He remembered that there had always been something wrong with her clothes. Today, in her white muslin dress with its delicate lace trimming and wide blue sash, she was a model of good taste.

Gottschalk could not understand how the dramatic critics could have called her voice thin. To him it was organlike. As she talked, he marveled at the richness of her vocabulary. "Do you read as much as you used to?" he asked. "Much more," she said. Then she went on to explain that she had never known how to read until the winter following their meeting. He had made her conscious of her ignorance, and she went back to Charleston determined to improve her mind. Under the guidance of her brilliant cousin, the poet Paul Hayne—five years older than she and the only relative for whom she had ever felt a sympathy—she learned the necessity of getting at the bottom of an author's thought. She would be forever in debt to Paul for teaching her how to read Shelley, the master whose philosophy of rebellion was now her philosophy and whose word music stirred within her what she called "a spiritual ecstasy."

She knew, she said, that her own verse was a dim and imperfect echo of Shelley's. Still she was confident that what it said came direct from her heart. At Gottschalk's request she brought three of her poems, clipped from the New York *Atlas*, and placed them in his hands. As she recited the pieces from memory, he listened and read.

She had made each the monologue of a woman in love. In the first, entitled "Lines to ——————," the speaker is lying on a couch, late at night, with her sleeping lover beside her, his head resting upon her breast. With a Shelleyan delicacy she describes the quiet rapture which possesses her and wafts her away to the realm where

There is no time, no life, no death!

In the second, entitled "To Thee Alone," the speaker is standing before her lover, replying to his taunt that her cooling passion is making her gloomy. If she is melancholy, she says, it is because of the excess of her love, not the lack. The third, "To Thee," is a lament. While the lover has gone away and has forgotten, the speaker is left behind to weep.

By the time Ada finished the first stanza of the second poem it was clear to Gottschalk that he was the man. The poems were telling him that Ada had been in love with him for two years, and her very presence was assuring him that her love was no trivial passion, that its power was immeasurable. It had led her to the determination to turn herself into the lady of elegance she had become. Realizing all this shook Gottschalk. When the reading was over he had difficulty in composing himself sufficiently to exclaim, "No American woman has ever before written verse of such frankness!"

Ada answered with the question, "Why shouldn't I be the first?" The ring of assurance in her voice brought him back to himself.

So captivating had she been from the moment of greeting that it was time to leave before he remembered to ask about her family. "You probably know as much about them as I do," she said.

Then, holding back nothing, she told of her last year in Charleston, the year following her meeting with Gottschalk. It was twelve months of family quarreling, all because of her decision to go on the stage, shine in the world, and be somebody. Her grandfather, her brother, her sister, her aunts and uncles, and her many cousins hounded her for her shamelessness. They called her names—a creature without pride, a disgrace to her people. Even Paul Hayne, the most understanding of the lot, called her a fool and then, seeing the grossness of the epithet, modified it by exclaiming, " A sublime fool! " She was one against many, but she fought and held her own until summer arrived and her brother became of age. In the settlement of her father's and mother's estates nearly everything went to him. But she and her sister each received a small income. At last independent, she fled to New York and, with good luck, got a part in Ware's production of *The Hunchback*. The break between her and her South Carolina relatives was complete. They would never mention her name again, and she would never mention theirs, except to some friend who had known them, some friend like Gottschalk.

" Ada McElhenney is dead," she said.

" Long live Ada Clare! " exclaimed Gottschalk.

A few days later he took her to the New York Philharmonic Society's first public rehearsal for the season. Just before the playing of the opening number the president mounted the platform and in a brief talk summarized the achievements of the organization during its thirteen years of existence and outlined the plans for the year to come. In closing his speech he read the list of the noted musicians who had recently been made honorary members. Those who were present rose when their names were called and bowed to the applause. Gottschalk was among them, and the acclaim he was given was more thunderous and more prolonged than that accorded any other.

While the New York correspondent of *Dwight's Journal* was forced to admit this, he, as usual, found fault with Gottschalk. The pianist from Louisiana, he said, continued to converse with the young woman he was escorting until long after the orchestra had begun to play. The correspondent's final word was: " Mr.

Gottschalk, however renowned, might well have benefitted from the admonition of an usher."

Those fortunate enough to have a view of Gottschalk's companion could see that there was a reason for his lapse from proper concert-hall manners. Ada Clare was a radiant creature on that occasion. Moreover she showed in the way she looked at Gottschalk that she considered him her god.

Just at this time she was involved in a theatrical venture about which there was a mysterious secret. She divulged nothing to Gottschalk; and he knew nothing until Wednesday, November 15, when the New York newspapers announced the première at the Metropolitan Theatre on Friday evening of a new American tragedy, *Love and Revenge*, by Wilson Bennett, with the author and Miss Ada Clare in the principal rôles. Following the tragedy Knowles's *The Wife* was to be given in an abridged version with Miss Clare in the rôle of Mariana. The notices contained no hint of a mystery, but for days Gottschalk and many another in New York had been hearing that there was an exciting surprise in store for those who had seats in the Metropolitan Theatre on Friday evening.

When Gottschalk, all alone, took his place in a rear row of the orchestra that night, he found the house packed. The opening of the play set a sombre mood, and he settled down for two hours of villainy, murder, and tears. But the first character who was killed refused to remain dead. He rose from his bier, explaining that he must appear in two more scenes. The secret was out: the play was a burlesque. From this point on everything went wrong, as planned. The scenery fell or was pushed over. At the end of each act the stage hands swung on the curtain to bring it down. For the death scenes, the musicians played jigs or polkas. The actors accused one another of stealing lines, fought with pistols or swords, killed one another, and came back to life for further clowning. No one among them, the critics said, was so pert and devilish as Miss Clare. It was she who kept the audience in suspense over what was to come and gave to the play a semblance of plot. Romping up and down the stage, laughing and crying, shouting and cooing, she was to Gottschalk the embodiment of delight. The evening was a brilliant success, made all the more effective by the straight playing of *The Wife* as an afterpiece. In this part of the evening's entertainment Miss Clare showed remarkable promise as a serious actress.

After the final curtain Gottschalk went backstage. He found Ada surrounded by a dozen young men, all congratulating her and expressing regret that, by its very nature, *Love and Revenge* could never be given a second performance. As Gottschalk stood looking on, sudden anger overwhelmed him, and he realized that he was within the toils of jealousy.

He could have been no tyro as a lover in the autumn of 1855. He was then well past the age of twenty-six. There are hints of a love affair in Paris when he was eighteen. It is possible, as gossip claimed, that his mysterious disappearance in Switzerland was due to an amorous adventure. It is almost certain that he was involved in an affair of the heart when he was in Spain. But as to his erotic experiences before his meeting with Ada Clare the positive records are silent.

By the time she came into his life he knew his temperament perfectly. For him love was a whirlwind, violent but soon spent. The woman who responded to his affection and expected it to endure was destined for grief. Either he was born to be as he was, or his devotion to his art made him that way. He had long since decided, he said, that the Muse of Music, ever fair and young, must remain his only bride.

All this he certainly told Ada.

But the month of November, 1855, had not progressed far when his words to her and her words to him had come to mean nothing. Both had been swept up by passion, a force that for the time being meant everything.

Love was a strong bulwark for Gottschalk. His fears for the future vanished. Backed by Mr. Hall and Mr. Chickering, he entered a period of great prosperity. Before the end of 1855 he knew that he would soon be able to pay the last cent of his father's debts.

On December 20—in Dodworth's Hall on Broadway, adjacent to Grace Church—he started the most illustrious series of concerts any artist had ever given in America. The last of the soirées, the sixteenth, came on June 7. The series began in a period of great cold and ended on an extremely hot evening. Whatever the weather, every seat in the hall was sold at each concert.

In the course of the series Gottschalk played all his old pieces and introduced to New York about forty new ones. From the works not heard before, the critics chose for special commendation "The Banjo," "María la O," and two Ossianic numbers, "Marche de nuit" and "Chant du soldat." "The Last Hope," demanded at almost every concert, came to be known as "Gottschalk's evening prayer." It was hummed or whistled throughout New York, and Mr. Hall could scarcely keep the music stores supplied with it. No one compared it with "The Maiden's Prayer." The critics spoke of it as a serious nocturne; one of them was sure that it was derived from an ancient Hebrew tune. Also popular were the Spanish and West Indian dances—the fandango, the jota, the jaleo, the cocoyé, the zapatacado, and the tango.

In these concerts Gottschalk depended less upon his own music than in any other series he was to give in the United States. With the violinist Edward Mollenhauer he played Mozart's sonata in A and with another violinist, Joseph Burke, Beethoven's *Kreutzer Sonata*. With Richard Hoffman he gave Schumann's "Andante with Variations" for two pianos. From Weber he played the sonatas in A and C and "The Invitation to the Waltz" in Liszt's transcription. He failed to give the Chopin concert as announced, but before the series was over he played Chopin's sonata in B flat minor, the scherzo in B minor, the impromptu in F sharp, the fantaisie impromptu, and miscellaneous études, preludes, waltzes, mazurkas, and polonaises. His playing of Henselt's "Si oiseau j'étais" was so well received that he repeated it on several programs. He gave Mr. Wallace's second concert polka and the étude entitled "La Rapidité." From William Mason—with whom, probably to the surprise of Mr. Dwight, he at once made friends— he played an étude and two mazurkas.

In each concert there were at least two assistants, usually a pianist and a violinist or cellist. Toward the end of the series the harpist Aptomas assisted on three or four occasions. Of the sixteen concerts only five included vocal numbers. Among the singers were Mr. Wallace's sister, Madame E. Wallace-Bonchelle, and the star of stars in opera in the new Academy of Music that season, Madame Anna de Lagrange.

The publicity Gottschalk received for his astounding successes at Dodworth's Hall meant full houses in the much larger theatres in which he played in neighboring cities—Brooklyn, Newark, New Haven, Springfield, Albany, Philadelphia, and Baltimore. He easily earned during the year between twenty and thirty thousand dollars, clear profit—far more than enough to satisfy his father's creditors.

After giving three or four highly successful concerts in Baltimore he experienced the one great mishap of the season. It was the time of the snow storm of January, 1856, one of the most calamitous ever known. At eight o'clock in the evening, when the train on which Gottschalk was a passenger left Baltimore, the flakes were falling lightly. No one dreamed of danger. But soon the clouds opened up and the flakes came down in a mighty avalanche. The train was stalled before midnight, and when morning came and there was no light the passengers realized that they were buried in snow. Gottschalk joined the trainmen who made their way to the top of a coach. They found the storm ended and the sun shining brightly upon a world completely white. Waving their hats and shouting, they finally attracted the attention of several farmers who were clearing a road.

Rescue was easy. But with all the telegraph lines down there was no way of sending a message to New York. When Gottschalk finally rejoined Ada, three days late, he found her sick in bed, completely overcome by anxiety.

Love, it appeared, brought material success to her as well as to Gottschalk. That winter she was engaged for an important rôle in a melodrama, *The Marble Heart*. When the run ended, late in May, she was employed to play Lady Mary in John Brougham's dramatization of *Jane Eyre*. Then at the end of June she joined a company organized for a summer production of Dion Boucicault's *The Phantom*, with Boucicault himself in the part of the Vampire. She was busy with the rehearsals for this play when Gottschalk

—with his Chickerings and his tuner, the great Madame de Lagrange, her Montenegrin husband the Baron de Stankowitch, her accompanist, and her maid—set out for a three months' tour of Canada, upper New York State, and the principal watering places. There was a tearful farewell between Gottschalk and Ada. Each promised the other a daily letter.

The tour was a fiasco. Try as Gottschalk and Madame de Lagrange might, they were unable to stir the Canadians. Gottschalk decided that those who made up the British half of the population were too stubborn to enjoy music and that those who belonged to the French half were too stupid. Whether in cities such as Montreal, Quebec, and Toronto or in smaller centers, the response to the concerts was the same—one tenth of the seats occupied by well-dressed persons whose faces throughout the evening of music remained studies in boredom. Much of the money that had poured into the pockets of Gottschalk and Madame de Lagrange the preceding winter and spring now poured out. Their luck was better once they were back within the borders of the United States. But too little time was left to make up for the losses incurred north of the St. Lawrence. When they returned to New York in September, neither could think of anything favorable to say of Canada.

Gottschalk had been too concerned over the failure of the tour to write to Ada every day. He expected to be chided for breaking his promise, but found on the contrary that his mistress knew how to be sympathetic. She understood perfectly his disappointment over the unfortunate summer. She understood also why he was worried about the future.

The newspapers had already announced the arrival of the great Sigismund Thalberg's Erard pianos. Within a few weeks the master himself would be on the scene to use the splendid instruments in a tour consuming an entire year. That Thalberg was coming had been a rumor for six months. Gottschalk had believed that it would remain a rumor. But now it was a certainty which must be faced.

He, as well as his manager Mr. Hall, knew that there was not as yet a sufficient number of music lovers in America to support at the same time two concert pianists of the first order. Gottschalk also realized that, in open competition, Thalberg—long a legend in the world of music and for Americans a novelty—would hold all the advantage. The only sensible procedure which Gottschalk and Mr. Hall could see was to yield the field as quietly and as gracefully as possible.

Gottschalk needed from twelve thousand to fifteen thousand dollars a year in order to live as he liked and at the same time fulfill his obligations to those he had promised to support. Friends in Paris assured him that if he returned to France he would be named the imperial court pianist and in such position be rich. Espadero and other friends in Havana wrote that the Cubans had not begun to open up their purses to him on his recent tour of their island and were now eagerly awaiting the chance to swarm to his concerts. Both Hall and Chickering advised him to try for a share of the gold of California and then follow down the Pacific coast for more gold in Peru.

The reunion with Ada meant more to Gottschalk than his friends realized. She was with a stock company booked for the autumn and early winter in the larger towns of Connecticut and New Jersey. After her performance every Saturday night she took the train to New York to be with her lover until Monday afternoon. He could not think of wrenching himself from the joys of these week ends.

In the middle of September his advertisement for pupils appeared in all the important New York newspapers. During the preceding Lent he had given lessons, and had asked for—and easily got—the high price of five dollars an hour. He now asked for six dollars an hour for individual instruction, eight dollars for a class of two, twelve dollars for a class of four, and sixteen dollars for a class of eight. The comment on these figures in *Dwight's Journal* was, "Neither Mr. Gottschalk nor any other professor is worth such fees."

Young New Yorkers ambitious to be virtuosos did not agree with *Dwight's Journal*. Within a month after the advertisement first appeared, all the hours Gottschalk had reserved for teaching were filled. And each pupil, prior to acceptance, had demonstrated his talent in an audition. For a studio, Gottschalk used the loft of Descombes' music store. It was attractively furnished, and was kept in order by a middle-aged Irish maid in constant attendance.

Among the pupils receiving individual instruction was a young woman in whose progress Gottschalk was especially interested. She was the nineteen-year-old wife of an Episcopalian clergyman, the Reverend William Wood Seymour. She and her husband lived in a Murray Hill mansion with her father, George Russell Ives, a New Englander who had made a fortune practicing law in New York. Gottschalk had been a guest in her home, and knew no house in America where there were so many handsomely bound books and well-chosen paintings.

The young wife was a blonde, tall and slender, distinguished in appearance rather than beautiful. She had talent for the piano, but Gottschalk was frank in telling her that she would never be a concert virtuoso. To give her an idea of her shortcomings he had his star pupil, Harry Sanderson, play for her.

" It would be foolish for you to aspire to be more than a good pedagogue," said Gottschalk after her third or fourth lesson.

" I might write about music," she said.

" If you do," said Gottschalk, " call yourself Octavia Hensel."

He had facetiously spoken the first name that came to mind, and straightway forgot it. But it was to remain in Mrs. Seymour's memory.

She had been under his instruction not more than two weeks when one day, without thinking of the effect the question might have, he asked her her Christian name.

" My father, my brothers, my husband, and my close friends," she said, " call me Mary Alice."

From that day on she to him was Mary Alice and he to her was Moreau. Ada called him Gottschalk, except when she addressed him with a term of endearment.

He took more and more delight in his talks with Mary Alice. He changed the schedule of the pupil whose lesson followed hers and kept that hour free, pretending to himself that he wanted those sixty minutes for rest. But he knew that what he really wanted was to hold Mary Alice at the studio for another hour of conversation.

He told her things he had forgotten to tell Ada. He spent thirty minutes of a lesson period relating the story of his meetings with America Vespucci, an alleged descendant of the explorer who provided a name for the continents of the New World. When a boy of twelve he had seen this romantic adventuress, clad in a golden velvet gown, standing on a balcony of the St. Louis Hotel in New Orleans. He was introduced to her in Madame Merlin's salon in Paris. Then the past summer in Ogdensburg, New York, he drank " a little glass " with her in the magnificent house which she had wheedled from a former American millionaire lover. He talked to her about the great world from which she had at last retired, and she in turn told him of her futile attempts to win a grant of money from the government of the United States on the ground of her descent from Amerigo Vespucci. The interview had impressed Gottschalk with the tragedy of old age. Ada would have used the story in an article for the *Atlas* or some other periodical, but when in her presence Gottschalk had never once thought of America Vespucci.

Toward the end of October his friend Richard Storrs Willis—amateur composer and music critic, brother of the editor of the *Home Journal*, Nathaniel Parker Willis—invited him to spend a few days at Idlewild, the Willis estate in the Highlands on the Hudson. In accepting the invitation Gottschalk made one reservation: he must not be away from New York on Tuesday. This was the day of Mary Alice's lesson. He made no reservation regarding Sunday, the day Ada was in town for their weekly rendezvous. Chance seemed to be on Ada's side, for Storrs replied that he and Gottschalk would go up to Idlewild by train Wednesday morning and return to New York by boat late Saturday afternoon.

Gottschalk made the trip as Storrs had planned it and got back to his apartment a few hours before Ada, after a fatiguing train ride from Hartford, joined him. He did not even tell her that he had been out of New York.

But for Mary Alice's ears on the following Tuesday he had a spirited account. The visit to Idlewild made possible an opportunity he had longed for, the opportunity to view the American autumn foliage in all degrees of light. The Willises were civilized hosts: they gave their guests the freedom to entertain themselves. Gottschalk rode up and down the mountainside on a big fiery horse, sometimes alone and sometimes with Storrs and the one other guest, a writer for the New York *Courier*. One day the three ventured deep into the wilds, where, according to Storrs, deer, bears, foxes, and rattlesnakes had their lairs. They had brought a lunch of sandwiches and wine, and feasted in the mouth of a cave. The drawing room at Idlewild was ideal for music. Every evening Gottschalk played for two or three hours, mainly Bach preludes and fugues and Beethoven sonatas. He surprised himself as well as Storrs when he used no music. Ten years had passed since he had so much as thought of some of the pieces he played.

On the last evening, about midnight, Gottschalk, Storrs, and the *Courier* man got into a discussion of aesthetics and the interrelation of the senses. Gottschalk told of a lady in Philadelphia who declared that when she heard his music she was overwhelmed with the odor of tuberoses. He confessed that for him the taste of pineapple belonged to the key of A minor and that when he played Chopin he saw and smelled heliotrope—great spreading fields filled with it and mountains covered with it. Storrs admitted that when he heard Mozart he fancied himself caressing plush and when he listened to "the music of the future" he felt himself pricked by thorns. The discussion lasted till morning. In the end the three agreed that sense perception was a science which man had only begun to investigate.

Mary Alice drank in every word. When Gottschalk came to the end of his monologue he asked, "What would I do if I didn't have you to listen to my twaddle?" Her answer was, "You never speak twaddle."

Ada could not have known of the existence of Mrs. Mary Alice Ives Seymour. But it is clear that she sensed some untoward influence at work upon her lover. She fought to retain his affection as she had fought to win it. The indirect method she adopted this time was to show him how powerful her pen could be when used in his defense.

She had never sympathized with his policy of quietly yielding the field to Thalberg. Nor had countless others, many of whom were writing to the newspapers championing Gottschalk as the greatest of living pianists. Ada, using the New York *Atlas* as her medium and signing her essays with the pseudonym Alastor, outdid them all. She had been reading Carlyle, and imitated his manner of satirizing. While she pictured Thalberg as the Fossil or the Intruder or the Automaton, she made Gottschalk the Spirit of Youth or the Poet of America or the Genius or the Laureate. She was at her cleverest in her treatment of the Gullibles, as she called the New Yorkers who rushed to buy tickets for Thalberg's concerts. Within a week after its appearance, her first essay was being quoted in newspapers throughout the East. Even the man on the street came to understand that music rather than politics was indicated when he heard someone called a Gottschalkian or a Thalbergian. Ada's use of a pseudonym meant nothing. It was said that she herself sent notices to newspaper editors far and wide asking them to announce that the Alastor of the New York *Atlas* was in reality the poet and actress Ada Clare.

The satires failed to accomplish their nominal aim. After Thalberg's début, on November 10, Gottschalk himself was numbered among the Thalbergians. On November 20, at a grand concert in the Academy of Music, he and Thalberg played together the latter's *Norma* fantasy for two pianos. The stock company with which Ada had been traveling was disbanded, and she was in the audience that night. She had never seen Gottschalk " glitter so superbly." Another who was present, John Huneker of Philadelphia, was to say years later to his musical son James Gibbons, " While Thalberg's scales were a string of pearls, Gottchalk's were glittering stardust." Ada gazed longingly at her lover in his splendor. He had been so occupied in preparing for this appearance with Thalberg that for two whole weeks he had not so much as written her a line.

Two or three mornings after the grand Academy of Music concert, when Gottschalk was in his apartment getting ready to go to the studio for a day of teaching, a servant brought up his mail. Among the letters was one from Paris, edged in black and addressed in Célestine's handwriting. " Can it be Edward? " Gottschalk asked himself, his face bloodless and his hands trembling. He tore the envelope open and learned that on Sunday, November 2, while Parisians with their arms filled with chrysanthemums were in cemeteries decorating graves in celebration of the Day of the Dead, his mother, in the salon of the pension on the rue des Filles-du-Calvaire, had succumbed to a stroke of apoplexy. She had not known that she was ill, and died without pain. One minute she was her usual self, and the next minute she was gone. Célestine had sent a notice of the death to New Orleans newspapers. She asked Moreau to have it reported also in New York and Philadelphia.

The shock plunged Gottschalk into a whirl of memories. He was in the nursery of the house on the rue des Remparts listening to his mother as she talked of Père Antoine; he heard her singing the first tune he had ever played; he was with her and his father in the St. Charles Theatre waiting for Fanny Elssler to emerge from the wings; and he was in his mother's arms as she begged for his promise that one day he would visit the Holy Land. The self-control which made it possible for him to give a concert in Boston a few hours after hearing that his father was dying now took possession. He hastily wrote a letter to his sisters and brothers, enclosed a bank draft to pay for his mother's funeral, and called a servant to post it immediately. He then sent by messenger a note to Mrs. Seymour, urging her to be at his studio that afternoon at three.

He spoke to no one that day of the sad news he had received. On arriving at his studio he teased, as usual, the Irish maid. He gave the scheduled lessons, and spent an hour or two working on a new composition promised to the Escudiers, a transcription for two pianos of the " Miserere " from *Il Trovatore*. But all the time he was waiting for three o'clock.

When Mary Alice finally came, he greeted her calmly and seated her on a sofa where the light was good. He then handed her Célestine's letter, forgetting that she was unable to read French. She looked at it, shook her head, and handed it back to him, smiling at what she took to be a joke. He then sat down beside her and translated the letter, word for word. When he got to the end and saw that tears were streaming down her cheeks, he rose, went to one of the pianos, and began to improvise. Until the maid showed in the four pupils due at four o'clock, he played without pause, not once lifting his eyes from the keyboard. As he ended with a major chord and looked up, he saw that Mary Alice was standing at his right. Her eyes were dry, and her face was a picture of resignation.

" You've taught me the power of music," she said.

His reply was a word of thanks for her kindness in coming.

Ada did not know of his mother's death until she read of it in the New York *Times*. She immediately wrote him a long letter of condolence. He answered with a brief note, saying at the end that he would see her soon. In a postscript he added: " Gottschalk once more thanks Alastor for her support and congratulates her on the brilliance of her satires."

A day or two later he received a call from Salvatore Patti. The onetime tenor, now impresario, immediately stated the purpose of his visit. He wanted Gottschalk to join him and his daughter Adelina, the child wonder soprano, on a two-year tour of the West Indies. Gottschalk asked for a week to consider the offer.

Arriving at a decision of such importance consumed him so completely that Ada heard nothing relating to him until she read in the newspapers that he was to leave soon with the Pattis for Havana.

The morning after the announcement appeared he received a letter from her. He *must*, she said, take her to Cuba with him. She would go in any capacity, perhaps as his secretary, or even as Adelina Patti's maid. His reply, dispatched immediately, was that she asked the impossible and that he was surprised to see Ada Clare in a beseeching mood.

He did not know her reaction to his rebuke until Sunday morning December 7, when he got a copy of the latest *Atlas*. He turned immediately to Alastor's column, thinking he would read another attack on the Thalbergians. But he had scarcely seen the title, "Whips and Scorns of Time," when he found that Ada had changed her theme. Then after going through the first three or four paragraphs he realized that she was telling the world the full story of their affair, depicting with eloquence the melancholy pass to which his coldness and neglect had led her. All New York had gossiped about their intimacy: there was no need to call him by name. But she had spared him nothing. In concluding she had written: "Young as I am, I feel as if my life was already closed. All that I had faith in seems to have glimmered out. Nay, the very world itself is like a dream, yet I perceive that Trigonometry, Carbonic Acid, and Gottschalk still exist. But what of that? The world plunges straight onward to its own dissolution, when shall remain but those two sole self-existencies, Necessity and Truth, which were omnipotent before Trigonometry had birth, or ever Gottschalk was."

There was no time to give way to resentment and anger. Gottschalk was getting ready for his farewell concerts, at one of which Thalberg was to appear with him in the *Trovatore* duo he had just completed. His decision was to ignore Ada's revelation, as he had always ignored unfavorable press comment.

Still on the next Sunday morning, December 14, he dropped everything to rush out for a copy of the *Atlas* as soon as he knew it was on sale. Ada's essay in this issue was the last in her series on the Gottschalkians and Thalbergians. It was as bold and as merry as the others had been. Gottschalk judged that it had been written in advance of the essay published the preceding week.

The December 21 *Atlas* carried nothing signed Alastor. But in the number for December 28 came the second of Ada's revelations, entitled "The Pangs of Despised Love." Gottschalk had not read far when he saw that Ada had never before written with such mastery. He admired the tenderness with which she told of a simple South Carolina country girl who died of a broken heart. Then he came to this passage: "Happy was she to lie there in the arms of Death, the quiet mother. Alas! how much happier than I—reserved to work out one grim and dreadful fate, which it drives me mad to think of. Yet, when it is over, and I have drunk of this cup, which cannot pass from my lips, shall she not—great, deep-hearted Nature, true mother of us all!—shall she not take me to her breast as fondly as a mother folds into her bosom her weakest child?" Gottschalk did not need to read the rest of the essay and see the paragraph on himself to know that Ada was admitting to him and all the rest of the world that she was pregnant. He at once sent her a note, saying that he would call that evening.

He did not find her the bedraggled woman whom the readers of the *Atlas* were conjuring up in their minds. In anticipation of his coming she had put on a light blue satin evening gown. She was paler than he had ever seen her, and the world-weariness in her eyes was deeper. She had never before appeared to him so beautiful.

They greeted one another in the manner of old friends. He thanked her once more for her brilliant leadership of the Gottschalkians and praised her witty prose. She complimented him on the success of his first farewell concert, just three nights before—the concert at which he and Thalberg played the *Trovatore* duo. She was ready to agree, she said, with Richard Hoffman, who asserted in a review of the concert that he had never heard such a volume of sound come from two pianos as in the passage where Thalberg had a double trill in the middle register while Gottschalk with the speed of lightning raced back and forth between low bass and high treble. Then she assured him that she would be present at the next Philharmonic Society concert, at which he was to play the Henselt concerto in F minor. "That staid old organization will give a lively evening at last," she said.

Gottschalk asked her point-blank, "Are you going to have a baby?"

"Yes," she said.

"The experience need not be a bitter cup," he said.

Since he was the man he is known to have been, it is certain that he then offered marriage, stating frankly that on his part there could be only a dead love.

It is certain that Ada rejected such a proposal. As to bringing into the world a child stamped with illegitimacy, she was to write: " Is Thalberg frowned upon because he's a bastard? Has Paris made a pariah of Emile de Girardin because he was born a natural son? Do the children of Franz Liszt and the Countess d'Agoult feel disgraced? Oh, it's time for us Americans to grow up! There isn't a woman in our land who shouldn't feel proud to bear an illegitimate child if the blood of a genius flows in its veins."

When Gottschalk asked her how much money she had, she was obliged to admit that her income from her South Carolina property was only about seven hundred dollars a year and that the little she made from acting and writing she spent on clothes.

" You've no reason to feel any longer the melancholy you felt when you wrote the *Atlas* revelations," he said. " It's now my turn to do the worrying."

The next afternoon he called again. He had a ticket on a steamer which was to sail for Le Havre within two or three weeks. He had money, and he had letters of introduction to friends who would receive her as the distinguished writer and actress she was and take care of her every need while she was in Paris. He had already written to them, and they would be expecting her. Then he warned that she must not try to brave the puritan prejudice which prevailed in America. She need not return to the United States for several years. Then she could bring the child and say it was adopted. He would, he promised, keep her at all times informed of his address, and he urged her to call upon him for any help he could give.

He escorted her to the pier when she embarked for Le Havre. As they walked up the gangplank they noticed that they were being pointed out and knew that the scandalmongers were saying, " There go Don Juan and his forlorn female of the *Atlas*."

Until the end of January, Gottschalk was aware of the gossip as he made his way along the streets. Then it shifted—to Thalberg! It was said from New Orleans to Boston that the aging virtuoso who looked like an English squire had taken as mistress the eighteen-year-old daughter of the great singer Madame d'Angri, one of his assisting artists. Certain ladies of Boston were so outraged that they reported the affair to Madame Thalberg, who was in Italy. That lady, it was said, was on her way to the United States to investigate. "Oh, these rakish pianists!" the American puritans were exclaiming.

On the afternoon of February 6, Gottschalk called on Mrs. Seymour in her Murray Hill home to say farewell. "Play your adieu to me," she said.

Seated on a sofa near the piano, she listened as he improvised for her once more. He poured into the music his sadness over his mother's death, his mingled feelings over Ada and the child that was to be born, and his pity for Mary Alice herself, who, he realized, was very unhappy in marriage. When he finally looked toward the sofa he saw that her head was buried in cushions and that her body was shaking with sobs. He stole out without attracting her attention.

In company with Adelina Patti, then just three days under fourteen, and her father, Salvatore Patti, Gottschalk sailed on the *Quaker City* for Havana the morning of February 7, 1857. The three reached the Cuban capital five days later. After several sensationally successful concerts there and Gottschalk's happy reunion with Espadero and the Edelmanns, he and the Pattis began a tour of the provincial Cuban cities.

He wrote regularly to Ada. She in turn passed on to *La France musicale* his reports on his Cuban concerts. She was also contributing articles on the Parisian theatre to the New York *Atlas*. In late May, not long after Gottschalk began his twenty-ninth year, he received a letter announcing the birth of his son. "I've decided to call him Aubrey," Ada wrote.

The night of June 6, 1857, the sailing vessel on which Gottschalk was making the voyage from Havana to the island of St. Thomas skirted the north shore of Haiti. Signor Patti, Adelina, and all the other passengers had gone below. But Gottschalk remained on deck. Though dark clouds fringed the southern horizon, a full moon shone unobstructed high in the heavens. The mountainous Haitian shore line was distinctly defined.

One peak towered above all the others. Gottschalk fancied that it was the very mountain upon which his grandmother Bruslé wandered after witnessing the horrors of the Cap François massacre —the mountain from which she sighted the British vessel standing by to pick up refugees and carry them to Jamaica.

As Gottschalk gazed towards the land, recalling long buried memories, he felt overwhelmed by life's ironies. More than sixty years had passed since three sailors from the British vessel rescued his grandmother. In his childhood he loved nothing better than to hear her tell the story of their courage and their kindness. She was still alive, telling the same story to great-grandchildren. But her daughter, his mother, was dead. No, not dead, Gottschalk reflected. No life with progeny ever really dies. His mother was living on within him—and also within his son, lately born in Paris.

Gottschalk was too full of his thoughts to think of sleeping when he went down to his stateroom. He spent the rest of the night in committing to paper his impressions on first viewing the mountains of Haiti. When he reached St. Thomas, he started the manuscript on its way to Paris. Before the end of the year it was to be published in *La France musicale*. It shows that if

Gottschalk had not given himself to music he might have attained distinction in literature.

He and the Pattis had intended to remain in St. Thomas only long enough to transfer to the schooner *Isabel,* on which they had booked passage to Caracas, Venezuela. But they found St. Thomas enchanting, even with yellow jack threatening. Moreover they heard of excellent theatres and a deep interest in music on neighboring islands. So they canceled their passage on the *Isabel* and put off until another day their trip to Caracas.

To Gottschalk, Charlotte Amalie, the one town on the island of St. Thomas, was as charming as its name. It reminded him of the papier-mâché villages which the toy-makers of Nuremburg manufactured and sent out to all parts of the world. The Danes, who held possession of the island and had built the town, were, he decided, a little queer. The editor of the newspaper made and peddled bath tubs. The tobacconist sold preserves and patent medicines as well as cigars and snuff. And the trails laid out by the founders formed a labyrinth without rhyme or reason.

Yet Gottschalk found these crazily twisting pathways delightful for horseback riding. He learned also that the Danes and other whites who inhabited the island were willing to pay well to hear good music. The concerts which he and Adelina gave in the theatre of Charlotte Amalie yielded each of them over twelve hundred dollars.

The next port they visited, San Juan, Puerto Rico, had a theatre which would not have been out of place on a Paris boulevard. They gave here also several well-attended concerts. In playing Spanish and Cuban dances Gottschalk made the Puerto Ricans realize that their own folk music was rich in promise. In time they were to look upon his visit with Adelina Patti as the first great event in their musical history.

Poncé, the important city on the south shore of the island, also heard the two artists in a number of concerts. Though less populous than San Juan, Poncé was a more advanced cultural center.

Gottschalk and the Pattis met there a wealthy couple who owned a great estate in the mountains of the interior. The hus-

band was a sugar planter, and the wife before her marriage had
sung in opera in Spain. They invited the visiting artists to spend
a month or two in their mountain retreat. To escape the intense
heat on the coast in the middle of August, Gottschalk and the
Pattis speedily and joyfully accepted the invitation. Their hosts
had another guest, a French doctor who might have been an
impressive tragedian. His great enthusiasm was Racine. There
were memorable evenings in the beautiful patio under the stars—
Gottschalk playing his echoes of Ossian, Adelina imitating Jenny
Lind and Madame Sontag or singing Rossini duets with her
hostess, and the French doctor reciting passages from *Phèdre* and
Andromaque.

It was autumn when Gottschalk and the Pattis sailed from
Poncé for Port-au-Prince. In this city, the capital of Haiti, Gottschalk played to the descendants of the blacks who had slain his
ancestors and taken their wealth. The facts about his Creole
background were made much of in the Port-au-Prince press. He
was hailed as a son of the island. Since he was a visiting artist
he had to be polite, but he was never to have much to say about
his sojourn in Haiti.

From Port-au-Prince he and the Pattis went to Jamaica, another
island of the Antilles which had figured in his family history. " I
owe a debt to Jamaica," he was to write. " It was the place where
my maternal grandparents met. If it had never existed, where
would I be? " After facing two very small audiences in Kingston,
the capital, he and his associates wished they had " burned " the
island. They had been told to pass it by. The miserliness of
Jamaicans was proverbial throughout the Antilles.

Gottschalk learned one evening however that Jamaicans could
be generous as well as tight-fisted. When out for a walk he
wandered into a poor section of Kingston and came upon a lighted
chapel. Hearing music inside, he entered and stood in the doorway, where he could see without being seen. When the singing
ceased, the minister, a Protestant missionary from the United
States, delivered a plea for money to relieve a group of ship-
wrecked sailors brought ashore that afternoon. As he concluded
his remarks with quotations from the Scriptures on giving, a hat

was passed around to the sixty or seventy worshipers. But when the minister poured the contribution on the table behind which he was standing only a few copper coins fell out, perhaps enough to make up a shilling. Gottschalk, sorry for the minister as well as for the unfortunate sailors, stole to the little organ at one side of the room and began to play. For five minutes he improvised, the worshipers all the while listening as if in the presence of a miracle. Then he himself passed around the hat. When the collection was poured on the table this time the congregation was so excited over seeing the pile of silver that no one noticed the disappearance of Gottschalk. He lingered in the shadow of the doorway long enough to hear the minister say, " Who knows but that the maker of music who opened up your hearts and your pockets was an angel sent by the Lord? "

The next port Gottschalk and the Pattis visited was Caracas, where the public had been awaiting them more than a year. It was not like the public of Haiti and Jamaica. It was sophisticated, elegant, music-loving, and pure Spanish. When Gottschalk faced his first audience he felt that he was again in Madrid.

Among the Venezuelans who were deeply impressed by his artistry was a public official and amateur pianist of talent, Manuel-Antonio Carreño. His little daughter Teresa, four years old, had already manifested a phenomenal gift for music. She was too little to go to concerts, but not too young to listen intently when her father, her only teacher, spoke of Gottschalk's incredible virtuosity. At many a lesson he was to say, " Gottschalk did it more like this." To her Gottschalk represented the ideal.

He and the Pattis went from Caracas into the Guianas and gave concerts in Georgetown, Paramaribo, and Cayenne. They then followed the coast of the Brazilian state of Pará, and stopped in every town where there was a theatre. At Belem their tour ended.

It was near the close of the year 1858 when Gottschalk saw Adelina and her father embark on a steamer bound northward. They did not reach New York until the year 1859 was well begun. Before its end Adelina was to begin at the Academy of Music her unparalleled career in opera.

Early in February, 1859, Gottschalk, alone except for his Chickerings, arrived in St. Pierre, Martinique. The picturesque little city, as French as a Norman coastal town, made him feel at home again. On his second morning there he went to a livery stable, rented a horse, and cantered over the slopes of Mont Pelée, the volcano which in time was to erupt and wipe St. Pierre out of existence.

He was soon meeting the Martinique musicians, among whom was an excellent French harpist, Frédéric Allard. Before the end of February he and Monsieur Allard gave the first of a series of concerts in St. Pierre's beautiful new theatre. The very next day Gottschalk began to receive requests for piano lessons. He was willing to take a few advanced pupils, he announced, but he would have to charge forty francs an hour. This was twice the fee demanded by Chopin, the most highly paid private teacher of the piano Paris had ever known. But five or six in St. Pierre paid it without protest. Two who offered the fee were given lessons for nothing: they were nuns, teachers of music in a convent.

Gottschalk remained in St. Pierre five months. He did not devote all his hours to concerts and teaching. The tropics had cast their spell upon him. He had learned to live, he said, according to tropical customs, which, "if not strictly virtuous, were, in retaliation, terribly attractive." In the native girls he saw again the New Orleans quadroons who had fascinated him in his childhood, nature's daughters, with red lips and brown bosoms. They were ignorant of evil, they sinned with frankness, they never experienced the bitterness of remorse, and they had no notion of telling the world about their relations with him in the columns of the New York *Atlas*. One of these black-eyed creatures, he admitted, would make him feel for a few days that he was living only for her. But then another would win his affection. He was to say: "All this was frightfully immoral, I know; but life in the tropics, in the midst of a voluptuous race, cannot be that of an American Presbyterian."

No one love was ever strong enough to conquer his interest in fresh musical fields. That summer the unveiling of the statue of the Empress Josephine in Fort-de-France, Guadeloupe, was made the occasion for fêtes lasting three days. Officials from other islands—British, Spanish, Danish, and Dutch as well as French—were the guests of honor. Gottschalk had let the Guadeloupe government know of his presence in Martinique, and he also was among the visitors of distinction. He provided the entertainment the third evening of the festival, and was paid an honorarium of twelve hundred dollars.

One of the numbers played by request at this concert was a medley of airs associated with the different nations represented at the festival. As a grand climax to the medley, in the main an improvisation, Gottschalk paid special tribute to England and France by playing at the same time, in loud octaves, " God Save the Queen " and " Partant pour la Syrie." On recognizing a strain of their national anthem the English officers leaped to their feet and then dropped to their chairs when the French tune came to the fore. Gottschalk was so amused at their bobbing up and down that for once when he was at the piano he came near losing control of himself.

After several more concerts in Fort-de-France, where he had the assistance of a soprano trained in the Paris Conservatoire, he moved on to Basse-Terre. Here, within a period of three weeks, he made eight appearances, each to an audience of at least five hundred. Requests poured in for a ninth concert. But the heat of Basse-Terre had become unbearable. Besides, Gottschalk had enough money to meet his varied responsibilities for many months to come.

Someone told him of an abandoned stone hut on one of the highest points on the island of Guadeloupe, Mount Matouba, an extinct volcano. Once he saw the place he fell in love with it—and stayed. He described it as follows: " Perched upon the edge of the crater, on the very top of the mountain, my cabin overlooked the whole valley. Level with my one room was a terrace, upon which I rolled my piano every evening at sunset. There, in view of the most beautiful scenery in the world, I played for myself alone, everything which my surroundings inspired—and what surroundings! "

He had a servant, a mulatto who had heard him play in Basse-

Terre. "He attached himself to me," Gottschalk said, "and loved me with that absurd and touching constancy which one only meets with in dogs and mad men." The mulatto, Firmin Meras by name, claimed that the Pope was his brother and the Emperor of the French his cousin, and wrote letters, sometimes in verse, to these personages. He had read Voltaire and Rousseau, insisted that he too was a philosopher, and called himself "the Prince of Thought." "In the midst of this intellectual ruin," said Gottschalk, "the love of music had remained balanced. He played the violin, and had an ear for true pitch. Although insane, he had never heard of Richard Wagner and knew nothing of 'the music of the future.'"

Firmin constituted Gottschalk's first audience for several compositions which were to figure prominently on his programs in the future. One was "Marche des gibaros," based probably on a Puerto Rican folk tune. Another was "Pastorella e cavalliere," a tonal narration of an old French pastourelle. Still another was "Ojos criollos," a Cuban dance written for two pianos. The eccentric servant also heard Gottschalk play much of his symphony "La Nuit des tropiques," and scenes from his opera *Charles IX* and from his cantata "Fête champêtre cubaine." After listening to these works "the Prince of Thought" could scarcely have approved of certain "teaching pieces" which his idol wrote while on Mount Matouba—pieces which Hall was to publish under the pseudonyms "Seven Octaves," "Oscar Letti," and "Paul Ernest."

By October, Gottschalk's conscience was hurting him. His destiny was to make music for great audiences, not for himself and a single servant. He wrote to his many correspondents that his next address would be Havana, in care of Nicolas Espadero. But with the approach of winter Mount Matouba became all the more fascinating. It was not until December that Gottschalk broke away. Firmin, whom kind treatment had made as sane as any other man, embarked with him in Basse-Terre for the voyage to Cuba.

When they reached Havana—early in January, 1860—Gottschalk found that his friend Espadero had many letters for him. There was a sad one from Mrs. Seymour, announcing the death of her only child, a boy less than a year old. Gottschalk's younger sisters—Clara and Augusta, pianists, and Blanche, a soprano—wrote that they were planning to go to England, where professional débuts were not so difficult to arrange as in France. Célestine would remain in Paris to look after Edward and Gaston. There were also letters from Mr. Hall and Mr. Chickering, reminding Gottschalk that the public quickly forgets a favorite and that he should not delay too long his return to the United States.

From Ada there were half a dozen letters and all the existing numbers of a new literary weekly with which she was associated, the New York *Saturday Press.* After Aubrey's birth Ada made a tour through most of Europe, and came to know Germany, England, and other countries unfamiliar to Gottschalk. Soon after her return to New York in the spring of 1859, she was engaged to play Iras in an elaborate production of *Antony and Cleopatra.* The run in New York was brief, but the play went on tour until summer. Ada was no longer in the theatre. She was giving all her time to the *Saturday Press,* which was edited by a man she was eager for Gottschalk to know, Henry Clapp, Jr. He was a native of Essex County, Massachusetts, and had begun his career as an abolitionist and teetotalist. But he had spent several years in Paris, had mastered French, and, said Ada, had become almost as " civilized " as Gottschalk himself.

Ada's letters made it clear that she had not returned to New York with head bowed in shame because of the child born out of wedlock. She had said, and continued to say, that any woman who refused in the name of morality the opportunity to bear a child to a genius of Gottschalk's stature was an enemy of society. What the world most needed, according to Ada Clare, was *quality* in the population. At Aubrey's conception, she said, three were present—she, Gottschalk, and God. To her the little boy was holy, and no ritual ordained by man could make him more holy. " The first lesson I'm trying to teach him," she wrote in one of the letters, " is *pride* in his paternity."

All these ideas Gottschalk found elaborately developed in Ada's weekly *Saturday Press* column, " Thoughts and Things." In it she also discussed the theatre, music, books, religion, politics, and travel. The column abounded in names. Gottschalk saw that his own, always mentioned with reverence, was the one which appeared most often.

In Ada's letters there was much comment on the informal suppers at which the contributors to the *Saturday Press* met weekly or more often. There was never any plan. They just congregated in the cellar of Pfaff's saloon, directly under Broadway near Prince Street. The good food and the excellent beer were cheap, and Herr Pfaff allowed no noisy rowdies in the place. There was talk, said Ada—hour after hour of wonderful talk. They had all read Murger's *La Vie de Bohême*, and because of that, Ada supposed, they called themselves Bohemians. Clapp was referred to as the King and she as the Queen. Among those who were just plain subjects was a story writer whom the Queen considered the equal of Poe, an Irish immigrant, Fitz-James O'Brien. There were two shy young poets, William Winter and Clarence Stedman. A young Westerner who frequently contributed verse to the *Saturday Press*, William Dean Howells, looked in one evening. Ada was afraid that her cigarette-smoking was too much for him: he never came back. The one among her subjects who interested her most was a Long Islander, a big shaggy individual who never wore a cravat and never thought to button his collar. Everybody was always glad when he sauntered in: somehow his presence made one feel better. The Queen, the King, and all the others loved him; but none of them, the Queen was sure, had read his volume of poems with any care. He was a journalist, and his name was Walt Whitman.

In a recent number of the *Saturday Press*, that for December 24, Gottschalk found a poem by Whitman, " A Child's Reminiscence," one day to be known as " Out of the Cradle Endlessly Rocking." Gottschalk read the poem entire—and reread it. Then he saw that Ada had said of it in her column: " Versifying would ruin the piece. It's right out of the poet's heart, and I like it just as it is." Gottschalk could not agree with her. He had labored too long and too hard to perfect his own art to accept Whitman's artless lines as poetry.

Both Ada's letters and printed essays proved that she had attained a certain happiness. Gottschalk admired her. She had had the courage to turn to her advantage a situation which to any conventional woman would have been a tragedy. Her success served as a spur to him just at this time.

He was deep in the labor of preparing for the "monster" concert—which he gave in the Teatro Tacón in Havana on the evening of February 17. The orchestra which he conducted on that occasion numbered more than six hundred. There were also a drum corps of fifty and a trumpet choir of eighty. There were fifteen vocal soloists and a chorus of a hundred. "All together," said Gottschalk, "I directed nearly nine hundred performers, each of whom seemed to explode with sound in the big climaxes." More than half of the long program was devoted to the music Gottschalk had worked on in Guadeloupe—the symphony "La Nuit des tropiques," the cantata "Fête champêtre cubaine," and a hymn and grand chorus from *Charles IX*.

He had at last proved to the world that as a composer he was not afraid to attack the large forms, and the music critics in Havana outdid one another in praising his new works. He himself never claimed that the gigantic affair raised his stature as a musician. He continued to insist that new music cannot be appreciated until it is given what he called "normal performance." In his opinion the public had not as yet heard his attempts at symphony and opera.

His real aim in putting on the "monster" concert was to prepare the way for a money-making tour of Cuba. The mobs who fought to gain admission to his concerts that spring in cities and towns throughout the island proved that he attained his aim in grand fashion.

The tour led to physical exhaustion. In Santiago he became so ill that his physicians despaired of his life. A rumor spread that he had died, and a Santiago newspaper published it as a fact. Newspapers in the United States picked up the lie, and it was printed far and wide. Gottschalk spent his convalescence writing letters to prove that he was not a corpse.

In Havana the following January he again became desperately

ill. Once more the doctors said that he had little chance to live. This time his friends saw to it that no alarming reports were circulated. Sickness, however serious, could not, it seemed, conquer him. By the middle of February he was able to begin rehearsals for a second "monster" concert.

It was given on the evening of Wednesday, April 17, and, as in the previous year, every seat in the enormous Teatro Tacón was occupied. The program opened with the performance of a one-act comedy. The first musician heard was Gottschalk's star pupil, Señorita Carrere, who played a fantasy on *La Sonnambula*. She performed before the curtain, as did Gottschalk, who followed her with three or four minutes of improvisation. He was still thrilling the audience with his roulades and trills when the curtain rose revealing thirty-nine pianos, a performer standing before each. With Gottschalk playing and also conducting, the ensemble gave his "Ojos criollos" and another Cuban dance which he had recently completed, "Ay, Pompillo, no me mates." After this "glorification of the piano," as one critic called it, Gottschalk was called before the curtain so many times that the orchestra, vocal soloists, and chorus—five hundred all together— had replaced the pianos when he made his last bow and the stage was again revealed. Closing the first half of the program, Gottschalk conducted "La Nuit des tropiques" and the hymn and march from *Charles IX*. In the second half of the program there were only two numbers. The first was Méhul's descriptive symphony "La Chasse royale," with trumpeters playing echoes in all parts of the theatre. The second was a "military fantasy," compiled by Gottschalk and conducted by the bandmaster to His Excellency, the Captain-General of the Colony of Cuba.

Gottschalk was never to have much to say to his New York musical friends about his "monster" concerts in Havana. As he had given the first to gain publicity for a concert tour, he gave the second to convince Cubans that his piano lessons were worth a very high price. Teaching in Havana and assisting other artists in concerts filled his time for the rest of 1861.

It was an upsetting year for him, as it was for every American. The Civil War had begun. His affection for his native state, where he had always been treated with the greatest kindness, was deep. But his hatred for slavery, which he saw as the fundamental problem in the conflict, was deeper. He declared himself for the North.

With his mind made up, he felt, he said, that he had no right to linger longer in the tropics. When Jacob Grau, a New York impresario, offered to sponsor him in a tour of the North, he sent an immediate acceptance.

A morning or two later, in company with his friend Nicolas Espadero, he went to the American consulate, renounced his fidelity to the state of Louisiana, and swore allegiance to the government headed by Abraham Lincoln. The way was cleared for his return to New York. He sailed from Havana on the steamship *Columbia*, January 16, 1862. Firmin, who proved indispensable as a valet, was with him.

In returning to the United States Gottschalk hardly knew what to expect. His American correspondents had been writing sober letters since the outbreak of the war, but they had said nothing about the social distress reported in the Cuban newspapers. Gottschalk had read repeatedly that Abraham Lincoln—pictured as America's Robespierre—was commandeering all public treasuries, taking over private fortunes, killing trade, crushing all enterprise, and creating unemployment, lawlessness, and famine. " How can you think of giving concerts to people who are hungry? " Gottschalk's Havana friends asked when they found out that he was on the point of leaving for New York. He was aware of the fact that Cuban newspaper editors printed what they were told to print by a government eager to see the collapse of the United States and every other republic in the world. But he had observed for himself civil war in France in 1848, and he knew that it could lead to social chaos and great violence. He was impatient to reach New York, mingle with the people, and make his own deductions.

He had been in Manhattan scarcely a day when he realized that the Cuban journalists were liars. Everywhere he turned he saw evidences of prosperity. Broadway was thronged with smartly dressed persons, all in a hurry. The shops were crowded with buyers. Visitors to the city taxed the capacity of hotels and restaurants. It was difficult to obtain seats in theatres.

But Gottschalk soon learned from Mr. Grau that those attending the theatres wanted only diversion. The war dominated everybody's thoughts and determined everybody's decisions. In order to forget it for a few hours thousands flocked every evening to the amusement places which offered melodrama, farce, comic songs, dancing, acrobatic feats, and every other type of variety entertainment.

They had no heart for grand opera, Mr. Grau was obliged to admit. He had come to New York from his native Austria the year of the opening of the Academy of Music, 1854. The great theatre had been the scene of one money-losing opera season after another. But Mr. Grau was sure that the current season, which he was managing, was the worst of all. His one hope of saving himself from financial ruin lay in the popular concerts in which he proposed to present Gottschalk as well as his leading singers.

Grau had the reputation of a hard taskmaster. Now in his desperation he was doubly hard. Gottschalk had scarcely set foot in New York when he was in rehearsal for his first series of concerts, announced to begin on the evening of Tuesday, February 11, the ninth anniversary of his American début. Yet in spite of the demands made upon him he found time for reunions with old friends—Richard Hoffman, Mrs. Seymour, Ada Clare, and many others.

Ada appeared to him more beautiful than ever, more gracious in manner, and more brilliant in conversation. She too had renounced her loyalty to her native state and had sworn allegiance to Lincoln's government. Her income, derived from investments in South Carolina, was wiped out. Furthermore, the *Saturday Press* was suspended. She had hoped to win fortune with a novel, announced several times for publication under the title *Asphodel*. But for some reason the book never got into print. After all, her profession was acting. Just now she was in rehearsal for a play intended for a long tour, a melodrama aimed at spreading propaganda in support of the war.

Aubrey, almost five now, was quite blond, like his mother. Gottschalk could see little of himself in the boy. Ada had not spoiled him. He was in all respects a lovable child. Though he had learned that a little boy should be seen and not heard, he answered questions with a precocity that amazed and delighted his father.

Ada was as frank as in the old days. She told Gottschalk that she still adored him, and vowed that he would always remain above all others in her heart, even above Aubrey. But she made no effort to renew the relationship of love with her onetime lover. When she invited him to her apartment there were always twelve or fifteen others present, all of whom were loyal subjects of Bohemia, on hand to do honor to their Queen.

One afternoon when she was holding court Gottschalk witnessed an interesting little scene. Ada was sitting on a sofa talking with a young poet who was evidently much in love with her. All at once she rose and left the drawing room. Within ten minutes she returned, leading Aubrey, who was dressed in a beautiful new drummer boy's costume. Everybody shouted greetings to the child, as to an old acquaintance, and then the conversations went on as before. Ada, still holding Aubrey by the hand, sat down beside the poet.

Gottschalk failed to catch a question the young man asked the boy, but he distinctly heard Aubrey answer, "Oh, when we're traveling I don't call my mother Mama, I call her Ada Clare."

"And why do you do that?" asked the young man.

"She thinks it better, on the whole," said Aubrey. "People don't understand us. They fail to recognize our real distinction."

When the young man made no comment, Aubrey said, "You see, sir, my father is the great Gottschalk."

"You must say why you think so," broke in Ada.

"Well," said Aubrey, "he sent me this drummer's suit yesterday. And when he was in Havana he sent me a sword and a gun and I don't know how many other things."

"That's a funny reason," said Ada, rising and taking the child in her arms. "And you're a funny boy."

On several evenings Gottschalk joined Ada and her court at their favorite rendezvous, Pfaff's saloon. The Queen's throne was a chair at the head of a long table. She was always quietly dressed, and maintained at all times the dignity of a lady. Still she drank much beer, smoked one cigarette after another, and spiced her talk with occasional risqué allusions. However antagonistic her courtiers might become in their arguments, she could restore peace with a gesture. Though she rarely raised her voice, every word she spoke could be heard at the foot of the table.

Gottschalk observed that an evening invariably ended with nostalgic talk about the *Saturday Press* days. The two most interesting subjects of Bohemia in that time were no longer to be seen at Pfaff's. Fitz-James O'Brien was an army officer, on the eve of receiving his death blow in battle. And Walt Whitman was on the eve of his extraordinary career as volunteer minister of mercy to wounded soldiers in Washington hospitals.

But Gottschalk met and made friends with Bohemia's King, Henry Clapp, Jr. The pianist and the journalist conversed only in French, and each was astounded at the other's eloquence.

Ada was on her tour when, on the evening announced, February 11, Gottschalk gave his opening concert. The critics hailed his return with enthusiasm. But two or three remarked that Mr. Grau was evidently less concerned with the pianist than with the two pianos the Chickering company had manufactured specially for his use. Each was ten feet long, with a tail three feet wide, and had seven and a half octaves. Both instruments were kept on the stage throughout the program, though they were used together only when Gottschalk and Richard Hoffman played the former's *William Tell* fantasy. Gottschalk used one and then the other in his solos—"The Banjo," his never-to-be-published *Rigoletto* fantasy, and two pieces new to New York, "Pastorella e cavalliere" and "Murmures éoliens." The singers for the evening were four of Mr. Grau's brightest opera stars; like Gottschalk, their accompanists shifted from one piano to another. One of the disgruntled critics wrote: "It was difficult to tell whether the applause was for Mr. Gottschalk or the pianos. To what is advertising leading us?"

Mr. Grau was too elated over the financial success of the concert to bother about this question. What counted with him was that Gottschalk had played to a house—Niblo's Saloon—without an empty seat.

More concerts followed in quick order, ten in as many days, in Brooklyn and Newark as well as in New York. Gottschalk introduced his "Ojos criollos," played with Richard Hoffman, and it immediately became a sensation. He also played for the first time in the United States his most recent Ossianic piece, " Apothéose," and several new works based on West Indian themes, including " Marche des gibaros."

Of the many singers selected by Grau to appear on these occasions only two threatened Gottschalk's priority as a public favorite. One was Carlotta Patti, who but for an unfortunate lameness would probably have outshone as an operatic star her younger sister, Adelina. The other was a South Carolinian, Clara Louise Kellogg, who, like Gottschalk and Ada Clare, had deserted her native South and taken her stand for the North.

On February 22, Mr. Grau tried the experiment of combining opera and concert. At the Academy of Music that evening he presented Miss Kellogg in Donizetti's *Don Pasquale* and Gottschalk in a half-hour recital of his own music. The public liked the idea sufficiently to fill the immense theatre. Miss Kellogg, the critics reported, was as usual superb. But they had to admit that Gottschalk was the one who stirred the house to a frenzy when, against a background of American flags, he played in honor of Washington's birthday his recently composed " Union," a fantasy based on " Yankee Doodle," " Hail Columbia," and " The Star-Spangled Banner." It was the first public performance of a work to be associated with the name Gottschalk until the end of the Civil War.

Mr. Grau immediately followed this highly successful experiment with two gala offerings of like nature. For each of these the Academy of Music was illuminated as it had been for the grand ball of the previous year honoring New York's royal guest, the Prince of Wales. On the first evening Miss Kellogg appeared in a performance of *Lucia* and then, to lighten the effect of a story of madness and murder, sang " The Clara Louise Kellogg Polka," composed for her by her colleague, the baritone Susini. Gottschalk, with a violinist and cellist, played first a trio entitled " Two Tarantelles," composed, said the program notes, while he was in the West Indies. He then gave " The Banjo" and " Union." On the second gala evening the opera was Donizetti's *Betley*, starring Isabella Hinckley. On this occasion Gottschalk repeated

" Union " and played with the full orchestra what was listed on the program as " A Fragment of Mr. Gottschalk's lately composed Concerto in F minor."

Apparently, he never again included either the trio or the fragment of the concerto on a program. Beyond the casual generalized praise of the critics who reported the evenings for the New York newspapers nothing is known of either work.

After two weeks of giving concerts with a quartet of Mr. Grau's singers in Philadelphia, Baltimore, and Washington, Gottschalk was back in New York for another series of appearances. He again served as an added performer at evenings of opera. Moreover he introduced to New York what Mr. Grau advertised as " matinees of instruction."

For these " teaching recitals," as the critics preferred to call them, Irving Hall, used mainly for dancing, was engaged. In the center of the immense room two Chickering grands were placed. Around them sat three or four hundred auditors, each with a clear view of one keyboard or the other. A typical program consisted of a slow movement from a Beethoven sonata, an opera fantasy by Liszt or Thalberg, a polonaise and a nocturne by Chopin, and two or three pieces of contrasting character selected from Gottschalk's own compositions.

Stopping often to repeat and analyze a given passage, Gottschalk first played each number in very slow tempo on each piano. Then on one instrument or the other he performed the piece without interruption in the tempo intended by the composer. His hearers, made up mainly of teachers and students of music, were thus instructed and entertained.

To gain admission one had to subscribe for the entire series of twelve matinees. The public response was such that all tickets were sold within three or four days after they were placed on sale. Then when the series was near the end requests poured in for an extension.

But Mr. Grau had booked Gottschalk for his first tour of the West. It was the middle of March when the pianist and his company set out for Philadelphia. The maestro of the troupe was Emmanuele Muzio, a former pupil and friend of Verdi.

The singers were Carlotta Patti, the tenor Brignoli, the baritone Susini, and the basso Mancusi. Also in the party were two or three accompanists, the tuner who looked after Gottschalk's two ten-foot Chickerings, and Firmin.

After several concerts in Philadelphia, Gottschalk and his associates traveled by train through the same territory he had traversed in 1853 by stagecoach and river boat. " One has only to enter a railway carriage in order to be near the war," he wrote in the diary in which he had begun to make regular entries. The cars were crowded with soldiers, drinking, shouting profanity, singing obscene songs. The presence of women in no way deterred them. They were even more rowdy when the train stopped at stations and girls came on board to serve cake, ice cream, and lemonade. The officers ignored the soldiers and their conduct. It was hard for Gottschalk to reconcile this display of brutishness with the war ideals so simply and so beautifully expressed by Mr. Lincoln.

At a series of concerts in Pittsburgh, Gottschalk drove the audience to patriotic frenzy with " Union." William Hall already had the fantasy in print and in music stores all over the country. Thousands of piano pupils were trying to surmount its technical difficulties. Gottschalk had dedicated it to General McClellan, and cherished the note of thanks he had received.

In Cincinnati, where there were evening and afternoon concerts, Gottschalk devoted his mornings to sight-seeing. He visited the library of the Young Men's Mercantile Association, and was happy to find a full collection of the great French classics on the shelves. In the rack reserved for periodicals he saw, to his surprise, the latest issues of Le Nord, Le Charivari, La Gazette d'Augsburg, and Le Figaro. He never dreamed that in Cincinnati he would be homesick for Paris. What interested him most in the Ohio city was the stockyards. Here he saw healthy grunting pigs enter a series of gates, to emerge from the last as hams, sausages, slabs of bacon, and buckets of lard. He marveled when he was told that nine hundred of the animals were dispatched every day. " The potentialities of this American inventiveness! " he put down in his diary.

At the concerts in Louisville, where the sympathy of the people was preponderantly for the Confederacy, there was no playing of "Union." Gottschalk felt like a foreigner in his native South. The calls he made on friends who had been kind to him in 1853 were very unsatisfactory. Neither he nor they dared mention the war, the subject uppermost in their minds. He was glad when the hour came to board the train for St. Louis.

Traversing southern Indiana and southern Illinois, he was at last in strange country. Since childhood he had pictured it as an endless savanna, the roaming ground for bands of Indians. But he was ever after to associate it with moving troops—on trains, on river boats, on stagecoaches, on horses, and on foot. They were all headed, he knew, for the Tennessee and Cumberland River valleys, where for weeks severe battles had been anticipated.

The train he and his associates were on was so delayed by the congestion that they were almost twenty-five hours late in reaching St. Louis. They barely had time to rush to a hotel, change into evening clothes, and dash to the theatre to give their first concert. It was Lent, and they had heard that St. Louis was almost entirely Roman Catholic. They therefore expected a small house. But at the theatre the local manager told them that every ticket for the six evenings and the one matinee for which they were booked had been sold.

Gottschalk was not surprised at the great interest in the concerts when he found out that many thousands of music-loving Germans had settled in St. Louis. They had, he was told, a philharmonic society capable of playing the symphonies of Beethoven, Mendelssohn, and Schumann. Aside from this German segment of the population Gottschalk saw little in St. Louis to admire. He spoke of the Western metropolis as "a dull tiresome city of two hundred thousand inhabitants."

His first morning there he read the full details of the great battle fought in the vicinity of Pittsburg Landing on the Tennessee River. Before the end of the week the wounded began arriving in St. Louis. One afternoon, when a light rain was falling, Gottschalk sat at his hotel window and watched as litter after litter, each bearing the broken body of some young man, was removed from a ferry boat, placed on a wagon or cart or any sort of vehicle, and started on the way to a hospital. He thought of the contrast between this scene and the scene of rowdiness and bluster he had witnessed on the train while traveling westward from Philadelphia. A youth destined for the hazards of battle, he now felt, should be forgiven everything.

Carlotta Patti also saw the wounded borne in the rain to hospitals that afternoon, and that evening she was scarcely able to sing. Every newspaper stressed the heavy Confederate casualties at Pittsburg Landing, especially in the brigade commanded by General Beauregard. In that brigade, serving as a bandmaster, was Carlotta's brother Carlo, as gifted for the violin as were his sisters for singing. As director of music at the Varieties Theatre, he had popularized "Dixie" in New Orleans; and he had been for a time concertmaster in the orchestra at the new French Opera House. When the war came, he enlisted in the Confederate army. He was then only nineteen, and could not have realized the seriousness of the step he was taking. Carlotta knew that his heart was not in the cause for which he was fighting. Always conscious of her own physical handicap, she kept saying to Gottschalk, "I can bear to hear that he was killed, but I can't bear to hear that he has lost an arm or a hand."

She received no news of her brother's fate until the next week, when the troupe arrived in Chicago. Waiting for her there was a telegram from her brother-in-law, Maurice Strakosch. Carlo, the message said, had been unhurt in the fighting but had been taken prisoner and was being moved to a prison camp somewhere in the North.

With Gottschalk her escort, Carlotta called at once upon the Archbishop of Chicago and put before His Grace the facts in Carlo's case. She insisted that her brother would follow Mr. Gottschalk's example and transfer his allegiance to the United States if given the opportunity. The Archbishop promised to do all in his power to have the facts brought to the attention of the proper authorities.

From Chicago—where Gottschalk found everything on a smaller scale than in St. Louis, including the attendance at the five concerts in which he appeared—the troupe went to Milwaukee. Of the Wisconsin metropolis he wrote: "This city has a philharmonic society probably better than that of St. Louis, a very handsome theatre, a cathedral, and a magnificent hotel. Do not forget that it is a thousand miles from New York, and very near the Indian territories." The chef at the hotel, a Frenchman who had heard Gottschalk play in Bordeaux in 1851, prepared special dishes for the members of the troupe. They showed their appreciation by conferring upon him the title of "Artist, First Class." Gottschalk had so much to say about the cook's delicacies, especially his salmis, that he failed to state in his diary whether the Milwaukee concerts were a financial success.

There was a return to Chicago, and then an engagement in Toledo. The hotel here was almost unbearable. Every morning about six the proprietor himself went up and down the corridors ringing a bell to summon all the guests to a breakfast few of them could eat. In Gottschalk's hotel room and also in his dressing room at the theatre was a placard inviting him to come to meetings at a certain church and find the *only* road leading to the gates of Heaven. He had noticed similar placards in other cities, and had about decided that the chief concern of American Protestants was proselytizing. The attendance at the concerts in Toledo was fair.

The troupe, advancing eastward, stopped for appearances in one city on the Great Lakes after another. They finally reached New York, only to give two big concerts at the Academy of Music and then travel southward for return engagements in Baltimore and Washington. On May 27, as they were crossing the Susquehanna River, Gottschalk jotted down in his diary: "Springtime. Health below zero." Fresh from five years in the tropics, he had been thinking in terms of the temperature for four months. Besides, he was very tired.

However, his contract with Mr. Grau was not fulfilled until he played in June at a summer season of opera at the Academy of Music. On the opening evening there was a performance of *Il Trovatore* with Miss Kellogg, Brignoli, and Susini. Between the second and third acts Gottschalk played, and between the third and fourth acts Mr. Hermann, a prestidigitator, gave an exhibition of his skill. On the remaining eight or ten evenings of the season the same pattern was followed. At the end Gottschalk very cheerfully said farewell to Mr. Grau.

Gottschalk's earnings since his return to the United States had been great. He was richer by a good many thousands of dollars. But he was in that state of mind when he did not care whether he was a millionaire or a pauper. His one thought was to get to Saratoga for a rest.

After a week of enjoying the quiet of Union Hall he submitted to requests for an evening recital and for one of his matinees of instruction. Then when he was asked to assist at an important concert to be given by his pupil Harry Sanderson in the Saratoga theatre he could not be so unkind as to refuse.

About the middle of August he received a letter from a Spanish friend in New York, Simon Camacho, a musical connoisseur whose judgments he respected. The letter told of an eight-year-old girl pianist named Teresa Carreño. Her father, a political refugee from Venezuela, had recently brought her to New York with the rest of his family. Señor Camacho had heard the child play, and considered her a musical phenomenon. She had been taught to regard Gottschalk as the ideal pianist, she played by heart practically all his published music, and since the day his name was first mentioned in her presence she had dreamed of attending one of his concerts. " I believe," wrote Señor Camacho in concluding his letter, " that if you will hear her play on your return to New York she will captivate you as she has captivated me. I even prophesy that you will wish to give her lessons."

Gottschalk had learned from experience not to waste time on reports about child prodigies. But he trusted Señor Camacho. Indeed, he was so impressed by the letter that he made the trip from Saratoga to New York for no other purpose than to meet Teresa.

He found her very natural, attractive enough, and bigger than the average eight-year-old girl. Her father was more perturbed than she over Señor Camacho's and Gottschalk's unexpected call. He was obviously a gentleman, but he was too effusive in describing the effect which Gottschalk's Caracas concerts had had upon him. In order to stop his extravagant praise Gottschalk abruptly asked Teresa to play.

When she sat at the piano, she hesitated for a few seconds, as if wondering whether she should attempt one of Gottschalk's compositions. She evidently decided that she had better not. For the piece she played was by another composer.

Gottschalk stood directly behind her, watching her hands. When she finished the piece, she swung around, looked up to him, and gave him such a smile as she might have given her father.

He bent down and kissed her on the forehead. Then he asked, "Shall I play for you?"

"Oh, yes," she answered, and ran and stood between her father's knees.

Gottschalk preluded a bit, lightly touching the keys. The magical tones were too much for Teresa. She fell in a faint against her father. The two or three women in the room shrieked, Gottschalk stopped playing, and there was great consternation. Señor Carreño held Teresa in his arms, head down, and someone sprinkled water in her face. Soon she was herself again, sitting in her father's lap, listening with mind, heart, and soul as Gottschalk played.

The little girl had had many wonderful hours of music in her life, but no hour like this. To do it honor she spent the rest of the day in composing a tribute to her idol. She called it "The Gottschalk Waltz." Gottschalk received a copy a day or two after his return to Saratoga.

He did not see the Carreños again until he came back to New York in September for a month of concerts at Irving Hall in association with the violinist and conductor Theodore Thomas. During this period he found time to give Teresa a few lessons.

On one occasion he took Mr. Thomas to hear the child. The violinist was so touched by her playing that the tears began streaming from his eyes. When Teresa saw them she stopped, and, turning to Señor Carreño, asked, "Father, why is that man crying?"

In December, when Gottschalk was in Cincinnati on a tour

under his new impresario, Maurice Strakosch, he received a letter
from Señor Carreño describing Teresa's sensational success at her
début in Irving Hall on November 25. A program was enclosed,
and Gottschalk saw that the last number was his *Jerusalem*
fantasy. She had worked on this extremely difficult piece under
his supervision, and he recalled that after five days she was able
to play it from memory with such finish that he had found little
to criticize. In a postscript Señor Carreño spoke of taking her to
Havana and asked for letters of introduction to Cuban musicians.

Gottschalk immediately wrote to his Havana friend Nicolas
Espadero: "Teresa Carreño is a genius. I have been able to give
her five or six lessons, and although she never had a teacher who
knew anything (this is between ourselves) she already achieves
a thousand miracles. I wish you to do all you can to help her
when her father brings her to Havana. She is a lovable, enchanting little girl." The testimonial which Gottschalk wrote for the
Havana press ended with the statement: "Teresa Carreño belongs
with the few upon whom Providence has lavished rare favors,
and I have not the slightest doubt that she will be one of the
greatest artists of our age." Within just a few years Gottschalk's
prophecy was to be fulfilled.

A day or two before Christmas, when he reached Chicago with
his troupe, he found an alarming letter from Célestine. Edward
was sick, and the doctors had diagnosed the trouble as consump-
tion. His condition was already grave. He seemed to be living
for just one purpose—to hear Moreau play once more. Surely,
Célestine wrote, the voyage to New York could not hurt him more
than the Paris winter. Gaston could travel with him, and she
could join her sisters in London. What did Moreau think? The
decision, Célestine concluded, was entirely up to him.

Gottschalk left his associates to give performances without him
during the holidays and hurried to New York. Once there he
sent letters and money to Célestine on the first mail steamer
departing for France. Edward and Gaston, he wrote, must sail
for America at once. He was counting upon their arriving by the
middle of February.

The rest of his time in New York—when he was not in bed

recovering from a cold—he spent looking for an apartment where he could make a home for Edward. He finally found a desirable place on Ninth Street, just east of Broadway.

On January 8 he was back with his troupe, ready for a concert in Springfield, Illinois, President Lincoln's city. A few days later he and his colleagues were in Indianapolis. In one of their concerts there Ralph Waldo Emerson was in the audience. The philosopher heard them with impatience: he wanted them to leave Indianapolis so that he could give a course of lectures in the hall in which they were appearing.

With concerts in Washington and Baltimore, the first and second weeks in February, the tour came to an end. Gottschalk hurried to New York. The ship on which Edward and Gaston were expected was due to arrive within a day or two.

The preceding October, when Gottschalk was engaged in the Irving Hall concerts with Theodore Thomas, he dared a return to Boston. Since his politics, from the point of view of New England, had become acceptable, his music was acceptable also. Even Mr. Dwight received him with open arms. Henceforth the "Hub of the Universe" was to be as kind to him as New York, Philadephia, and Baltimore. Several Bostonians were to be numbered among his best friends. Among them was Francis G. Hill, a pianist.

During the few days Gottschalk waited in the Ninth Street apartment for the arrival of Edward and Gaston, Mr. Hill was his guest. On the morning he faced the ordeal of reunion with a brother who he knew was dying, his Boston friend gave him the support he needed.

The ship bringing Edward and Gaston docked at eight o'clock. Moreau, who had been told that it would not get in before eleven, was about ready to leave for the pier with Mr. Hill when, at ten, a servant came up and told him that his brothers were at the foot of the stairs.

Edward was too weak and tired to mount the single flight. Gaston—a robust full-grown man, though only seventeen—took him in his arms and bore him up the steps as if he were an infant. Mr. Hill, seeing that each of the brothers was too full of emotion to speak, drew Moreau to the piano and said, "Do some improvising and you'll feel better."

But Moreau did not improvise. He collected himself and played "Bamboula," "Le Bananier," the dances from "El Sitio de Zaragoza," and other lively pieces associated with his years with

Edward. Then Gaston said, "Play your 'Berceuse,' and I will sing it." As Moreau heard for the first time his younger brother's rich baritone voice and realized that a born musical insight was back of the singing, a smile of great satisfaction spread over his face.

His release from tension was shared by everyone else in the room. When Edward, sitting in comfort before the fire, said, "Now I know I'm going to get well," even Mr. Hill was ready to agree with him.

Whatever decisions Gottschalk made that spring were determined by his concern over Edward's welfare. The physician entrusted with Edward's care was one of the most celebrated of American lung specialists. Moreau relinquished Firmin to Edward because he knew that no better nurse could be found. Gaston was still full of adolescent spirit. When Moreau noticed that his boisterousness sometimes got on Edward's nerves, he made arrangements for him to live with the Italian couple who were training his voice. Gottschalk let all his friends know that he would accept no invitations to social affairs. He spent his free hours in reading to his sick brother, or playing for him, or just talking.

He turned down offers from Strakosch and other impresarios for out-of-town appearances. But he did give, again in association with Theodore Thomas, two series of concerts in Irving Hall. New York musical critics were for many years to hold up as an ideal performance his and Mr. Thomas' rendition of Mozart's A minor sonata for piano and violin. Another performance at Irving Hall that spring also drew exalted praise from the critics— his and William Mason's playing of the *Trovatore* fantasy which he and Thalberg had played. But the program which attracted the biggest audience was the one featuring Gottschalk's arrangement for four pianos of the march from *Tannhäuser*.

With the coming of June and warm weather Edward showed such improvement that Gottschalk saw no reason to refuse when Strakosch proposed a brief summer tour of central New York, central Pennsylvania, and New England. Carlotta Patti—who, whether or not through the offices of the Archbishop of Chicago, had finally seen her brother freed from a prison camp and made a United States citizen—was now in Europe, dividing honors with Adelina. The place filled by Carlotta on Gottschalk's two Western trips was to be taken on the projected summer tour by her elder sister, Strakosch's wife, a contralto known to the public as Amalia Patti-Strakosch. Strakosch himself was to play her accompaniments and appear in piano duos with Gottschalk. The three artists were to travel without attendants. Strakosch was to find a tuner to care for Gottschalk's Chickerings in each of the towns visited.

The tour opened with a very successful concert in Utica the first week in June. The good luck continued until Gottschalk and the Strakosches reached Williamsport, Pennsylvania, late Monday morning, June 15. When they stepped from their train, they observed great agitation on the station platform. Then they saw that a man was pasting a placard on a bulletin board. They pressed forward, and were among the first to read the communiqué, the announcement that General Lee had begun an invasion of the state of Pennsylvania and was moving his army toward the capital, Harrisburg.

They were scheduled for a concert in the county courthouse at Harrisburg the evening of June 16. Madame Strakosch, thinking of the possibility of being cut off from her children, and Gottschalk, thinking of his sick brother, were in favor of playing the Williamsport engagement and taking a night train for New York. Strakosch said, "We'll wait and see."

Though the receipts that evening were slight and the news bulletins issued at midnight reported that Lee was overcoming all resistance in his move northward, Strakosch, a believer in the tradition that "the show must go on," said bluntly, "We've been booked to give our next concert in Harrisburg, and we're leaving at six in the morning to get there in time to give it."

They found themselves that morning three civilians on a train packed with the military. The farther south they advanced the more they realized that they were speeding into the city from which those who were unable to fight were fleeing. The highways were solid streams of refugees headed northward, in every type of vehicle, on horses, on mules, and by foot.

When the train came to a halt in Harrisburg, Gottschalk discovered that the car in which he and the Strakosches were riding was right in the middle of the bridge over the Susquehanna River. Still the conductor shouted, "End of the run." The three artists joined a line of soldiers moving forward through the train, and when they reached the engine they saw that it was possible to alight on a cinder path. Between them and the station, a distance of half a mile, there were countless locomotives, all moving backward and forward in what appeared to be the greatest confusion. By sticking to the path Gottschalk and his companions finally made their way out of the smoke and noise.

The more questions they asked in the station the more terrifying were the answers they received. The bombardment of Harrisburg was expected to begin at any moment. Lee's advance regiments could not be more than twelve or fifteen miles away. The defense of Harrisburg was wholly inadequate. Troops were being rushed in, but they could never arrive in sufficient number to save the city. Its fall was just a matter of hours. Blundering through the crowded station, hearing such rumors of doom, Gottschalk and his friends came upon the two Chickerings, in their boxes, unhurt and sound.

The unexpected meeting with Gottschalk's "two brave companions" under such circumstances struck the three artists as ludicrous and they all began to laugh. On the spot Gottschalk composed a little apostrophe to the instruments: "Poor pianos! Exposed to bombardment or attack by assault! Perhaps by to-morrow your lives will have ended. Tonight you will probably serve to feed the fire of some obscure Confederate soldier, who will see with an indifferent eye your harmonious bowels consumed without any regard for the three hundred concerts which you have survived and for the fidelity with which you have followed me in my campaigns in the West."

Strakosch saw his wife safe for the time being at the Jones Hotel, and then, with Gottschalk at his side, set out to find a means of getting out of the city into which he had foolishly insisted upon coming. A concert, with Gottschalk playing his "Murmures éoliens" and Madame Strakosch singing his "Berceuse," in Harrisburg that night? Every inhabitant left in the city had one thought—defense! Gottschalk saw a group of Roman Catholic priests digging trenches and constructing breastworks. Aged men, women, and little boys were building barricades in every street. No one seemed to be in command. The whole city was in a state of panic. When Strakosch and Gottschalk spoke to an army officer or an official of any sort about transportation for New York, they were looked upon as deserters.

By chance Gottschalk learned that his cousin Leonard Myers— now a member of Congress and a major in the Union army—had been sent to Harrisburg with a unit of the Pennsylvania militia. After hours of searching, Gottschalk found him, and soon had the permits to buy transportation for three on a train which was to leave for Philadelphia early in the evening.

Before the nine-car train departed, Gottschalk and his companions found out that at least two thousand other persons had also obtained permits. The pianist, standing in an aisle wedged between two enormous men, managed to get out the notebook in which he was keeping his diary. "We are like herrings in a barrel," he wrote. "The women are sitting on each other, the men are all on their feet, and the children are everywhere. There's not one inch of room which is not occupied. We're almost dead from thirst, and I can't see how we are going to endure the heat." It was not until two o'clock the next morning that the train reached Philadelphia.

Confusion prevailed there also. So great was the demand for cars in which to move troops into the vicinity of Harrisburg that Gottschalk and the Strakosches had to wait until six that evening to get a train for New York.

They were due to arrive at nine. But every five or six miles they were shunted onto a siding to make way for a troop train dashing westward. The journey of only ninety miles required the whole night.

Gottschalk, again with Edward on Ninth Street, expected every day for two weeks to hear that the capital of Pennsylvania had fallen to the Confederates. But in the newspapers of July 3 and 4 he read that General Lee was turned back at Gettysburg in the most desperately fought battle of the war. The estimates of the casualties varied, but in each the number was appallingly great. Gottschalk wondered how many of the young men in uniform he had seen on their way to the battleground came out of the holocaust alive and whole. His rejoicing over the great Union victory was mingled with sorrow.

At the same time he was reading reports in the newspapers which filled him with alarm—reports of the growls and threats over conscription of New York's enormous Irish immigrant population. He feared that he might see in the city on any day such outbreaks of violence as he had seen in Paris in 1848. He had no sympathy for the stand taken by the Irish. If there were any gratitude in their hearts, he said, they would not shirk the chance to fight for the country to which they owed rescue from starvation and the privilege of citizenship. But despite his emotions, he had to face the fact that the dissatisfaction of the Irish over the draft law was rapidly leading them to open insurrection.

The New England part of the summer tour had been announced for the last two weeks in July. Strakosch, deaf to the warnings of his wife and Gottschalk, made plans to meet every engagement. The three artists left New York the morning of July 13 and gave a concert in New London that evening.

Four days later—after concerts in Fitchburg, Nashua, and Manchester—they were back in New York to look after their charges. The draft riots had begun, and there was evidence that they had been far better organized than anybody had thought possible. The building in which the drawing for conscripts was under way had been burned. The *Tribune* building, the Harlem railroad bridge, and the main telegraph office had also been fired. The rioters were reported to be well armed. Everyone expected that with the arrival of the troops who were being rushed into the city there would be battles in the streets. While the Strakosches fled with their children into northern New Jersey, Gottschalk succeeded in getting Edward, Gaston, and Firmin on a train bound for Saratoga.

The railroad journey seemed to benefit Edward. On reaching Saratoga he insisted upon going by foot from the station to Union

Hall, where a suite of three rooms had been reserved. Since his reunion with Moreau he had not once spoken of dying. Now, with the beauty of the Saratoga trees all around him, he felt as well, he said, as he had felt at any time in his life. He had studied music for his mother's sake and then had shifted to law because of Moreau's influence. But it was not until he turned to writing that he had put his heart into his work. He had met encouragement. Two periodicals in Paris, Le Siècle and La Revue de la famille, had paid money for his contributions. He now discussed his various literary projects with Moreau, and actually spent an hour or two every day at his writing table.

Moreau devoted a good deal of his energy toward keeping Gaston's spirits properly subdued. The Chickering company had sent up a piano for his use, and he found that the best way to quiet the boy was to play. At the same time he knew that his music was always a delight to Edward.

One of the guests in the hotel was a blind Protestant minister, a man of learning and great charm. Soon he and the Gottschalk brothers were the best of friends. Since he could not keep from dropping bits of food, he disliked eating in the main dining room, especially at dinner, when everybody was in evening clothes. So it was arranged for him to have his meals in the Gottschalk suite, where the food was brought up on trays and served by Firmin.

The minister gave two morning lectures at Union Hall, the first entitled "What a Blind Man Saw in England" and the other "The Poetry of John Milton." Before each talk Gottschalk played three or four solos. There was a fee of twenty-five cents for admission, and—because of Gottschalk—the receipts all together amounted to more than two hundred dollars. When the minister proposed sharing the money, Gottschalk said, "Why, you've already paid me. I understood that my music was to count for my admission to the lectures. I gave no money at the door."

After August 15 the mornings in Saratoga began to be chilly. Edward took a cold, and the doctor ordered him to stay in bed. He remained cheerful in spirit until the afternoon near the end of the month when he suffered a severe hemorrhage. After that his coughing spells came more frequently and caused great pain. The doctor advised that he be taken back to the warmth of New York at once. This time Edward made the railway journey on a cot in the baggage car, with Moreau seated on one side of him and Firmin on the other.

For a full two weeks after the return to Ninth Street Edward seemed at least to be getting no worse. Moreau passed many hours every day playing for him or sitting at his bedside talking gaily of the time when they would be, respectively, a retired rich musician and a retired rich author. One evening he spoke of the trip they would take to the Holy Land in fulfillment of the promise they had each made to their mother. Suddenly he noticed that Edward was having difficulty in breathing.

Firmin was sent at once to bring the doctor. When the physician arrived and glanced at Edward, he advised Moreau to summon a priest.

The next day—Wednesday, September 23—Gottschalk dispatched the following letter to Mr. Hill: "I have not written to you this long while on account of poor Edward's illness. He is fading away, gradually, and, alas, will leave this world for another—better, I hope—ere the week is over. The doctor has just told me that he may perhaps not last so long, that at any moment he may——(I cannot write the dreadful word). You can imagine my feelings; my pen can't describe them. Adieu, dear friend."

Edward died the following Monday, September 28. Two days later, at nine o'clock in the morning, New York's musical world gathered on Ninth Street to join Moreau and Gaston as they followed their brother's body to St. Stephen's, on East Twenty-Eighth Street. At the requiem Mass, sung by a full choir, the church, said the New York *Times*, was filled to the doors. The interment was in Calvary Cemetery in Brooklyn.

Forced once more into grief, Gottschalk again turned to his loyal friend Mrs. Seymour for comfort. A few days after Edward's funeral they were together at a Philharmonic Society rehearsal. The symphony was Beethoven's *Eroica*. When the orchestra began the dead march, Mrs. Seymour, thinking not only of her lost child but of three brothers killed in the war, was unable to hold back her tears. Gottschalk reached over, took her hand, and held on to it. His face, terribly set and drawn, was, she said, as complete an expression of sorrow over the world's woes as was the music to which they were listening.

Gottschalk had learned that work is the best panacea for grief. Two days after his brother's funeral he signed a contract with Strakosch to appear every Saturday in a six weeks' season of orchestral matinees which Theodore Thomas was to conduct at Irving Hall. The prospectus said: "Mr. Thomas' programs will consist of full symphonies, overtures, selections from the operas, waltzes, polkas, and quadrilles. Mr. Thomas will do in New York what Musard has done in Paris, Strauss in Vienna, and Alfred Mellon in London. His orchestra will number more than sixty players. He has in addition the cooperation of the greatest pianist now before the public, Mr. Gottschalk, a host in himself."

At the first matinee, on October 10, the orchestra gave Beethoven's *Prometheus* overture, the third of Mozart's symphonies in E flat, a potpourri of melodies from Verdi's *Un Ballo in maschera*, and a polka and a quadrille by Strauss. Mr. Thomas and the first cellist of the orchestra played a duo with piano accompaniment. Gottschalk played two groups of his own compositions, one made up of Cuban dances and the other of opera fantasies.

Before the last matinee was given Strakosch had organized a troupe which Gottschalk was to head on a projected tour of the West. Madame Strakosch, who was expecting another baby, had been replaced by a soprano new to America, Mademoiselle Cordier. But the Patti family was represented in the company by the violinist Carlo, ex-Confederate soldier. The tenor Brignoli was again a colleague of Gottschalk. There was an accompanist, a German named Behrens. And there was Strakosch to serve as maestro of the troupe. Gottschalk, as usual, had Firmin and a tuner. Brignoli had a valet, and Mademoiselle Cordier a maid.

Gottschalk formed ideas about his fellow troupers, and put them down in his diary. Strakosch, he said, was a jerky man, never still a minute, and was feared because of such stubbornness as he manifested in rushing into trouble in Harrisburg and then in ignoring the threats of the draft riots in New York. But Gottschalk admitted that Strakosch was an excellent musician and regretted that his compositions were not better known. Mademoiselle Cordier, Gottschalk said, had been taught at the Paris Conservatoire and could actually read music. "Her maid," he wrote, "is a young, thin, sentimental German woman, who paints flowers, can sleep standing up, is very ugly and pays not the slightest attention to her appearance." Brignoli, blessed with a seductive voice, reminded Gottschalk of Mario. "His valet," Gottschalk wrote, "is an old sailor who reads Renan's *La Vie de Jésus*, and is enraptured with the beauties of the style." Gottschalk said of Behrens, who played second piano with him in duos, "He is a young man from Hamburg, too fond of making puns and too fond of food." Gottschalk's nickname for Carlo Patti was "Sunshine."

Of all his extraordinary family Carlo was the most spectacular. "His flair for adventure," wrote Gottschalk, "has led him to California and Mexico. In New York in his eighteenth year he experienced both marriage and divorce. In New Orleans, where in his nineteenth year he served as concertmaster and also as substitute conductor at the French Opera, he remarried, it is said. It is certain that in that city he enlisted as a private in General Beauregard's brigade, became a bandmaster, was killed and resuscitated in many battle bulletins, and is as well today as all the other Pattis, none of whom are ever sick."

Carlo brought the latest news of Gottschalk's Spanish foster son, Ramon. He too had enlisted in General Beauregard's brigade, just when his years of dependence upon Gottschalk ended and he was ready to make his own way in the world—as a master barber! General Beauregard got acquainted with his skill and made him his orderly. The hand which once molded a little clay bull for the Queen of Spain was now being used to beautify the long hair and spreading beard of a great Confederate warrior.

" I knew that some sort of glory awaited my adopted son! " exclaimed Gottschalk. Both he and Carlo prayed that that glory would not be suddenly stopped by a Yankee bullet.

" Strakosch might have been a great geographer," said Gottschalk. The impresario knew the precise location of every town of five thousand or more on the network of railroads extending from New York to Milwaukee, and halted his troupe for a concert in each. " We are no longer human beings," wrote Gottschalk. " We are machines." From two to ten hours every day he and his colleagues listened to the rolling of car wheels. Then when they were exhibiting their art in theatres or town halls or courthouses or churches the roar of the rolling wheels was still in their ears. If they found heat in the main lobby of a hotel they considered themselves lucky. Their beds were always icy; and once they warmed them up with their bodies they were likely to warm also armies of bed bugs. When, in spite of all, they went to sleep, they dreamed of being on trains. Sometimes they were unable to get to bed before three in the morning. Nevertheless a jangling gong awoke them between six and seven to summon them to an inedible breakfast—tough beefsteak, soggy soda biscuits, rancid butter, weak coffee, and the inevitable molasses in a dirty glass jug on the center of the table. An artist in America in the year 1863? " If he survives," wrote Gottschalk, " he travels. And if he travels he is no longer an artist. He is a machine, set to running by two unreliable engineers, an anxiety-driven impresario and a war-weary public."

Near the end of December the troupe reached Chicago and enjoyed a week free of railroads. But three days after Christmas, Gottschalk was sent alone to Rockford to give a matinee of instruction. As he got off the train in this small Illinois town, his eyes fell upon a Fahrenheit thermometer on the station wall. It registered eighteen degrees below zero. He had to wade through snow three feet deep in order to reach the sleigh sent to carry him to the young ladies' seminary where he was to play, a full two miles from the station. " Those cruel miles! " he wrote in his diary that night. " The wind cut my fingers, my nose, and my lips, and left me just enough heat to enable me to feel my sufferings. Several times the inexperienced driver came near hurling me from the sleigh into a snowbank. I was too far gone to care. I'm a son of the tropics, and was never intended to endure the cold of the North. When I see snow, I see death."

Three days later, when he and his colleagues were on their way from Chicago to Madison, Wisconsin, they were stopped by a blizzard in the village of Harvard, Illinois. The temperature had dropped to twenty-five below zero, and the conductor of the train dared venture no farther. Strakosch announced that the population of Harvard was less than five hundred. His artists shuddered at the thought of stopping in such a place. It was past noon, and they were hungry. What sort of dinner could they expect?

The one hotel in Harvard turned out to be a surprise. It was clean, and in each of the two public rooms there was an immense wood stove, red hot. The proprietor had gone hunting the day before and had killed a deer. There was venison roast for dinner, and for supper that night there were broiled venison steaks.

But there were just enough beds for the women in the troupe. The men had to go to the postmaster's house, next door. Though the distance was only about a hundred feet, the fury of the blizzard made it seem a mile. Again Gottschalk found a clean house in Harvard, deep in the back country. He found also a charm in the simple hospitality of the young postmaster and his wife. As Gottschalk lay in his bed that night, in all his clothes except his shoes, he felt that he had at last come into that West of which Abraham Lincoln had made all America deeply conscious.

Early in the night the blizzard wore itself out, and the next morning the sun was shining. The cold was no longer bitter. After a breakfast of ham and buckwheat cakes at the hotel Gottschalk and his companions crunched over the snow to the station. The train they had left the day before was now ready to go on to Madison. A concert date had been missed, but Gottschalk knew that Strakosch would manage to make up for it with an extra matinee somewhere.

It was the first of February before the troupe got back to New York for a three weeks' vacation. "A machine has to be over-hauled and re-oiled from time to time," said Gottschalk.

He and the rest of the troupe—all except Mademoiselle Cordier, who had been replaced by Richard Hoffman's sister-in-law, American-born Madame Viviani—were in good trim when on Washington's birthday they began to function again. After a month of daily concerts in New York and New England they found themselves in the national capital, at the Willard Hotel. On the morning of March 24 Gottschalk heard the three sharp raps on his door which meant Strakosch. The wiry impresario was out about as soon as he was in. He had just dropped by to let Gottschalk know that the President and Mrs. Lincoln would be at the concert that night and that he must include "Union" among his encores.

Gottschalk had been waiting for this announcement for two years. On his every appearance in Washington he had hoped to have the President in his audience. He had actually felt a bit envious of little Teresa Carreño when her father wrote that she had played at the White House for Mr. and Mrs. Lincoln only, and had devoted herself to Gottschalk music until the President asked for "Listen to the Mocking Bird." Now that the desired opportunity was at hand, Gottschalk experienced a touch of stage fright. He kept telling himself that playing for a great man who was ignorant of music was far harder than playing for a Chopin or a Thalberg or a Victor Hugo or a Louis Napoleon. He longed for the hours to pass quickly and end the ordeal which lay ahead of him.

Not since his concerts in Madrid had he seen a more colorful audience than the one which welcomed him that evening when he appeared on the stage for his first number, a duo with Behrens. But he scarcely noticed the generals, admirals, foreign diplomats, and other personages in resplendent uniforms. His eyes were fixed on the first row, where sat the President and Mrs. Lincoln in company with the Secretary of State, Mr. Seward. Mrs. Lincoln was overdressed, and looked bored. Her husband appeared exactly as Gottschalk had seen him pictured hundreds of times—very ugly. He had on evening clothes, but the sleeves were too short and he had forgotten his gloves. About his shoulders was the inevitable black and white shawl.

Gottschalk knew that there were a great mind and a great heart within that ungainly body. But the music he made that night never once got into communication with either. The playing of "Union" seemed to stir everybody in the house except the President. He appeared to Gottschalk at the end of the concert as he had appeared at the beginning.

When Gottschalk got back to the Willard, he wrote in his diary: "I played very badly." He was furious at himself.

The rest of the spring of 1864 was for him and every other member of the troupe a test of endurance. Strakosch demanded too much of artists who were already near exhaustion. In Norfolk, Virginia, they spent two weeks, entertaining every night the thousands of soldiers stationed there and suffering their vulgarity during the day. In Pennsylvania they were molested by a "jinx" which forced them into the necessity of defending themselves against rioters in Easton, engaging in a free-for-all fight on a train between Bethlehem and Allentown, giving half a concert in a hall without lights in Reading, and putting on a program in Pittsburgh with only one small upright piano available. Later, as they roamed back and forth in Canada and New England, Gottschalk discovered that overwork had led him into a nervous habit dreaded by every pianist—the habit of unconsciously biting the finger nails. To keep from incapacitating himself for playing he wore heavy gloves, even when he was sleeping.

He knew that rest was the only cure for the habit. So when at last the troupe disbanded, near the end of June, he shut himself in his Ninth Street apartment in New York and stationed Firmin at the door to ward off all callers. After a month of isolation he was himself once more. He had had his warning: he was never again to allow an impresario to drive him into such a state of nervousness.

He spent August at Saratoga, a guest at Congress Hall. His days were passed in what he called "laborious idleness." What he meant was that instead of playing he composed several pieces for the young and completed three essays which he had been asked to write for the *Atlantic Monthly*.

Emmanuele Muzio, onetime lieutenant to Jacob Grau, was now an independent impresario. In the autumn Gottschalk came under his management, and began still another nation-wide tour. The artists sent out with him were the Italian baritone Morelli, the German violinist Döhler, and the American soprano Lucy Simons, Signor Muzio's fiancée.

The tour was not advertised as the pianist's farewell. But, for a reason which Gottschalk could not explain, he felt as he departed from one familiar city after another that he would never see it again. At his every performance he gave as a final encore "The Last Hope." To tens of thousands of Americans the image of Gottschalk seated at one of his Chickerings playing this "evening prayer" had come to symbolize the trying period of the Civil War, like the image of John Brown's body dangling in the air at Charlestown in Virginia or the image of Lincoln delivering the "Gettysburg Address."

Early in December the troupe gave three concerts in Boston. In contrast to Gottschalk's fiasco there eleven years before, each of his present appearances was a triumph. The last, a matinee, was before an audience which filled every seat in immense Tremont Temple.

That evening Gottschalk was the guest of honor at a reception given by the editor of the *Atlantic Monthly*, James T. Fields, and his wife, Annie Fields. The Brahmins of Boston and Cambridge were present in numbers, and all paid homage to the pianist who had delighted them in many a concert. Gottschalk enjoyed greatly his chat with Oliver Wendell Holmes.

Early the next afternoon, when he returned to his hotel room after a visit to his friend Francis G. Hill, he found a card under his door. It bore the name "Henry Wadsworth Longfellow." Gottschalk was to regret for the rest of his life that he had missed a call from the poet who was then universally looked upon as America's greatest.

On a train bound for Pittsburgh that night Gottschalk wrote in his diary: "Adieu, Boston! I once said that you were stiff, pedantic, and exclusive, that Mr. Dwight was your oracle. Your enemies still say that you are cold and morose. I, your friend, say that you are intelligent, literary, and polished."

Not too much molested by snows and blizzards this year, he said farewell with his " evening prayer " to Pittsburgh, Cleveland, Detroit, Chicago, Milwaukee, Cincinnati, and St. Louis. Then, when he was in the middle of a concert in Toronto on January 3, he received a telegram which meant trouble. His barber in New York, a Frenchman, had been arrested on a charge of embezzlement. Gottschalk had been quixotic enough to put up several thousand dollars to bail the fellow out of prison. Now, said the telegram, the man was making plans to skip the country within three days. Gottschalk spent an anxious twenty-four hours dispatching messages to New York, seeing all the while much of the money earned under great hardship slipping through his fingers. But some resourceful friend in New York saved the day for him and got the barber safe in jail once more.

In February, when Gottschalk had said his adieus to Canada and was playing in the towns on the border between New York and Pennsylvania, the first of his *Atlantic Monthly* articles appeared in print. The other two were to follow in March and April. The general title, "Notes of a Pianist," suggests the informality of the essays. They are simply a record of a few of Gottschalk's observations as a concert pianist in Europe and the New World. He was very proud to be known as a contributor to America's greatest literary periodical. Those who were to build up publicity for him in the future were careful to remind the world that he belonged among the writers for the *Atlantic*.

Ada Clare—accompanied, as always, by Aubrey—had spent most of the year 1864 in California. She went to the distant West, not as an actress, but as a staff writer for the *Golden Era*. She sent copies of her contributions to Gottschalk, and he found in them numerous allusions to his greatness as pianist and composer. He also found much on the musicians and other entertainers who had sought fortune in California—Henri Herz, Strakosch, and Ole Bull in earlier years, and Ada Isaacs Menken and Paul Julien, both of whom were there when Ada Clare arrived. Gottschalk had thought seriously about going to California at the time he was striving to make money to pay his father's debts. Ada's articles—and also her personal letters from San Francisco—reawakened his curiosity about the Golden State.

He talked with Muzio and Miss Simons, and learned that they too had been playing with the idea of challenging luck in California. A small audience in each of the cities in which they appeared during the last two weeks in February doubtless influenced the three to make up their minds. On the first day of March they entered into a contract to leave for San Francisco as early in April as possible.

In New York, on the morning of April 1, Gottschalk witnessed the marriage of Signor Muzio and Miss Simons. That afternoon, at the Academy of Music, he gave the last of his New York concerts. That evening the program was repeated in Brooklyn. The next morning—after bidding Gaston goodbye and commending him anew to his voice teachers—he embarked with Firmin and the Muzios on the steamship *Ariel* for the voyage to Aspinwall, on the Isthmus of Panama.

Signor Morelli was also on board, but he was no longer under contract to Muzio. He was going to San Francisco with four other opera stars, one of whom was the celebrated Boston contralto, Adelaide Phillips. The quintet had been engaged by telegram to head an opera company which Tom Maguire, the Barnum of the West Coast, was organizing to offset an opera season put on in San Francisco by an Italian impresario who for some trivial reason had won his ill will.

The important war communiqué in the newspapers for April 2 was that the speedy fall of Petersburg, just below Richmond, was certain. The passengers on the *Ariel* knew that almost a month would pass before they could find out the significance of this Union victory.

Suffering as usual from seasickness, Gottschalk remained in his cabin the first four days of the voyage. On the fifth day, when the ship was nearing tropical waters, he appeared on the promenade deck. But he found no comfortable spot on the old, dirty, crowded *Ariel*. He had never been so eager to see land from the prow of a vessel as he was on April 13 when Aspinwall was sighted, about eleven o'clock in the morning.

The landing, the rail journey across the isthmus to Panama City, and the trip by lighter to the waiting steamship *Constitution* occupied the whole afternoon. It was just seven o'clock when Gottschalk was shown to his commodious cabin on the most luxurious liner he had ever boarded.

But the heat was almost unbearable. At dinner he was further discouraged by the very poor fare. The thought of his beautiful cabin cheered him. But in the night he discovered that it was infested with bed bugs. He knew that almost two weeks of torture lay ahead of him.

On April 17 the *Constitution* called for coal at the Mexican port of Acapulco. Gottschalk went ashore to inspect the town. As he walked up the principal thoroughfare he felt at the same time disgust for the squalor and admiration for the picturesqueness. He entered the cleanest restaurant he could find, hoping to get at last a good meal. The proprietor turned out to be a New Orleans Creole. He and Gottschalk fell into one another's arms, and for an hour talked about home. Finally the proprietor mentioned Paul Morphy, the famous chess player.

" There's a glory for Louisiana! " the man exclaimed. " But from childhood he showed what he'd be some day. He's not like that other little prodigy, named Gottschalk. He promised marvels enough, and his father sent him to Europe in hopes of making a great musician out of him. Nobody I've met has ever heard of him since. Have you? "

Gottschalk answered, hesitatingly, " Yes, I've heard of him. He still works at music, I think."

The excellence of the dinner, said Gottschalk, was adequate compensation for the blow at his pride.

On the afternoon of April 23 the *Constitution* met a sister ship, the *Golden City*, which was only two days out from San Francisco and communication by telegraph with the East. When the passengers on the *Constitution*, four hundred in number, saw a boat coming from the *Golden City*, they all gathered on a lower deck to hear the latest reports on the war. As the cry

"Lee has surrendered!" rose from the boat, the passengers broke into a demonstration of joy and had to be quieted to hear the second cry, "Lincoln has been assassinated!" They refused to believe the tragic announcement until they saw it confirmed in the newspapers brought on board.

Gottschalk said of his reaction, "It seemed impossible to me that such news could come on such a day—the sea so calm, the sky so blue, and the sun so resplendent." When he got his hands on a newspaper and learned that John Wilkes Booth was the assassin, he felt all the more let down. He had seen Booth act in Cleveland in a play in which Ada Clare also had a part, and had greatly admired his performance.

"Of what import now," Gottschalk wrote in his diary that night, "are those frivolous judgments on the man whom we are weeping for today? His ugliness, his awkwardness, and his coarse humor are forgotten now that he is dead. Purity of heart, honesty, and greatness rise up today and in their radiancy transfigure him whom we called 'the common rail-splitter.' Oh, eternal power of the true and beautiful! Yesterday his detractors were ridiculing his huge hands without gloves, his enormous feet, his blunt speech. Today this man whom we found grotesque appears to us on the threshold of immortality. We understand by the universality of our grief what future generations will see in him."

The evening of the next day a memorial service was held in the grand salon. Crewmen as well as ship's officers and passengers were present. Justice Stephen Johnson Field, of the United States Supreme Court, who was on his way to his home in Marysville on the Sacramento River, delivered a eulogy. Signor Morelli and the three Italian artists with whom he was traveling sang "The Battle Hymn of the Republic" to Gottschalk's accompaniment. Adelaide Phillips sang "The Star-Spangled Banner," and Gottschalk played "Union."

The *Constitution* was scheduled to dock in San Francisco the morning of April 25, a Tuesday. On Monday evening Gottschalk made all preparations to land. But upon nearing the Golden Gate the ship ran into a fog so dense that the captain gave the order to drop anchor. Two full days passed before he considered it safe to proceed. It was noon on Thursday when Gottschalk at last disembarked. As he set foot on the soil of California he wondered whether the delay in arriving was an omen of bad luck.

From this person and that, particularly from Ada Clare, he and Muzio had heard what they might expect in San Francisco. The Californians, except for the few of European origin, knew nothing about music. Yet, like all the new rich, they wished to appear before the world as men and women of culture. Any skillful advertiser found them easy prey.

A man who had mastered every trick to induce them to dig into their pockets to buy entertainment was Tom Maguire. What his life had been before his arrival in California in the days of the gold rush no one knew. He turned up in San Francisco as a prize fighter, saved his earnings from the ring, and when he was too old to box opened a gambling house. The venture prospered, and he opened another. Soon he owned gambling houses throughout San Francisco and in every town of importance on the West Coast. By 1860 he was a millionaire.

Convinced that more millions could be made in "show business," he built theatres in centers where he had gambling houses and imported companies and individual artists from the East. Now, in the spring of 1865, he controlled four theatres in San Francisco, each with a seating capacity of fifteen hundred or

218

more. The only one he did not control was the Metropolitan, where the Italian impresario whom he was determined to force out of business was putting on three or four performances of opera each week.

The year past had been for Maguire a year of money-making, mainly because of Ada Isaacs Menken, who, like Gottschalk, came from New Orleans. Night after night for five or six months the men of San Francisco paid enormous prices to get into Maguire's Academy of Music to see la Menken exhibit her nudity in *Mazeppa* or assume lewd masculine poses in *Black-Eyed Susan* or flash her nimble legs in a fencing match in *The French Spy* or do her imitations of Lola Montez. According to Maguire's advertisements, la Menken was the most gifted woman who had ever " gone on the boards."

On meeting Maguire early in the spring of 1864 Ada Clare recognized at once that here was an ingenious disciple of P. T. Barnum. She won his favor by devoting much of her column in the *Golden Era* to eulogies on la Menken's art, and, in return, he presented her as the star in a sumptuous production of *Camille*. But the rôle of the consumptive courtesan was too much for Ada Clare. Overcome by stage fright on the opening night, she provoked laughter instead of tears. Maguire, outraged over the fiasco, told her at the end of the performance that she was a disgrace to his Academy of Music and declared their contract void. When she threatened to put the matter before the courts, he said, " When it comes to show business, I'm the courts in the state of California." Realizing the truth of this, Ada Clare left San Francisco and, after a hurried trip to the Sandwich Islands, returned to New York.

In acquainting Gottschalk with her West Coast experiences, she had held back nothing. Her final admonition was, " Get Maguire's good will and hold on to it."

Neither Gottschalk nor Muzio had any idea of doing anything else. The two had been in San Francisco scarcely a day when they called on Maguire. He received them with the greatest cordiality, and declared that there was a place for them in his plans. His opera company—made up of the quintet of artists who arrived on the *Constitution* and a chorus and orchestra recruited in San Francisco—would occupy the Academy of Music only three or four nights a week. The other nights it was at the disposal of Signor Muzio. If he found it too large another theatre would be made available. Maguire might wish to borrow Gottschalk or Miss Simons to put on as an extra attraction on a night when a short opera was billed. In turn Signor Muzio might wish to use Miss Phillips or one of the other Maguire artists from time to time. "We'll all work together like a big happy family," said Maguire. Before the interview ended it was agreed that Muzio would present his wife and Gottschalk in their début concert at Maguire's Academy of Music on the evening of May 10.

The concert was given as scheduled. There were a few vacant seats in the balconies, but the boxes and orchestra were filled. Gottschalk, mindful of the times, opened the program with his paraphrase of "The Battle Cry of Freedom." He could not have made a happier choice. His playing of the fantasy captivated his more than two thousand hearers, and until the end of the concert he was free to work upon their emotions as he willed. While Miss Simons pleased them, Gottschalk drove them wild. Many times before, he had heard an audience produce every noise possible with mouth, hands, and feet; but never before had he been obliged to make his bows at the back of the stage to avoid being hurt by the gold and silver coins rained upon him.

Californians, he was told, were accustomed to show their appreciation of an artist in this way. He insisted they should be taught better manners. Therefore, Signor Muzio announced in the newspapers that any money thrown upon the stage at Mr. Gottschalk's future concerts would be donated to charities. "Capital advertising!" Maguire exclaimed.

At one or another of the Maguire theatres in the course of the next three weeks Gottschalk and Miss Simons gave eight concerts, each as triumphant as the début; and on several opera nights at the Academy of Music Gottschalk gave brief recitals between acts.

The first day of June he and the Muzios set out on a tour of Maguire's provincial theatres. They appeared successively in Oakland, San Jose, Sacramento, Stockton, and Virginia City,

Nevada. They were delighted with the comfortable steamer on which they traveled up the Sacramento River to the state capital, but from the hour they set out for Stockton they experienced little except hardship. The only means of transportation was the stagecoach, and the roads were rough trails. Ada Clare had made the same trip the year before. In Virginia City two charming young men called on her, introducing themselves as Mark Twain and Dan de Quille. The good times they showed her during her sojourn in the great center of gold and silver were ample compensation for the physical sufferings endured to get there. There were no compensations for Gottschalk. Every woman he saw in Virginia City was a slattern and every man a boor. Gottschalk liked nothing about the city perched on the side of a treeless mountain except the magnificent brilliance of the stars at night.

The return journey, by way of Dutch Flat and Grass Valley, wore so heavily upon his strength that when he arrived in Sacramento he had to be helped up the gangplank of the steamer that took him back to San Francisco. As soon as he was in his hotel room he had Firmin fetch a doctor. The physician assured him that he was not really sick, that all he needed was a few days of rest.

During July and August he permitted himself to be lionized by wealthy San Franciscans. He made friends with the French consul, Henri de Cazotte, who was looked upon as an arbiter of gentility in the best San Francisco society. Though Gottschalk gave a concert or a recital or a matinee of instruction in one of Maguire's theatres every week, he passed most of his time with the set into which Monsieur de Cazotte introduced him. He was a guest at dinners, balls, and picnics. He joined parties on long horseback rides into the country and went on moonlight sails in luxurious yachts. To have the charming Mr. Gottschalk accept an invitation became the desire of every fashionable San Francisco hostess.

He discovered that in matters moral San Francisco was not unlike Boston. The puritans were in control. He played the organ in churches as often as he danced in ballrooms.

To his embarrassment, admirers showered him with presents.

Those sent by anonymous givers—canes, umbrellas, watch chains, and the like—were turned over to some charitable organization. If a package bore the name and address of a sender unknown to Gottschalk, it was returned unopened. If it came from someone in whose home he had been a guest, he of course had to keep it and send a note of thanks.

One of his hosts honored him with a gift he was very happy to keep. Indeed, he was so proud of it that he lent it for exhibition in the show window of one of San Francisco's leading shops. The beautiful object was an immense rug specially woven for Gottschalk. His monogram served as the main motif in the pattern, and musical symbols provided the embellishment. The giver of the rug was the designer and manufacturer. He had learned his art in his native Flanders. Now his carpet factory in San Francisco was rated the largest west of the Allegheny Mountains. On the card which came with the rug was written: "To the musician of musicians, who is also the talker of talkers."

The newspapers made much of this honor, and of another accorded to Gottschalk on the occasion of his fête, August 25. That day, in San Francisco's grandest hotel, he was given a testimonial banquet by forty of the most prominent men of the city. Seven of them made speeches, paying tribute to his greatness as an artist and his amiability as a gentleman. "Mr. Gottschalk," said the *Alta California*, "replied with the modesty and tact which characterize him." Then a committee, headed by the mayor, presented him a magnificent medal of California gold. On one side was a crown of laurel set with rubies and, below it, in diamonds, the initials "L. M. G." On the reverse were the arms of California wreathed with diamonds and the inscription: "To Gottschalk: a token from his California friends. 25 Aug. 1865."

The San Franciscans were very sociable and very kind. But they were not, said Gottschalk, very musical. The composition of his which they favored above all others was one he had never publicly acknowledged, "The Dying Poet." He had written it for the young, and Hall had published it as the work of "Seven Octaves." No one in the East paid any attention to it except the Carreños. They discovered that it was by Gottschalk, and

Teresa included it in her repertoire. It was among the pieces she played at the White House for Mr. and Mrs. Lincoln. Gottschalk would never have dreamed of including it on a program in an Eastern city. But at his first matinee of instruction in San Francisco, when his audience was made up largely of music pupils, he played it. San Franciscans took it to their hearts, wept over it, and called for it on his every appearance. Young girls found it much easier to play than any of his other pieces. The music stores had difficulty in keeping it in stock. Wherever one turned in San Francisco he was sure to hear the air, played on the piano or some other instrument, or hummed, or whistled.

Gottschalk also learned that San Franciscans liked sound and fury. At Maguire's Academy of Music on the evening of August 24 he and nine other pianists, each at a separate instrument, played the march from *Tannhäuser* and the soldiers' chorus from *Faust*. The novelty was received with Western enthusiasm. The great theatre reverberated with yells, the stamping of feet, and the clang of silver dollars hitting the strings of the ten Chickering grands.

Before Gottschalk and Muzio left the Academy of Music that night they decided to give San Franciscans still more sound and fury. The next morning the newspapers announced that at his grand farewell concert, to be given before the end of September, Mr. Gottschalk would present an ensemble of thirty pianists playing thirty pianos in his symphony, "The Battle of Bunker Hill."

That afternoon as he was relaxing in his hotel room Gottschalk received a call from Maguire. The millionaire had come with an ultimatum: any further multiple piano playing in his theatres, he said, must be done on instruments other than the Chickering. His reason? He disliked the local piano dealer who served as the West Coast representative of the Chickering company. That was all. And that was that.

Gottschalk's answer was, " I have a contract with the Chickering company, and I have no notion of breaking it."

" Then you will not play again in one of my theatres," said Maguire, and stalked out.

Gottschalk was not a fighter. But this was a challenge he would have to accept. He even felt a certain joy at the prospect of a clash with Maguire. To him the millionaire represented the one American type he scorned—the rich American marked by vulgarity, intolerance, and fundamental littleness. He saw clearly that his adversary was without honor; he realized that he would have to be on guard against a stab in the back. Yet he went into the struggle with confidence in himself and with the belief that his many San Francisco friends and admirers would lend him their support.

Before the day was over Gottschalk and Muzio found two places for future concerts—Platt's Hall, much like Irving Hall in New York, and the Metropolitan Theatre, where the Italian impresario detested by Maguire was still holding his own.

But before a concert was announced for either house Gottschalk learned that Maguire had stolen the Muzios. The pianist knew nothing of the treachery until he read in the newspapers that Signor Muzio had been added to the staff of conductors at Maguire's Academy of Music and Miss Simons to the group of leading sopranos. When Gottschalk faced them, demanding an explanation, they said that he would surely not be so unkind as to deprive them of the biggest opportunity of their lives. Mr. Maguire, they declared, was going to build up the greatest opera company the world had ever known and they would be among the original members. When Gottschalk reminded them that they had broken a contract and had given him ground for legal action, they told him to go ahead if he dared, showing by the intonation of their voices that they had in mind Maguire's declaration to Ada Clare, "When it comes to show business, I'm the courts in the state of California."

Gottschalk did not miss the Muzios. The owner of Platt's Hall gladly took over the management of his concerts, and the impresario at the Metropolitan Theatre provided him with assisting artists. Within the ten days beginning Wednesday, August 30, he made eight appearances, each to a packed house. To the hundreds of San Franciscans backing him in his fight against

Maguire his victory seemed sure. They could conceive of no way in which the millionaire showman could strike.

But Fate turned against Gottschalk.

Sunday afternoon, September 10, he and a young Market Street hatter with whom he had become friendly hired buggies from a livery stable and took two society girls on a secret drive into the country. The girls—a blonde and a brunette of the same age, about eighteen—were roommates in a fashionable female seminary on South Park Street. As a guest in the home of the brunette, Gottschalk had fallen under the fascination of her beauty and believed that she was emotionally interested in him. The blonde was engaged to the hatter. It was he who made the arrangements for the clandestine outing, probably at the brunette's suggestion. The drive, it is certain, was innocent. The two buggies were at no time out of sight of one another, and neither made a stop. The road was crowded with San Franciscans out to take the air. Gottschalk returned to his hotel feeling only that he was better acquainted with a very charming young woman who attracted him.

The next three days he was busy rehearsing the twenty-nine pianists who were to assist him at his farewell festival concert, announced for September 20. He was also making preparations for the luncheon he was to give on Friday for the forty gentlemen who had honored him on his fête. He was so occupied that he forgot the lovely brunette.

But on Thursday morning he was brusquely reminded of her. The hatter called at his hotel, bringing news about the aftermath of the buggy ride. The two girls were a few minutes late in returning to the seminary, and the preceptress caught them slipping up to their quarters by a back door. She found out that they had not been in their homes since four that afternoon, and questioned them until she got all the facts. The brunette, in hysterics, shouted that she loved Gottschalk and would do anything in the world to be with him. The blonde kept saying that the drive was an outing with her fiancé and that she had no regrets over taking it. The preceptress allowed the girls to remain at the seminary over night, but the next morning she expelled them and sent them home.

"We must get the girls back into the seminary," said Gottschalk, "and see that the affair is hushed up."

"Everybody in San Francisco knows of it by now," said the hatter, as he produced a roll of morning newspapers.

Only the *Alta California* and the *Bulletin* failed to report the affair. As Gottschalk read the account in the *Call*, he envisioned Maguire threatening, browbeating, and bribing the editor. The article warned San Franciscans of two satyrs in their midst. Very late on Sunday evening, it stated, the fiends abducted from a boarding school two virgins, of thirteen or fourteen, and took them into the country in buggies. The girls succeeded in escaping with honor intact, and walked five miles back to the city, in the darkness. The police knew the identity of the satyrs, and the readers of the *Call* would probably be informed of arrests within a day or two. Then the names of the malefactors would be made public. The other printed reports of the affair were in substance the same.

Gottschalk assured the terrified young hatter that he need fear neither arrest nor the loss of his fiancée. "The man back of these lies," said Gottschalk, "has no interest in hurting you. His aim is to ruin me, not only in California but in all America."

In the Friday reports in the scandal sheets—one of which carried illustrative drawings of the supposed abduction—a note of humor was injected. The two opera troupes singing in San Francisco that summer had familiarized the public with Mozart's *Don Giovanni*. So everybody knew what was meant when the satyrs were referred to as Don Giovanni and Leporello. Two of the reports reminded San Franciscans that they were acquainted with one of Don Giovanni's Elviras, the New York writer and actress who had come to the West the preceding year in company with her beautiful little boy, a half brother to her seducer's countless bastards.

That Friday was the day for the luncheon which Gottschalk had planned with such great care. At noon he was in a private dining room of his hotel awaiting his guests. Of the forty who accepted his invitation only Monsieur de Cazotte and two others turned up. They came to advise Gottschalk to remain in his hotel room until they could smuggle him aboard the steamer *Colorado*, sailing for Panama City on Monday morning. The word-of-mouth lies spread by Maguire's agents were, said Monsieur de Cazotte, far more provocative than the newspaper stories. Gottschalk was convinced that if he appeared on the streets he was running the risk of assassination.

By Sunday evening he and Firmin were ready to depart. The two Chickering grands brought from New York were left at the Metropolitan Theatre, where on Thursday evening Gottschalk had made his last San Francisco appearance. The beautiful gift from the carpet manufacturer was also abandoned. But Gottschalk could carry in his pocket his happiest memento of California, the medal given to him on his fête. His trunks had been taken to the *Colorado* one at a time at different hours on Saturday.

Between two and three o'clock Monday morning he, Firmin, and Monsieur de Cazotte left the hotel, entered the closed carriage waiting for them, and drove to the ship without mishap. Once on board, they were conducted to the cabins which had been reserved.

"I was promised that you would have your meals here," said Monsieur de Cazotte. "And remember that you are not supposed to leave these staterooms. If you do, you'll be laying yourself open to insult or violence. This ship will be crowded with San Franciscans."

"I understand," said Gottschalk, not unobservant of the fact that the friend who was aiding him in his enforced flight from his native land was a citizen of France.

The San Francisco scandal sheets on Monday afternoon and Tuesday morning carried varied accounts of Don Giovanni's ignominious exit from San Francisco. Gottschalk's name was given, but not the hatter's. According to one report, the celebrated pianist was seen stealing on the *Colorado* in the disguise of a Chinaman. According to another, Gottschalk turned up at the gangplank Sunday night in the dress of a miner and bribed the guards with gold. Still another report had Gottschalk costumed as an elephant and hoisted on board with several other wild animals. All the accounts agreed that since the rake was not named in the published passenger list he was on the *Colorado* as a stowaway.

Articles vilifying Gottschalk continued to appear in the California press for weeks. In newspapers all over the United States—in cities and towns where Gottschalk's playing of his "evening prayer" was to thousands a precious memory—the lies were reprinted.

A New York druggist clipped the most lurid and kept them on display in a show case in his shop. When Gaston Gottschalk, with tears in his eyes, begged him in the name of truth and justice to withdraw the exhibit, the druggist laughed in his face and asked, "And keep away the dozens of possible customers who come in here every day to read them?"

Maguire's victory was complete.

The *Colorado* dropped anchor off the shore of Panama City on Sunday, October 1. Gottschalk and Firmin had suffered from seasickness, bad food, intense heat, and isolation for exactly two weeks. They did not leave the steamer until all the other passengers had gone ashore. The train for the Atlantic side of the isthmus was departing just as they touched land.

Though weeks were to pass before Gottschalk received letters from New York, he knew that the story of his flight had already been spread throughout the United States. He knew that there was no longer any section of the country in whose concert halls he would find a welcome, that the lies sent out from San Francisco had made his name odious everywhere.

On the long tormenting voyage he had thought more than once of returning to France. But he could not bear the prospect of meeting those to whom he must be a disappointment, such men as Hector Berlioz and Monsieur Marmontel. Equally repugnant was the thought of encountering those who had looked up to him as a superior but who were now far in advance of him in the world of music—Jacques Offenbach, Camille Saint-Saëns, Georges Bizet, and Ernest Guiraud.

The road he decided upon was the one William Vincent Wallace had followed as a vagabond music-maker twenty-five years before. But while Mr. Wallace traveled up the west coast of South America in the direction of civilization, Gottschalk would be traveling down toward primitivism. He would always be drawing nearer the region of snow—which to him was one with the nescience of death.

He spent ten days in Panama City, a guest at the Aspinwall

Hotel. His first dinner was fair, he said, though he found flies in the soup and in the omelette. One evening he gave a concert in the city hall to an audience of one hundred and forty, each of whom paid the equivalent of an American dollar for admission. The soirée was under the patronage of the highest government official in Panama, a mulatto who took great pride in telling the world that his father was a bishop, pure Spanish. The piano Gottschalk used was an upright, probably the product, he said, of an illicit union between a jew's harp and a big kettle. The man who had tuned it was a clerk in the French consulate, an unfortunate with half his face eaten away by cancer.

But all in Panama City was not squalor and misery. Gottschalk could see from his hotel room into a seamstress' shop across the street. The woman's helper was an Indian girl of about sixteen, with black eyes, carefully combed glittering black hair, round yellow shoulders, and supple body. She reminded Gottschalk of a timid doe, and he soon had the habit of sitting where he could look out and watch her at her sewing. One afternoon in the market district he purchased a yard of pink ribbon, put it in his pocket, and kept it there, unwrapped. Two days later when he was returning from a promenade he found the girl in the doorway of the shop teaching a little naked boy his a, b, c's. " Is the little one your brother? " asked Gottschalk in his gentlest voice, as he took the ribbon from his pocket and held it out to the girl. Trembling with fright, she dashed behind the shop. Gottschalk made no more advances. Afterwards when he met the girl on the street he never showed that he saw her. Still he spent hours every day sitting where he could gaze at her wild eyes and warm yellow shoulders as she moved about the shop in bare feet. Commenting on the experience in his diary, he wrote: " Fortunately for me, my desire to conquer is never so great as my fear of being conquered."

He left, he said, a bit of his heart in that seamstress' shop when, on October 10, he embarked with Firmin on a small freighter bound for Callao, Peru. The only other passengers were half a dozen French Sisters of Mercy and a young Peruvian priest recently ordained in Rome. " May this holy cargo ensure calm seas!" said Gottschalk when he found out who his traveling companions were to be. Apparently his wish was granted.

The ship arrived at Callao on the afternoon of October 18. That evening Gottschalk was installed in a comfortable room on the first floor of the best hotel in Lima. The capital—all Peru, in fact—was alarmed over a revolution then in progress. For ten years Gottschalk had dreamed of harvesting a share of the gold of Lima. Back in the spring of 1855 when he was trying to pay his father's debts, the New Orleans press reported that he was shortly to leave for Peru. Later, the same report appeared from time to time in New York newspapers. Now that he was finally there, the city of Inca gold was on the verge of being turned into a battleground.

On an evening early in November he played for a small gathering in the home of a musician. His last number, an improvised development of the air "Bénédiction des poignards," turned out to be most appropriate for the occasion. Just as he played the last note, a messenger hurried in to announce that the revolutionists were approaching. Several of the guests were officers in the army of the existing government. They grabbed their swords and rushed out to join their regiments.

Gottschalk was in his hotel room sleeping soundly when, at four the next morning, Firmin woke him and said, "They're fighting here, sir." Gottschalk knew that the hotel was very near the government buildings and judged that it would probably be right in the center of the battle. He felt, he said, no fright. He calmly dressed himself, and stood behind the shutters, looking out.

There was light enough to distinguish color. A troop of cavalrymen, in round yellow hats and red ponchos, filled the street. If he had opened the window and reached down, he would have touched heads. At first there was silence. Presently it was broken by the booming of the big guns which Gottschalk had noticed the afternoon before in front of the government buildings. A number of the cavalrymen dashed forward, and in a few seconds he heard a clashing of swords up the street. Just as he opened the shutters slightly for a better view, a cannon ball struck the balcony and imbedded itself in the masonry. Gottschalk had no thought of danger. He was too fascinated by the sight below. Where mounted cavalrymen had stood there were now fallen horses thrashing the pavement in their death agony, the mangled bodies of men, blood streaming in every direction, and cries of the dying, " Jesus! Maria! Dios! "

He saw a priest dash from the hotel entrance and kneel beside one moaning figure after another. Then he saw four men rush out with a stretcher. As others followed with more stretchers, Gottschalk and Firmin joined them and helped in moving the wounded into the hotel patio. Doctors, nurses, and priests turned up from no one knew where. Shortly after daybreak the report came that the revolutionists had taken the city. Nobody seemed to care. Gottschalk decided that to the average intelligent Peruvian all governments were alike corrupt.

Within ten days Lima was quiet enough for Gottschalk to begin a series of concerts. Acting as his own manager, he found his assistants among the city's amateurs. The soirées were given in the municipal theatre until an earthquake made it unsafe. The best of the other halls was a place where every Sunday, said Gottschalk, veiled women and their lovers indulged in a sort of dancing which, though very picturesque, was considered indecent even in Peru. How could public prejudice against such a hall be overcome? Gottschalk, remembering Barnum, answered this question by announcing in the newspapers that because of the superior acoustics in the hall where he was to continue his concerts the price of admission would be doubled. To hear Señor Gottschalk in the place of ill repute immediately became fashionable. He did not give his farewell soirée until the middle of January.

By this time he had received many newspaper clippings from Gaston and others, and had seen with his own eyes what was being said of him in the press of his native country. Monsieur de Cazotte in San Francisco, Mr. Hall and Mrs. Seymour in New York, Mr. Hill and the Chickering brothers in Boston, his cousin Leonard Myers in Philadelphia, Léon Escudier in Paris, and a dozen more who knew that he was incapable of the villainies charged against him had written begging him to come back to the United States and enter libel suits against his detractors or at least make some sort of statement to the press. His answer at first was that his friends could not possibly believe the calumnies and that he had no interest in what others believed. But when his defenders became more insistent, he agreed to the publication in a New York periodical, *Watson's Journal*, of letters stating his version of his San Francisco experiences. After they appeared in print excerpts were quoted in newspapers as far away as Paris, and gave rise to considerable editorial comment in favor of Gottschalk.

But he knew that where a hundred read the good said of him a thousand had read the evil. The two months following his Lima concerts he spent at Chorillos. In this beautiful resort he reveled, he said, in the delights of idleness. Yet between the lines of the journal he kept while there he admitted his defeat as a musician, his hopelessness as a man, and his indifference toward living.

On March 20, 1866, he embarked at Callao on the steamer *Limena*, intending to land at Islay and then travel by mule to Arequipa, the most important Peruvian city after the capital. But when he was told that the journey over the mountains was very difficult and that he would find in Arequipa only a roofless theatre in which to give concerts, he changed his mind and remained on the *Limena* until he reached Arica, the northernmost city in Chile. From here a railroad ran to Tacna, the southernmost city of Peru. Gottschalk spent five or six weeks shifting from one place to the other, giving concerts in each.

It was May when he moved on to Valparaiso and Santiago. Once more he was in cities where he saw few faces which were not white. But the high rate of illiteracy in these two urban centers appalled him. When after a number of concerts in each city he decided to make his farewell to Chile with a mammoth festival in Santiago, he discovered that of the five hundred forming the chorus a hundred could neither read nor write. Yet they had good ears and loved music. He taught them to sing with effectiveness the choruses from *Fidelio*, *Le Prophète*, and *Tannhäuser*.

From the beginning of the year 1867 until the end of April he was in Copiapo, a Chilean coastal resort four hundred miles north of Santiago. An experience he had while there was to haunt him for the rest of his life. In the hotel where he stayed he made friends with a fellow guest, a French engineer, an aristocrat who had become what Gottschalk called a " social wreck." The man was unhappy, very thin, shabby, and obviously ill. Gottschalk was not surprised when at four o'clock on the afternoon of February 12 he heard that the engineer had suddenly died. According to Chilean law, burial must take place within twenty-four hours after death. The manager of the hotel arranged for the funeral that same night, and Gottschalk, as close to the Frenchman as anyone else in all South America, attended as a sort of chief mourner.

" I was never present," he said, " at the interment of a foreigner who had died far from his native country and his family without having my heart torn with grief." This time—for a reason he was unable to explain—his feeling was terror rather than grief. The cemetery, on the side of a mountain, was reached by a mile-long twisting road. The coffin was on a cart drawn by a bedraggled horse. The driver, swishing his poncho as he walked beside the cart, prodded the beast constantly. When half the distance was covered, the harness broke and had to be repaired. Then, after another hundred yards, the horse gave out completely. From this point on the cart was pulled and pushed by Gottschalk and the ten or twelve others who made up the funeral party. Finally the coffin was taken into the cemetery chapel and left in the care of a tottering old man in a black cap. " Was it all an awful dream? " wrote Gottschalk in his diary when he got back to the hotel.

On April 26 he sailed from Copiapo on a steamer bound for Buenos Aires. A call at Valparaiso afforded a brief respite from seasickness, but soon the vessel was pitching again on the open sea, and Gottschalk was back in his cabin suffering again from extreme nausea.

By the time the ship entered the Strait of Magellan, his appetite had returned and the voyage had become a pleasure. The remoteness of his situation both frightened and fascinated him. "I cannot," he wrote in a letter, "explain with my pen the strange feeling I experienced on landing at Punta Arenas, on the Strait of Magellan in Patagonia, one hundred miles from Cape Horn, at the antipodes of civilization." Since it was still early in the autumn, there was as yet no snow. After he met the governor of the island and saw two or three Patagonian families in their strange costumes, he felt comfortable enough.

When the ship reached Buenos Aires—in May, an autumn month in the Argentine Republic—the passengers obtained full reports of the cholera epidemic that had ravaged the capital since the beginning of summer. Only a few on board were daring enough to land. Gottschalk was among them. He hoped to remain on the La Plata River for at least a year or two, dividing his time between Buenos Aires and Montevideo. He was tired of the life of a wandering exile.

But he did not settle down at once within the boundaries of pestilence-stricken Buenos Aires. He found lodgings in a small town thirty miles up the La Plata and stayed there for a month. Then, after a few frosty days had made the capital safe, he came back and surveyed the possibilities for a series of concerts. The people, he was told, were still afraid to assemble in crowds.

So he went over to Montevideo, where the cholera had been much less severe. Here the musicians whom he met were encouraging, and he soon had a date set for his first concert, to come early in August.

On arriving in Montevideo he took rooms at the Hotel Americano. He had been there only a few days when he met his next-door neighbor, Luiz Fors, a young journalist who had been driven from his native Spain because of his attacks on the government and on the Jesuits. The two exiles became fast friends. For almost two years they traveled back and forth together between Montevideo and Buenos Aires, and in each city they always stayed at the same hotel.

Fors was editor of a revolutionary newspaper which the Church in both Uruguay and Argentina was fighting to suppress. Though he devoted many of his columns to the discussion of civil abuses, neither government had as yet seen fit to silence him. He was vital, full of enthusiasm over his dreams of making the world perfect, and he was unafraid. He talked with all the abandon and extravagance of the Latin who feels that he is fulfilling a great destiny.

His influence over Gottschalk was extraordinary. The despair which had possessed the pianist since his departure from San Francisco gradually gave way to hope. He became once more an ambitious musician. In brilliant concerts in Buenos Aires and Montevideo he manifested all of his old zest. He returned to composition and wrote a grand tarantelle for piano and orchestra and a new symphony. The latter, entitled "Montevideo," was the featured number at his farewell festival concert in the Uruguayan capital on October 9, 1868. He composed a number of smaller works, among which was the popular elegy for piano, "Morte!" In the cheerful letters to his friends in the United States he spoke of coming back and touring the country with a full orchestra. After rehabilitating himself in his native land he would, he wrote, go to France and compose with the powers of maturity. He was particularly impatient, he said, to finish the books and the music of the two operas he had under way, *Charles IX* and *Isaura di Salerno*.

The fiery young Spaniard even induced Gottschalk to become a social reformer. The parochial school, according to Fors, was the main cause of the degradation of the people of South America. No topic was more frequently discussed in his journal. Finally he persuaded Gottschalk to write letters to various newspapers on the free schools in the United States. "You're a public idol," said Fors, "and your voice will carry far." Fors was right. The letters were widely quoted, and led to invitations to Gottschalk to address clubs and other groups. He accepted those for which he had time. In a letter to Léon Escudier he wrote: "I have to think twice when I set out for an appointment in order to make sure whether I'm to give a concert or a talk on education."

His heart was in what he said to his auditors about the advantages of the public school over the parochial. From the time of his short stay in Panama City he had been a very close observer of the part played by the Church in South America. He had met a few priests whom he thought of as his mother had taught him to think of Père Antoine. But his diary is witness that he considered many of his clerical acquaintances corrupt in the extreme. That the Church authorities overlooked their viciousness filled him with indignation.

Not long after reaching the east coast of South America he received a copy of Ada Clare's novel, *Only a Woman's Heart*, published in New York late in 1866. His opinion of the book as a work of art could only have been that of the American critics, who without exception condemned it as too unfinished for publication. But Gottschalk saw that as a narrative of his and Ada's love it had the strength of frankness and spontaneity.

One of Ada's letters of 1868 was the announcement of the death of Aubrey, who had reached the age of eleven. As to the particulars and as to Gottschalk's reaction, nothing is known. All that may be said with certainty is that Ada had the child buried in the Presbyterian cemetery in Hammonton, New Jersey. For the rest of her life she was to say that when Aubrey died Ada Clare died also.

She had taken a new name, Agnes Stanfield. As such, she was billed in the most important rôle she had ever played, that of Mistress Page in James H. Hackett's New York production of *The Merry Wives of Windsor*. At the present—in the fall of 1868—she was with a stock company touring the South. One of her fellow troupers, M. J. F. Noyes, had made her an offer of marriage. She had accepted, but only after telling him frankly that the Agnes Stanfield who would be his wife was no more than a dim shadow of the Ada Clare who loved Gottschalk.

At the time the pianist received this news he was under the spell of a Basque actress and singer who had come to South America with a French light opera troupe. She was known on the stage simply as Clelia, and it is doubtful whether Gottschalk ever learned her full name. She had heard him play and had fallen in love with him before their mutual friend Luiz Fors brought them together. Gottschalk found her beauty and seductiveness irresistible.

Fors spoke of her medium height, her slenderness, her small hands and feet, her long silky yellow hair, her immense black eyes, her white skin, and her pink mouth. She had the manners of an aristocratic lady, was a lively conversationalist, and spoke Spanish and Italian as well as she spoke French. A man had only to see her toss her head or hear her laugh to perceive her ardent disposition and her passionate heart. " She was," Fors said, " a dangerous volcano for those who came too near her enchantments."

At first, Gottschalk found her inspirational rather than dangerous. He met her just three days after his great Montevideo farewell festival. During the months that followed he devoted himself almost exclusively to composition. In a letter of April 6, 1869, to his Boston friend Francis G. Hill, he spoke of having recently finished " three études de concert, a scherzo, a septour for piano and strings, a capriccio, and several songs." It was in all respects an optimistic letter. Near the end came the request: " I hope you will keep the Boston public informed about poor old Gottschalk, who has been ill used very often, and is certainly not half as bad as some would make him out to be." In closing Gottschalk declared that he was seriously considering an offer from Strakosch and the Chickerings to return to the United States.

By the time he wrote this letter to Mr. Hill, Gottschalk was tiring of Clelia. Once again he realized that the Muse of Music, ever fair and young, must remain his only bride. But he could not bring himself to be unkind to his mistress. He felt too sorry for her. She, too, was all alone on a strange continent. As her passion for him gained in ardor, he pretended that he was still the enraptured lover. But such shamming was an unremitting strain upon his nerves. By the last week in April he was the victim of insomnia and a complete loss of appetite.

One night, in company with Luiz Fors, he crossed over to Buenos Aires. The next morning he consulted successively two physicians, each of whom drew from him the facts about his liaison with Clelia. They had the same diagnosis for his trouble: they told him plainly that if he valued his life he would break with his mistress.

He went back to Montevideo determined to flee. With the greatest secrecy he and Firmin made all preparations to leave for Rio de Janeiro. But when on the last night in April they embarked on the steamer which was to carry them to Brazil, Clelia was with them. At the eleventh hour Gottschalk's sense of pity had prevailed. As it held him in its power, the indifference toward living which he had felt during his first two years in South America came back in full force.

Gottschalk suffered his usual attack of seasickness. But by May 8, the day he reached the age of forty, he was well enough to have dinner with Clelia and drink to the pleasures of youth. When she proposed a bumper to long life, he said, " I've a feeling that I shall never see another birthday."

On the morning of May 10 the ship reached Rio de Janeiro. Within less than a week Gottschalk was summoned to the imperial palace. To a friend in Paris he wrote of his meeting with the Emperor Dom Pedro II: " His Majesty received me most graciously in the great audience room of the palace. We stood and talked for five minutes, the usual time for this intro-ductory ceremony. Then the Emperor told me that the Empress and Princess Imperial wished to see me. So I was committed to a gentleman in waiting, who conducted me to the Empress and her eldest daughter. They also were most gracious. Both ex-pressed their happiness in making the acquaintance of the author of compositions which had been bringing them pleasure for years. I was then taken again to the Emperor, whom I found in a small study at the end of a private apartment. He bade me sit down beside him, and said that he wished to have a long talk with me. We conversed for nearly two hours on politics, travel, the United States, spiritualism, the music of the future, Offenbach's operettas, fine arts in general, manners, and customs."

Very different in tone was his letter of a few days later to Luiz Fors. In it he said: " I've brought my illness with me. To tell the truth, I don't wish to stop being ill. I'd like to write you much, but I can't. Neither the imperial court, which entertains me, nor my memories, which assail me, nor *she* will give me the

240

time. Of art, nothing; of illusions, nothing; of sadness, an ocean; of pleasures, an infinity."

Preparing for his Brazilian début, under the patronage of Their Majesties, he was too busy to give much time to his mistress, whom he had installed in an apartment remote from his hotel. At the concert, which came near the end of May in a theatre in Rio de Janeiro, he was assisted by the German Choral Society, a group of amateurs led by a musician he had met many years before in Springfield, Massachusetts. The evening was another triumph. But if Clelia expected more of his attention now that he had made a very successful début, she was to be disappointed.

Two more concerts followed immediately. At the second, which came the evening of June 3, Gottschalk was so weak that he was scarcely able to hold out to the end. As he made his final bows, he clung to the piano to keep from falling. At the hotel he went straight to bed, and, on the orders of a doctor, stayed there two weeks.

Reminded in this forceful manner of what the physicians in Buenos Aires had told him, he brought his common sense into control and began pitying himself rather than Clelia. He saw less and less of her, and by the end of July the break between them was complete.

He was free of the spell of her black eyes. But his letters to Luiz Fors and others show plainly that he was not free of the conviction that he was a doomed man.

On the evening of July 30 he played at court for the first time. " At my previous visits," he said, " the Emperor had always had the delicacy to refrain from asking me to play, for he considered the pianos at the palace unworthy of me." On this occasion Gottschalk and his assisting pianist used the two Broadwood grands supplied by a local music house. The soirée was a big function. In addition to the imperial family and the ladies and gentlemen of the court there were a hundred and fifty guests. Gottschalk gave only request numbers—" Ojos criollos," his fantasy on the Brazilian national hymn, his étude " Tremolo," " Pensée poétique," and " Morte! " At the close of the program, the Emperor drew the pianist into a secluded recess of the great chamber and questioned him about the Mormons. " I was able to satisfy his curiosity completely," said Gottschalk, " as I had just read Dixon's *New America*."

It was four o'clock in the morning when Gottschalk left the palace. He had to wait in rain several minutes to get a carriage, and he became thoroughly chilled. The next afternoon he was running a temperature. It mounted with the days, and on August 4 his doctors reported to the press that he was a victim of yellow fever and that his condition was grave.

Late the next afternoon he sank so low that they thought he was dying. But he never lost consciousness, and was to describe his feelings as follows: " It seemed that the fever had enveloped me in a very hot cloud. I could see nothing except the grim face of Death, come to hurry me away from the pomp and vanities of this world. Yes, I was philosophical—and terribly distressed. No friend, save my faithful Firmin; no family; no loved hand to clasp mine and make me feel in one last pressure that my life was still dear to someone."

His doctors brought him through the crisis. In his words, " They got me out of the mal passo, which I dread only because it would separate me, perhaps forever, from those I love."

When he was strong enough to leave the hotel for short walks, they advised that he pass his convalescence in the mountain town of Valenza, five hours by rail from Rio de Janeiro. He took the journey, and felt none the worse for it. He found that Valenza was cordial as well as picturesque. His arrival at the private home where he had engaged rooms was greeted with music. " It came at first," he said, " from a clarinet, a cornet, and a big drum. Then, as I stood on my balcony looking out upon the smiling populace, I saw a trombone coming at a run, a flute all out of breath right behind him, and a bassoon turning a corner. The three who were late joined the three who had begun to play, and my ears were regaled with a romantic-eccentric symphony which even the great harmonist Monsieur Fétis would have difficulty in analyzing." Gottschalk was told by his host that this orchestra of six was in demand on every grand occasion in Valenza. The hospitality of the villagers and the pure mountain air worked a complete convalescence within three weeks. He had arrived in the mountains on August 22, and on September 12 he took the train back to the capital.

The first duty he performed when he was once more in Rio de Janeiro was to call on the Emperor and Empress and thank them for their concern and their kindnesses to him during his illness. Either on this occasion or a few days later he presented to Dom Pedro a copy of the conductor's score for a composition dedicated to His Majesty, " Marche triomphale " for orchestra.

In a letter to Mr. Hill, dated September 24, Gottschalk began: " Though I'm recovering slowly, I'm not yet strong. But, thank God, I'm in good health." He then wrote of his great esteem for the Brazilian Emperor, and added: " If you can speak of all this in the newspapers, you will please me much by doing so. I would like for our people to know that there is one emperor in the world who is not a tyrant and who is a friend of the Americans."

At the time he dispatched this letter he was in the middle of a series of soirées, in each of which he was assisted by an ensemble of thirty pianists and a full orchestra. Dom Pedro or some other member of the imperial family was present at every concert. The series was so successful that it was repeated on the evenings of October 5, 8, and 11.

Gottschalk paid no attention whatsoever to the warnings of his doctors against overwork.

On October 24 he dispatched two letters to the United States.

One was to Mr. Hall, to whom he had already sent a manuscript copy of " Morte! " It had proved to be a " succès de larmes " in South America, he said, and was neither better nor worse than " old ' Last Hope.' " He left to Mr. Hall's judgment the position on the title page of the translation of the title, " She is Dead! " He asked that the proofreading be done with great care. Finally he suggested that in advertisements the piece be listed as a lamentation rather than as a nocturne or reverie. It was to appear in print as opus 60.

The other letter, to Mr. Hill, was devoted wholly to his plans for his great Brazilian festival concerts to be given the last week in November. He would not, he said, produce such volume of sound as Patrick Gilmore had brought forth at his recent Peace Jubilee in Boston with an orchestra of a thousand and chorus of ten thousand. " But," wrote Gottschalk, " if rehearsing counts, I'm going to make good music with my handful of eight hundred performers, led by a corps of eighty drummers." The Emperor had placed at his disposal four hundred musicians from army and navy bands, and he had found that they required special training. He was obliged, he said, to direct rehearsals all day and spend the evenings preparing orchestral scores for copyists.

The first of the festival soirées came on November 24. Though the price of tickets was twice that charged for any previous Gottschalk concert in Brazil, every seat in the immense opera house of Rio de Janeiro was taken. The Emperor and Empress were in the imperial box. After the " Marche triomphale," which ends with the Brazilian national anthem, there was a great patriotic demonstration.

The second concert was billed for November 26, a Friday. That morning Fate, which had been springing surprises on Gottschalk all his life, sprang another: he was attacked by a severe pain on the right side of the abdomen.

Afternoon came, and evening, but the pain had not abated. Gottschalk insisted it was nothing serious and refused to call a doctor. At half past eight he was at the opera house determined not to disappoint the thousands who had paid high prices for tickets. The program opened with a comedy, which lasted about twenty minutes. Then when the curtain rose after a short intermission, the audience saw nothing on the stage except a Broadwood grand piano and a table on which stood a vase of heliotrope. Soon Gottschalk appeared, responded to the applause, sat at the piano, and slowly removed his gloves. He was to play a group of solos, the first of which was " Morte! " But he had gone through no more than half a dozen bars when he fainted and fell to the floor.

Several of the men and women standing in the wings were at his side in an instant. Before the curtain could be rung down they had him restored to consciousness. His first words on coming to were, "Tell the assistant conductor I expect him to carry on the program to the end."

Gottschalk was borne on a stretcher to his hotel. All that night he moaned with pain. In the morning the opiates the doctors administered brought some relief. He was able to dictate the following note to Luiz Fors: "My forebodings are turning into reality. I should like to see you and tell you much about myself. It will be a great disappointment to me if you can't come. For I find myself in the prestissimo del mio finale."

He was manifesting—and continued to manifest—the symptoms of the affliction which doctors of the future were to call appendicitis. But the two physicians attending him knew only that he was suffering from some sort of abdominal abscess. They tried to keep him comfortable. Each day they made the dosage of opiates a little stronger. On Wednesday, December 8, when the Brazilian summer brought the first oppressive heat wave, they moved him to a hotel in Tijuca, a suburb on an elevated plateau less than three miles from the center of Rio de Janeiro. The coolness of the higher altitude seemed to help.

When the doctors called the next Tuesday, December 14, Gottschalk said to them, "I'm no longer in pain." As soon as they checked his temperature and saw that it was very high, they knew that the abscess had broken. They now faced the problem of keeping the patient strong enough to fight off the poison which his blood was carrying to every part of his body.

He was delirious that afternoon and during most of the days and nights which followed. At times he sang, jumbling melodies in such fashion that neither Firmin nor the hotel servants who were in attendance as nurses could tell what they were. He made speeches, intermingling English, French, and Spanish. He often cried, and he often talked with his father or mother or Edward.

In the intervals when his mind was clear he invariably asked when Luiz Fors would arrive. It was evident to Firmin and the nurses that he was worried over matters he was willing to disclose only to his young friend—probably matters relating to his music manuscripts, his money, his sisters, and Gaston.

When he asked about Fors on Friday afternoon and was told

that no word had as yet been received, he said, " I'm afraid he's going to be too late." Near midnight, when his mind was again clear for a few moments, he said, " Get a lawyer to take down my will. I'll die when the clock strikes four in the morning."

The lawyer, with his papers and seals and professional air, came at one o'clock. Gottschalk was already in the coma from which he never awoke. He died just eleven minutes before the hour he had specified.

It was Saturday, December 18, 1869.

Luiz Fors, who had sailed from Montevideo as soon as possible after receiving his friend's alarming letter, arrived in Rio de Janeiro about noon that day. As he stood on deck waiting for his turn to descend the gangplank, he heard someone call out from the pier, "Gottschalk died at four o'clock this morning." Luiz refused to believe that he was too late until he got hold of a newspaper and saw the report confirmed.

He was one of the thousands who filed into the hall of the Philharmonic Society of Rio de Janeiro that afternoon to view Gottschalk's body. He saw near the bier the Broadwood piano on which the artist had begun to play when he fell prostrate on his last public appearance. The instrument was draped in black.

Luiz next went to Tijuca, had a long talk with Firmin, and got Clelia's address.

Late that evening he called at her apartment. When she opened her door and saw that Luiz was her visitor, she said, "He killed himself!" She appeared a grief-stricken wreck. Her rooms were in the greatest disorder. Luiz stumbled over trunks and traveling bags on his way into the tiny salon. "I'm sailing for Bordeaux day after tomorrow," she explained.

When the two were seated face to face, Luiz asked, "What did you mean when you said he killed himself?"

"He knew he was working himself to death," she answered.

Luiz wanted to say, "No, you killed him." But he lacked the heart to bring more sorrow to one who was already the embodiment of anguish.

She had, she said, a strange request to make. The last after-noon she and Gottschalk had spent together—months in the past—

they had taken the horseback ride to El Corcobado, the mountain peak which looks down upon Rio de Janeiro. As they stood side by side on the summit, Gottschalk, with the abandon of a little boy, exclaimed, "Think of it! We're on top of the city, in the clouds!" It was her wish to view the funeral procession from that spot. "Will you get horses and take me there?" she asked Luiz, pleadingly. He would try, he said.

It was already near midnight. In compliance with the Brazilian custom of speedy burial, the Philharmonic Society, which was directing the funeral, had arranged for the interment at an early morning hour. Luiz had little time. But he was lucky enough to find a livery stable open, and he and Clelia reached the summit of El Corcobado as day was breaking.

With the aid of spyglasses they were able to see the crowd filling the streets in the vicinity of the hall of the Philharmonic Society. They did not have to wait long before they saw a military band emerge from the hall, each man holding an instrument to his lips or beating a drum. They were too far away to catch even the slightest sound. But they knew from the published announcements that the music was Gottschalk's own "Marche funèbre." Following the band came the coffin, borne on the shoulders of eight prominent Brazilian musicians. Next came the members of the Philharmonic Society, in a body. Then came numerous other societies. Trailing all the rest was the host of Gottschalk's admirers, most of them carrying flowers.

Luiz and Clelia knew that somewhere in the crowd was Firmin, the only one among the thousands whose grief was akin to theirs. They knew that it was he, also a hard critic of the priesthood of South America, who had seen to it that the Church had as little part as possible in the funeral.

They watched until the last of the procession rounded a hill and was lost to sight. It was a relief to be far away from the Cemetery of San José Baptista, where the committal was to take place. They had many a time heard Gottschalk pour out his contempt for funeral eulogies. Yet two celebrated Brazilian orators, strangers to him, had been appointed by the Emperor to speak at his grave.

Luiz and Clelia did not get back to Rio de Janeiro till near noon. At the livery stable where they returned their horses they parted. She was to embark for France within twenty-four hours, and in the years to come was no doubt to remember Gottschalk only as one in a long chain of lovers. The young Spaniard, on the contrary, was to regard his friendship with the musician as the richest experience of his life and was to commemorate it in his book *Gottschalk*, published in Havana in 1880.

Gottschalk's death was reported in American newspapers the middle of January. It seemed that editors had forgotten the San Francisco scandal. From the number of laudatory obituaries which appeared in print one might have gathered that Gottschalk was a prominent politician or a general.

His sisters, all in London, and his brother, then singing with an opera troupe in Mexico City, did not learn of his death until the end of January. They immediately began proceedings to have his body brought back to the United States. Firmin—feeling no doubt that he was acting as his late employer would have wished—fought to keep the body in the Cemetery of San José Baptista in Rio de Janeiro. But he fought in vain. The coffin reached New York, where the sisters and brother had assembled to receive it, at the end of September. On October 3 in St. Stephen's Church—the scene of Edward's funeral just seven years before—Cherubini's *Requiem* in C minor was sung over Gottschalk's remains. Then the body was committed to a tomb in Greenwood Cemetery in Brooklyn. Beside it was placed Edward's body, which had been disinterred and brought from Calvary Cemetery. The sisters and brother marked the tomb with an elaborate marble monument.

They also made plans to honor Gottschalk's memory by publishing his music manucripts and his diary. Nicolas Espadero, to whom the editing of the music was entrusted, was in time to add more than twenty-five opus numbers to the list of sixty which Gottschalk himself had seen printed. The diary was to be brought out in Philadelphia in 1881 as *Notes of a Pianist*.

Since Gottschalk had died intestate, his sisters and brother were declared his sole heirs. Firmin was denied the legacy he swore his employer had promised. He then tried through the Brazilian courts to obtain some sort of pension, basing his claim upon ten years of service. Once more he was unsuccessful. He doubtless felt that he had a good reason for making no effort to see that the personal property left by Gottschalk was dispatched to the heirs. Agents of the police had taken possession of it at the time of Gottschalk's death, and Firmin allowed them to dispose of it as they saw fit.

In New York Gottschalk's sisters talked freely of what they called the valet's ingratitude. They also spoke of their failure to recover from the Rio de Janeiro police even the clothing that had belonged to their brother. They complained that those who saw him die—the doctors, the hotel manager, Firmin, and other servants—had persistently refused to answer questions regarding his last hours. It was clear that they suspected something sinister behind the mysterious silence.

What they were saying came to the ears of newspaper reporters. In certain printed items on matters musical there were hints that Gottschalk's death resulted from causes as yet unannounced to the public.

Then an American traveler arrived in New York direct from Rio de Janeiro. He had talked, he said, with the two physicians who attended Gottschalk in his last illness. Both, the traveler declared, were convinced that the abscess which killed the pianist was caused by a blow from a sandbag received one night when he was fighting off a gang of schoolboy rowdies who were trying to play some sort of brutal prank on him and Firmin on a dark street near the Rio de Janeiro opera house. The traveler communicated his story to the press, and it was printed throughout the United States.

It was dramatic—but not dramatic enough to satisfy the newspaper reporters who recalled Gottschalk's flight from San Francisco. They converted the schoolboy wielder of the sandbag into a hot-blooded Brazilian husband who believed that Gottschalk had stolen his wife's affection. The pianist's wickedness, these reporters wrote, had at last caught up with him: he was murdered, no less, and his slayer used the time-honored torture weapon, the sandbag. This was the fiction that lovers of the sensational were to keep alive for many a year.

At the time the story began to circulate—near the end of 1870—Mrs. Seymour's *Life and Letters of Louis Moreau Gottschalk* appeared in print. The book—artificial, sentimental, exaggerated, and very badly written—did more harm than good to the memory of Gottschalk. Reviewers everywhere, disgusted with its mawkishness, took delight in reminding readers that after all Gottschalk was known to be a Don Juan. A number went so far as to hint that the author herself had been one of his mistresses. Mrs. Seymour, then the respected widow of a clergyman who had risen to a position of importance in the Episcopalian Church, was no doubt glad that the book was published under a pseudonym—Octavia Hensel, the name suggested by Gottschalk so long ago.

Ada Clare had nothing to say in print on Gottschalk's death. Indeed, after the fiasco of her novel, *Only a Woman's Heart*, she ceased to be a writer. As Agnes Stanfield she became a perpetual trouper, traveling always with her husband, M. J. F. Noyes. In New York at the end of January, 1874, she was bitten by a mad dog. Four weeks later, when she was on the stage in a performance of *East Lynne* in Rochester, she suddenly became so ill that the curtain was rung down. Her husband brought her to New York that night. The doctor who was called the next morning saw at once that she was a victim of hydrophobia. After suffering pain far more excruciating than Gottschalk had endured, she died—on the afternoon of March 4. She was buried in Hammonton, New Jersey, in a grave adjacent to little Aubrey's.

"When I'm dead," she had said, " I'll be again Ada Clare, the Queen of Bohemia." But the public of 1874 was interested in neither her name nor her title. Only two New York newspapers mentioned her death—one with a brief obituary and the other with a tribute in verse written by a former loyal Bohemian, William Winter. Ada Clare was already on the brink of oblivion.

It seemed in the 1870's and 1880's that Gottschalk could never be forgotten. Teresa Carreño and other pianists were captivating audiences throughout the world with his music. His posthumous publications were pouring from presses not only in the United States but in Germany, France, England, and South America. Reminiscences written by those who had tales to tell of his deeds as a Don Juan as well as by those who had criticism to offer on his achievements as a musician were being printed in French and American newspapers, magazines, and books. The appearance of *Notes of a Pianist* in 1881 made such a stir that the music house which issued it turned the distribution over to a popular publisher.

But in the 1890's the eclipse of Gottschalk began, and by the end of the period of the first World War he had joined Ada Clare in near oblivion.

Today, only a few Americans know that he ever existed. And the majority of these invariably associate his name with two compositions. If he is mentioned in their presence, they smile superciliously and exclaim, "The man who wrote 'The Last Hope' and 'The Dying Poet'!" When they are told that they have been reverently singing the theme of "The Last Hope" all their lives, usually to the hymn "Lord, as We Thy Name Profess," they are surprised.

Gottschalk will remain on the brink of oblivion until that time arrives when his compatriots have developed what Mr. T. S. Eliot calls "the historical sense." By then they will have learned that there is no understanding of the present without an understanding of the past. They will surely also have learned how to evaluate the importance to their culture of the highest of the arts, the art of music. Then, and then only, they will grant to Gottschalk the place he deserves in their memory, a place of honor among the great American pioneers.

Among the Gottschalk music manuscripts in the New York Public Library there are several pages marked with marginal notes (scraps of verse in French or English or Spanish, funny asides embellished with drawings, and the like). I have found these random jottings, most of which are undoubtedly in Gottschalk's hand, most revealing. There are also in the New York Public Library several of Gottschalk's letters, all brief. A few more, likewise brief, are to be found in the Howard Library in New Orleans, the Tulane University Library, and the Library of the National Conservatory in Paris. I know of the existence of no other Gottschalk manuscripts.

Records of births, baptisms, marriages, and deaths in the Gottschalk and Bruslé families from 1805 up to and including the pianist's period are, with two or three exceptions, in the archives of either the St. Louis Cathedral in New Orleans or the New Orleans Board of Health.

The most important printed source on Gottschalk is his diary, *Notes of a Pianist* (Philadelphia, 1881). This work—written in French, translated into English by Robert E. Peterson, and prefaced with a fifty-page biography (very inaccurate) by Clara Gottschalk—covers only the years 1857-1869. However, the frequent flash-backs give much rich information on Gottschalk's earlier years. His contributions to *La France musicale* (1853-1868 *passim*), the Havana *Diario de la Marina* (1857-1861 *passim*), the *Atlantic Monthly* (March and April, 1865), and *Watson's Art Journal* (November 1865) are in the main autobiographical. Many of his letters are given in P. Arpin, *Biographie de L. M. Gottschalk* (New York, 1853); Octavia Hensel, *Life and Letters of Louis Moreau Gottschalk* (Boston, 1870); Luiz Fors, *Gottschalk* (Havana, 1880); and Clara Gottschalk's introduction to *Notes of a Pianist.* Letters, or quotations from letters, are also to be found in Léon Escudier, *Mes Souvenirs* (Paris, 1868); A. Marmontel, *Les Pianistes célèbres* (Paris, 1878); E. Fétis, *Histoire générale de la musique* (Paris, 1876); William Mason, *Memoires of a Musical Life* (New York, 1902); and Ada Clare's contributions to the New York *Atlas* (1856), *La France musicale* (1857-1859), the *Saturday Press* (1859), and the *Golden Era* (1865).

Gottschalk was a public figure. Therefore, much of the matter which I have used in telling his story was gleaned from the daily press of New Orleans, Paris, Geneva, Madrid, New York, Boston, Philadelphia, San Francisco, Havana, and the other important cities to which his wanderings led him. I also gleaned many revealing facts from the musical journals of Paris, New York, and Boston. All newspapers and periodicals which served me as sources are named in the text.

I have of course made use of the appropriate maps, directories, and guidebooks of Gottschalk's time; and I have found encyclopaedias, the general biographical dictionaries, musical dictionaries, and historical surveys of music most helpful.

In picturing the New Orleans which Gottschalk knew I have drawn from the following books: Mrs. Houstoun, *Texas and the Gulf of Mexico* (Philadelphia, 1845); A. Oakey Hall, *The Manhattaner in New Orleans* (New York, 1851); Theodore Clapp, *Autobiographical Sketches and Recollections* (Boston, 1858); George W. Cable, *The Creoles of Louisiana* (New York, 1884) and *Strange New Stories of Louisiana* (New York, 1889); Louise Livingston Hunt, *Memoir of Mrs. Edward Livingston* (New York, 1886); Alcée Fortier, *Louisiana Studies* (New Orleans, 1894); Grace King, *New Orleans: the Place and the People* (New York, 1895); Eliza Ripley, *Social Life in Old New Orleans* (New York, 1912); Lyle Saxon, *Fabulous New Orleans* (New York, 1936); Celestine M. Chambon, *The St. Louis Cathedral* (New Orleans, 1938); and Edward Francis Murphy, *Père Antoine* (Garden City, 1947).

Much of the background matter on Pass Christian is from John H. Long, *History of Harrison County, Mississippi* (Gulfport, 1936) and H. S. Fulkerson, *Early Days in Mississippi* (Baton Rouge, 1937).

The following biographical works were of help to me in projecting Gottschalk's Paris: Frederick Niecks, *Frederick Chopin as a Man and Musician* (New York, 1902); Camille Saint-Saëns, *École buissonière: notes et souvenirs* (Paris, 1913); Paul Landormy, *Bizet* (Paris, 1929); Siegfried Kracauer, *Offenbach and the Paris of His Time* (London, 1937); Adolphe Boschot, *La Crépuscule d'un romantique: Hector Berlioz 1842-1869* (Paris, 1912); and Jacques Barzun, *Berlioz and the Romantic Century* (Boston, 1950).

In relating Gottschalk's experiences in Spain I used facts drawn from Fitzgerald Molloy, *The Romance of Royalty* (London, 1904) and Francis Gribble, *The Tragedy of Isabella II* (London, 1913).

Of the following books several contain passages on Gottschalk and all were of aid in shedding light on his life after his return to his native country: Arthur Pougin, *William Vincent Wallace: étude biographique et critique* (Paris, 1866); Herman Klein, *The Reign of Patti* (New York, 1920); Marta Milinowski, *Teresa Carreño* (New Haven, 1941); Clara Louise Kellogg, *Memoirs of an American Prima Donna* (New York, 1913); Rose Fay Thomas, *Memoirs of Theodore Thomas* (New York, 1911); M. Strakosch, *Souvenirs d'un impresario* (Paris, 1887); George C. D. Odell, *Annals of the New York Stage*, Vols. VI-VIII (New York, 1931-1936); John Tasker Howard, *Our American Music* (New York, 1931); and Mary Wilhelmine Williams, *Dom Pedro the Magnanimous: Second Emperor of Brazil* (Chapel Hill, 1937).

Material on Ada Clare's family relationships was drawn from wills, deeds, and indentures in the archives of the District and County Courts in Charleston and from the extensive account of her grandfather, the Reverend John McElhenney, in George Howe, *History of the Presbyterian Church in South Carolina* (Columbia, 1870). While most of the rest which I have on Ada Clare was based on her own published writings (cited in the text), I must express my indebtedness to the following works: Odell, *Annals of the New York Stage*, cited above; T. Allston Brown, *A History of the New York Stage* (New York, 1903); Charles Warren Stoddard, "Ada Clare, Queen of Bohemia," *National Magazine* (September, 1905); Albert Parry, *Garrets and Pretenders: a History of Bohemianism in America* (New York, 1933); and Francis Wolle, *Fitz-James O'Brien* (Boulder, 1944).

There are three extensive collections of Gottschalk's published music—in the New York Public Library, the Library of Congress, and the Library of the National Conservatory in Paris. The list given below was compiled from all three. The order is, so far as I have been able to determine, chronological according to date of publication. The opus numbering which I have adopted is that of Gottschalk's French publisher, Escudier. There was evidently carelessness in the opus numbering used by the German publisher (Schott of Mainz) and the American publisher (Hall of New York). Unless otherwise indicated, all works are for piano solo.

The pieces published before Gottschalk's return to the United States, in 1853, are *Polka de salon*, op. 1; *Bamboula, danse de nègres, fantaisie*, op. 2; *La Savanne, ballade créole*, op. 3; *Ossian, deux ballades*, op. 4; *Le Bananier, chanson nègre*, op. 5; *Colliers d'or, deux mazurkas*, op. 6 (these two pieces were originally published separately as op. 6 and op. 7); *La Moissoneuse, mazurka*, op. 8; *Le Songe d'une nuit d'été, caprice élégant*, op. 9 (based on motives from the opera by Thomas); *Chasse du jeune Henri, à deux pianos*, op. 10 (paraphrase of the overture to the opera by Méhul); *Le Mancenillier, ballade créole*, op. 11; and *Danse ossianique*, op. 12 (a rewriting of *Polka de salon*, op. 1).

The pieces issued in 1853-1857 are *Jerusalem, grande fantaisie à deux pianos de l'opera de Verdi*, op. 13 (the opera is *I Lombardi*, produced in Paris with the title *Jerusalem*; the fantasy was also issued as piano solo); *La Jota aragonesa, caprice espagnol*, op. 14 (an excerpt from the work for ten pianos, *El Sitio de Zaragoza*); *Le Banjo, caprice américain*, op. 15 (an arrangement for small orchestra was published after Gottschalk's death); *The Last Hope, méditation réligieuse*, op. 16 (the theme has been used for published songs, both sacred and secular; arrangements for orchestra and military band have been published); *Marche de nuit*, op. 17; *Pensée poétique*, op. 18; *L'Étincelle, mazurka sentimentale*, op. 21; *Souvenirs d'Andalousie, caprice de concert sur la Cana, le Fandango, et le Jaleo de Jerez*, op. 22; *Chant du soldat, caprice de concert*, op. 23; *Sospiro, valse poétique*, op. 24; *Forest Glade, polka brillante* (published in Philadelphia in 1853 without opus number, issued a few months later in Paris as *Les Follets*, op. 25); *Tournament Galop* (published in New York in 1854 without opus number); *Ricordati, méditation*, op. 26; *La Naïade, polka de salon*, op. 27; and *Reflets du passé, rêverie*, op. 28.

During his continuous sojourn of five years (from early in 1857 to the beginning of 1862) in the West Indies and the northern coast of South America Gottschalk saw these pieces in print: *Apothéose, marche solenelle de concert*, op. 29; *Minuit à Seville, aubade*, op. 30; *Souvenir de Porto Rico, marche des gibaros*, op. 31; *Pastorella e cavalliere, scène*, op. 32; *Danza*, op. 33; *Columbia, caprice de concert*, op. 34; *La Gitanilla, caprice caractéristique*, op. 35; *Fântome de bonheur, caprice*, op. 36; *Ojos criollos, danse cubaine à deux pianos*, op. 37 (also issued for piano four hands and piano solo); *Manchega, étude de concert*, op. 38; *Souvenir de la Havanne, caprice de concert*, op. 39; *Printemps d'amour, mazurka de concert*, op. 40; *God Save the Queen, morceau de concert*, op. 41; *La Chute des feuilles, nocturne sur une mélodie de N. Espadero*, op. 42; *Polonia, caprice de concert*, op. 43; *Jeunesse, mazurka brillante* (copyright U. S. 1860, in Escudier's list as op. 70); *Les Ardennes, mazurka* (copyright U. S. 1860, not in Escudier's list).

The works published during the years of Gottschalk's Civil War tours are *O ma charmante, épargnez-moi!, caprice*, op. 44; *Suis-moi, caprice*, op. 45; *Murmures éoliens*, op. 46; *Berceuse*, op. 47 (*Slumber on, Baby Dear*, a song with *Berceuse* the melody, was in print by 1863; an arrangement for military band was published after Gottschalk's death); *Union, a concert paraphrase on the airs Star-Spangled Banner, Yankee Doodle, and Hail Columbia*, op. 48; *La Colombe, polka*, op. 49; *Di que si (Répondsmoi), danse cubaine*, op. 50; *Home, Sweet Home, caprice*, op.

51; *Miserere du Trovatore, paraphrase à deux pianos,* op. 52 (also issued as piano solo); *La Gallina, danse cubaine,* op. 53; *Impromptu,* op. 54; *Le Cri de délivrance* (after George F. Root's *The Battle Cry of Freedom*), op. 55; *William Tell Overture* (for two pianos, piano four hands, and piano solo); *The Dying Poet* (published originally in New York under a pseudonym, then in many editions with Gottschalk's name and with varying opus numbers); *Hurrah Galop, for General Grant* (published under the pseudonym "Seven Octaves"); *L'Amour chevaleresque, caprice élégant en forme de schottische* (signed "Seven Octaves"); and *Radieuse, valse de concert* (copyright U. S. 1865).

The only other compositions which Gottschalk saw in print are *Caprice élégiaque,* op. 56; *Grand Scherzo,* op. 57; *Tremolo, étude de concert,* op. 58; *Pasquinade, caprice,* op. 59; and *Morte!, lamentation,* op. 60.

The posthumous publications brought out with opus numbers (most of them under the editorship of N. Espadero) are *L'Extase, pensée poétique,* op. 61; *Dernier amour, étude de concert,* op. 62; *Bataille, étude de concert,* op. 63; *Marche funèbre,* op. 64; *Solitude,* op. 65; *Ses yeux, polka* (ed. A. Napoleon), op. 66; *Tarentelle, tutti d'orchestre,* op. 67 (the manuscript was probably sent to the French publisher before Gottschalk's death; there are arrangements for two pianos, for piano four hands, and for piano solo); *Pensive, polka redowa,* op. 68; *Grande Fantaisie sur l'hymne national brésilien,* op. 69; *Orfa, polka,* op. 71; *Scherzo romantique,* op. 73; *Souvenir de Lima, mazurka,* op. 74; *Souvenir de Cuba, mazurka,* op. 75; *Marguerite, valse sentimentale* (ed. Clara Gottschalk), op. 76; *Rayons d'azur, polka de salon,* op. 77; *Chant de guerre,* op. 78; *Caprice-polka,* op. 79; *El Cocoyé, caprice cubain de bravoure,* op. 80; *Mazurka rustique,* op. 81; *Deuxième Banjo,* op. 82; *Oberon Overture,* op. 83; *Sixième Ballade,* op. 85; *Danse de sylphes, caprice,* op. 86; *Septième Ballade,* op. 87; *Hercule, grande étude de concert,* op. 88; *Le Carnaval de Venise,* op. 89; *Huitième Ballade,* op. 90; and *L'Hymne portugais, variations de concert* (ed. A. Napoleon), op. 91.

The posthumous publications without opus numbers are *Le Chant du martyr, caprice réligieux; Dans les nuages, schottische;*

The Dying Swan, a romance; Esquisses créoles pour piano à deux mains (an arrangement for small orchestra has also been published); *Fantasy on airs from La Favorita; The Maiden's Blush,* concert waltz; *La Mélancolie, étude caractéristique; Souvenir du bal, caprice élégant; Yearning, a Romance;* and the andante from the romantic symphony, *La Nuit des tropiques,* for orchestra, the first of two movements, published about 1937.

In 1937, musicologists thought that the second movement (allegro moderato) of this symphony was lost. But in the collection of Gottschalk manuscripts acquired by the New York Public Library since then a piano score was found, and the full symphony was given its first performance in the United States by the Columbia University Orchestra, under the direction of Howard Shanet, on May 5, 1955.

There is one more work to which I must call attention. Though it has not yet appeared in print, it is known to the thousands of Americans and Europeans who have attended performances of the New York City Ballet. It is one of the most popular ballets in the repertoire of this company, *Cakewalk,* the music for which was adapted by Hershy Kay from a number of Gottschalk's Negro and Creole pieces.